The Comfort of Strangers

The Comfort of Strangers

SOCIAL LIFE AND LITERARY FORM

Gage McWeeny

OXFORD

UNIVERSITY PRESS

OXFORD
UNIVERSITY PRESS

Oxford University Press is a department of the University of
Oxford. It furthers the University's objective of excellence in research,
scholarship, and education by publishing worldwide.
Oxford is a registered trademark of Oxford University Press
in the UK and certain other countries.

Published in the United States of America by
Oxford University Press
198 Madison Avenue, New York, NY 10016, United States of America

© Oxford University Press 2016

Library of Congress Cataloging-in-Publication Data
Names: McWeeny, Gage.
Title: The comfort of strangers : social life and literary form / Gage McWeeny.
Description: New York : Oxford University Press, [2015] | Includes bibliographical references
and index.
Identifiers: LCCN 2015021433| ISBN 9780199797202 (cloth) | ISBN 9780199797288 (updf)
Subjects: LCSH: English literature—19th century—History and criticism. | Social change
in literature. | Strangers in literature. | Community life in literature. | Social psychology in
literature. | Literature and society—Great Britain—History—19th century.
Classification: LCC PR468.S57 M39 2015 | DDC 820.9/355—dc23 LC record available at http://
lccn.loc.gov/2015021433

1 3 5 7 9 8 6 4 2
Printed in the United States of America
on acid-free paper

For My Parents, Johnna and Philip McWeeny

{ CONTENTS }

{ ACKNOWLEDGMENTS }

A book about the comfort of strangers can't let those who made it possible remain unknown. And, a book this long in the making accrued many debts along the way. I am happy to be able to acknowledge, without hope of repaying, some of them here.

First, to Jeff Nunokawa, whose friendship, care, and guidance has had, and continues to have, a transformative effect upon both how I think and how I live. He knew what this book, and even its writer, could be long before I did. This book was made far better than it would have been otherwise, especially in its final stages of writing, by my good fortune in the friendship, conversation, and readings of Theo Davis and David Kurnick in particular.

I have been lucky to have many excellent teachers. The thinking for this book had its first inkling in a graduate seminar with John Guillory, and I was fortunate to get reading of early work from Amanda Anderson. Deborah Nord, who saw this through its first stages as a dissertation at Princeton University, knew how to both spur me on and keep me honest. Elaine Showalter's mentoring and friendship made it all much more enjoyable and glamorous, whether in New Jersey or London. Diana Fuss and Craig Dworkin modeled scholarly fun, while Mike Jennings helped ensure a very nice roof over my head. More and more do I admire the generosity and critical intelligence of Michael Wood, whom I hope to come back as in another life. Thanks as well to Starry Schor, Jeff Dolven, and Susan Wolfsen. I am grateful to Princeton for the support I received on a year-long Hyde research fellowship in London, as well as an APGA grant for summer research. Many friends made graduate school an enjoyable and even thrilling place to be: Amada Sandoval, Sally Bachner, and Stuart Burrows, in particular. Chris Rovee, Paul Kelleher, Tamara Ketabgian, Julie Park, Sarah Churchwell, Karen Beckman, and Heather O'Donnell were the best sort of friends and interlocutors. Thanks to Dan Novak for his astute reading of a draft of the chapter on Wilde. Among the many post-graduate school enlivening partners in conversation during the writing of this book, I was especially lucky to find David Russell and Heather Love.

Working on this book gave me the opportunity to engage with scholars whose work I admire and am inspired by, a number of whom were generous enough to respond in varied contexts as I tried to work out the arguments of this book. In particular I wish to thank Tanya Agathocleous, James Buzard, Amanda Claybaugh, Elaine Freedgood, Richard Kaye, Seth Koven, Christopher Lane, Sharon Marcus, Jesse Matz, Kevin McLaughlin, Elsie

Michie, Andrew Miller, John Plotz, Kent Puckett, Carolyn Williams, and colleagues at Villanova University. I am also grateful to the anonymous readers from Oxford University Press for their illuminating suggestions for revision. Audiences at MLA, NAVSA, NVSA, MSA, the CUNY Victorianist Seminar, and Rutgers University gave invaluable responses to my work-in-progress.

Williams College and the English Department in particular have been the richest of intellectual environments for me. I had the good fortune of many conversations with colleagues as I worked out my thinking. To name only a few who make it so rich, and who made rural New England seem like not such a crazy place to write a book largely about urban social forms: Pat Malanga, Bernie Rhie, Katie Kent, Peter Murphy, Jim Shepard, Karen Shepard, John Limon, Steve Fix, Steve Tifft, Larry Raab, Sherron Knopp, Dorothy Wang, Jessica Fisher, Anjuli Raza Kolb, and Walter Johnston. Along with their extraordinary friendship, Karen Swann, Chris Pye, Christian Thorne, Anita Sokolsky, and Alison Case provided insightful comments and challenging readings of this manuscript at crucial stages. Thanks to a year-long fellowship at the Oakley Center, I was able to revise in a stimulating and beautiful environment. Many kept me going in ways they couldn't know: Gretchen Long, Stefanie Solum, Peter Starenko, Ben Weaver, Peter Low, Molly Polk, Karin Stack, Richard Scullin, Guy Hedreen, and Liz McGowan, among others. Cindy Nikitas supported the completion of this book with childcare and good cheer in ways she does know. I tried out some of this material in seminars with my students, and I'm grateful for their patience as well as their questions and suggestions. And those who were there from the beginning, Morningside Heights in the early 1990s, a place and a time that has left an invisible watermark upon this book and its interests: Ben Alsup, Liz Craft, and Lou Wilson. I wish Mike Feldman was still alive to arch an eyebrow over it.

I have been very fortunate to work with the excellent Brendan O'Neill at Oxford University Press. An extraordinary editor from first to last, he and his assistant Stephen Bradley have been expert and gracious at every step, calibrating the pressure points at just the right moment. Thanks to Lynn Childress for her careful copyediting. Chelli Riddiough is a force to be reckoned with, but especially in the speed and cheer with which she helped in the preparation of the final manuscript.

I am lucky to have grown up in a family that not only cared about books and ideas but also encouraged me in my endeavors, even one as iffy as becoming an academic. My parents, Johnna and Philip McWeeny, have given me all the love and support that one could imagine, or even hope for, over the long arc of this book's writing and well before it, knowing with parental intuition just when to urge me on and when to remain tactfully silent. One of the many pleasures of having three loving elder brothers is they never let you forget you're the youngest. John, Peter, and Mark, thank you for allowing me to turn that from taunt into bragging right. Thanks too to those who improved upon those brothers: Katie, Abby, and Dwyer. My grandmother, Lorraine Suerth, saw me through many years of graduate study and beyond before she passed away; I am only sorry not to be able to share this book with her. The Berry family's generosity and love has been a great gift, one that I try not to take for granted. Mary Lynn Berry helped with this book in countless ways—from astute reading suggestions and alarmingly on-point questions, to childcare and giving over a floor of her house during multiple summers of writing.

Finally, those who lived with this book just about as long as I did: my wife Wendy, and our four children, who form a happy crowd of their own. Charlie, Clara, Lucy, and Nico—beautiful and vivid—you make life meaningful. Wendy, your love, intelligence, faith, commitment to a better world, and outrageously unyielding good humor (in the face of innumerable revisions) are a joy every day. From La Caridad to the Purple Valley, you make everything possible, you make everything worthwhile.

A part of Chapter 1 previously appeared as "Crowd Management: Matthew Arnold and the Science of Society," in Victorian Poetry 41(1) (Spring 2003): 93–111. An early version of a portion of Chapter 2 appeared as "The Sociology of the Novel: George Eliot's Strangers," in Novel: A Forum on Fiction 42(3) (Fall 2009): 538–545. I am grateful to both of these journals for permitting me to publish this material here.

The Comfort of Strangers

Introduction

THE COMFORT OF STRANGERS

A sociology of occasions is here advocated. . . . At issue [is] a "social gathering," but this is a shifting entity, necessarily evanescent, created by arrivals and killed by departures.

—ERVING GOFFMAN, *INTERACTION RITUAL*

I think people one hasn't met are charming.

—OSCAR WILDE, *THE IMPORTANCE OF BEING EARNEST*

In his 1888 essay "London," Henry James confesses himself smitten, although by nobody in particular. Instead, it seems James is losing his heart to the whole city of London. Describing lulls in "the Season" when the city's fashionable residents decamp for country homes, "when everyone he knows is out of town," James discovers that he finds London oddly vivified, even repopulated by its seeming desertion—a city less barren than bustling. In these regular periods of social low tide, with friends and acquaintances far removed from the precincts of the city, James discovers unexpectedly that "the exhilarating sense of the presence of everyone he doesn't know becomes so much the deeper." While his circle of London friends is "finite," he writes "the other, the unvisited London is infinite," a sublime of social potentiality.[1] In his preference for the many over the few, the impersonal intimacy of strangers over those who are friends and acquaintances, James's pleasure in getting away from those who are closest to him is also hard to distinguish from a social desire that is as vast as London itself. In James's account, having a circle of social intimates in London occludes a far wider scene, the social vastness and density of the city in its entirety. A taste for taking the occasional vacation from the friends and acquaintances who constitute London Society might seem an unlikely appetite for social reclusiveness in Henry James. He was, after all, a writer dedicated as much to frequenting as he was to depicting the social world whose dramas he considered the great theater of fiction. The season of London's abandonment by Society friends, however, is James's occasion not to become a shut-in, but to increase his social circle through a social promiscuity expansive enough to take nothing less than all of London as its ambit. In the absence of the parties and dances of High Society, James discovers a social life that is as broad as society itself.

As if a taste for the "exhilarating presence" of strangers were in need of a good alibi, however, James goes on in this essay to quickly sketch out the professional benefits accrued by swapping out his friends for time with "everyone he doesn't know." Such social holidays from his intimates are more like a working vacation, he assures his reader: the intensified "sense" of "everyone he doesn't know" is also the ideal social condition for writing fiction. In mustering the excuse of working on his novel in order to play social hooky from close friends—the familiar image of the solitary author—James, however, links the genre of the novel with a social impulse that is equal parts reclusive and promiscuous.

James's association of the novel with the social vastness of London might also remind us of the more familiar way in which the novel and other print publications—plays, newspapers, poetry—were used by inhabitants of newly urbanized crowded nineteenth-century spaces: to discreetly screen one's glances at fellow passengers in the public spaces of the train or the omnibus. In the everyday life of a regular Londoner, no less than in James's work as a novelist, a novel might afford its reader a sense of solitude or privacy amidst strangers and an alibi for one's interest in them. As Georg Simmel would note at the start of the twentieth century, "before the appearance of omnibuses, railroads, and streetcars in the nineteenth century, men were not in a situation where for periods of minutes or hours they could or must look at each other without talking to one another."[2] Among the novel's modern functions, then, was as a socially acceptable means of remaining detached while in public, as what Erving Goffman would later call an "involvement shield."[3] Seemingly immersed in a novel while slyly glancing across the aisle, such readers might thus be said to immerse themselves in two socially multitudinous environments at once: the realist novel's densely populated pages, which often brimmed to overflow with a multitude of characters, and the crowded public places that were a new fact of life in nineteenth-century cities, places where one might experience the exhilarating presence of those one does not know.

In James's confession of "a preference for the great city ... at periods of relative abandonment" by Society, one justified by getting some work done, writing his novels also functions as a kind of involvement shield. Like the screen placed between Bartleby the reclusive scrivener and his employer in Herman Melville's story, it is by means of James's writing, as *Bartleby*'s narrator puts it, that "thus, in a manner, privacy and society were conjoined."[4] Yet, James's love of a London both emptied of intimates and socially vast underscores not just how the activity of writing a novel might cover for a wish to be alone, and how that wish is hard to tell from more socially promiscuous impulses. It also suggests a continuity between the lived experience of social expansiveness and the densely peopled fictional social landscapes of the realist novel, what James calls in his preface to *Portrait of a Lady*, "that spreading field, the human scene." James's preference for writing within an immense socially anonymous setting becomes faintly visible as a desire to transmute context into text, to bring all of London into a Henry James novel. To write a novel about "everyone he doesn't know" would be, impossibly, to generate a literary form that could figure forth a socially "infinite" London. It would be, in short, to write a novel that is adequate to the newly dense social landscape of nineteenth-century Britain.[5]

Taking up James's conjunction of the novel with social numerousness, this book is about the charm of people one has not met and how nineteenth-century literary form responds to the figurational challenges posed by the unmet and the unknown: strangers. With London's population passing the one million mark by 1800, the very quantity of the city's inhabitants brought new experiences of social multiplicity into daily life. Living among strangers became a regular feature of everyday experience for inhabitants of cities like London, one that was at once utterly novel and totally routine. With Britain's rapid population growth across the nineteenth century and that population's continued concentration in urban areas, making it the world's first predominantly urban society in the world by 1871, and with new forms of transportation that enabled people to move rapidly across great distances, Britain is arguably, in James Vernon's words, the world's "first society of strangers."[6] This book studies a set of nineteenth-century literary works as they register this transformation in varied ways and shows how they are animated by the relation between the thin social attachments instanced by strangers and more lasting varieties of social life. Bringing out what I call that literature's sociological imagination—its efforts to account for the modern social complexity particular to a society of strangers—I locate that imagination amidst a range of social impulses that seem to take no single person as their object, or, that are so evanescent or attenuated as to hardly be recognizable as social experiences. Life amidst strangers on urban streets, in markets, and public squares produced public social experiences that were both alluring and fearsome, at once a mark of epochal social transformation and as routine as the daily walk to work. Literary works sought new ways to register and figure forth those experiences, even as those experiences seemed to flicker by so rapidly as to flummox efforts to name or figure them in literary forms such as the novel.

Of course, strangers were to be found in cities of earlier periods in history. But, it is in the nineteenth century that the stranger becomes the distinctive figure both of and for modernity, both a condensation of modernity's anonymous settings and the bearer of new forms of collective social experience. In Zygmunt Bauman's representative account, one that coheres with a well-known strand of thinking about modernity that I will be drawing on in this study, "strangers are not a modern invention—but strangers who remain strangers for a long time to come, even in perpetuity, are."[7] From the early classical social theory of thinkers like Georg Simmel to more contemporary thinkers such as Bauman, strangers have carried a great deal of the figurative weight in theorizations of social life in modernity. Strangers most frequently operate as the central emblem of the impersonality, transience and fluidity, or the traumas, of urban, public space that many in the sociological tradition ally with modern life.[8] As the bearers of a social experience that is both unprecedented and quotidian, however, strangers appear throughout this study not as figures of modern alienation or shock-inducing encounters with the utterly Other. Instead, strangers are simply an everyday fact of life in the city, less the occasion of a traumatic encounter than a routine grazing of shoulders, exchanging of glances, or delicate averting of eyes on the way to the market or work. In short, strangers are not so much the Other, in my account, as they are others, the invisible dark matter that constitutes the nineteenth-century social universe, a matter that exerts a powerful gravitational effect upon its literature's sociological imagination.[9] The hope of this book, then, is to make apparent the effects—at once vast and hard to detect—of that dimly perceived dark matter upon social and literary form in the nineteenth century, to understand how literature of this period registers the society of strangers less as traumatic encounter, than as the steadily felt, tidal presence of those unknown.

The works I study here constitute something like an out-of-doors account of Victorian literature in a period traditionally dominated by histories of the novel that emphasize its dedication to figuring the domestic, as well as its delineation of the private sphere more generally. Although this study is not limited to the novel, the story I want to tell here is about a realist form that is pitched as counter to the usual accounts of the novel in this period as being driven and structured by the psychologically individuating forms of sympathy and comity, with a corresponding sense of novelistic plots as interesting themselves in durable forms of social relations, such as the marriage plot, that are energized by the psychic inwardness of characters. In concurring accounts by diverse thinkers, the story of public life in the nineteenth century most frequently is told as one of its decline and disappearance, subsumed into the rise of a middle-class power organized around domestic space and psychic interiority.[10] And in many accounts the realist novel is the literary form whose apogee correlates to the privatizing trajectory of the nineteenth century. The novel, by these lights, is dedicated to the story of individual rather than collective experience, and to transforming the realm of the everyday and sexuality, as well as its domestic social space, into the sphere in which meaning can be found.[11]

By distinction, I argue that the works in this study register a counter-tendency of characters, or even narrators, to lose interest in those who are intimates, finding themselves diverted instead into intensities these works locate in the public world of strangers and the modern forms of sociality they emblematize. As a project interested in the nineteenth-century realist novel and desire, this study bears a debt to Nancy Armstrong's influential account in *Desire and Domestic Fiction* of the novel's role in the transformation of subjectivity and its reorganization around female sexuality, as well as the novel's association with the space of the domestic and psychological interiority. More recently, Armstrong has reiterated an understanding of the nineteenth-century novel as irremediably individualistic, and that in the novel's transformation from an eighteenth- to a nineteenth-century form it "abandoned the task of imagining an increasingly democratic nation."[12] My aim here, however, is to mark out in nineteenth-century realist form a lingering preoccupation with strangers and collective life—its affects and political possibilities, as well as its challenges for literary form—that a critical focus on individualism, domesticity, and interiority necessarily does not account for. To shift our understanding of the novel and the novelistic over to the stranger-filled streets and away from the home is not, of course, to make a claim for the novel's constitutive dedication to populism or even democracy in England. It is, however, to make the case for the democratic aspirations of its form, however mitigated, its working principle that any life, however ordinary, however unhistoric, might find itself figured within the novel's pages. It is this ethos Jacques Rancière associates with the novel's epochal shift in the subject matter of art, from "the great names and events" of tragedy, for example, "to the life of the anonymous."[13] It is also to mark out a set of impulses in these works allied with what Zygmunt Bauman has called—with reference to people who have been displaced semi-permanently into refugee camps and whose disenfranchisement extends to their being beneath notice or even discernment—"the right to be imagined."[14] This book's interest in strangers generally, rather than the specific category of the refugee, distinguishes the philosophical and ethical aims of Bauman's project from my own. But the stranger's "right to be imagined" does describe a political and aesthetic pressure generated within these works by the vivid sense of social multitudinousness I argue shapes them.

Taken together, the variety of texts in this book constitute a countercurrent to long-standing critical associations of the realist novel in the nineteenth century with privacy and interiority, a countercurrent I call the literature of social density. Primarily focused on a group of works by Matthew Arnold, George Eliot, Oscar Wilde, and Henry James, writers of the mid- to late nineteenth-century period of Britain's becoming a "society of strangers," my project shows these works to be occupied by a Victorian social imaginary increasingly understood as thickly populated, as well as by the social and aesthetic challenges posed by new understandings of social complexity. What brings this group of works together is their particular, if sometimes surprising, attunement to the collective and transient forms of social life carried by strangers, forms of social relationality that turn away from the inward and the individuating.

In its turn toward strangers rather than intimates, and in particular in its turn from that great Victorian value, sympathy, this book might seem to promise its reader a history of literary figurations of callous indifference, an unexpected and alarming efflorescence of cranky Victorian misanthropes, shut-ins, and antisocialites.[15] Instead, I mark out in these texts an ascendant sensitivity that is calibrated less to the sympathized-with individual or the interpersonal than to the more expansive site of the social itself. These works, then, register not just new forms of attentiveness, but also, crucially, modes of disattending and reverie, or strategies for losing interest in individual people, that develop amidst a densely peopled world. Alongside that sensitivity, I trace the development of new formal literary techniques and social modes suited to navigating and managing the complex, multitudinous social environments of Victorian modernity, arguing that literary form bears the imprint of the society of strangers. The social affiliations I discover in these works are often too minor, too impersonal, or too ephemeral to register in critical understandings tuned to the frequency of the more readily codified attachments that are usually understood as structuring realist literary form, such as marriage and friendship. Instead, I find that stranger relations often produce unexpected torsions in literary form, opening onto narratives and affects that are otherwise foreclosed by the demands of particular genres, such as the realist novel's reliance upon the courtship plot. These torsions—places where the sense-making work of realist literary form begins to bend under the gravitational effects of social dark matter—mark out modes of impersonal social life less scripted by the individuating energies associated with realist narrative, or the exigencies of novelistic plots of social and romantic convergence, at times making a libidinal object of social complexity itself.

It is significant to the story I tell in this book that the generically diverse set of works at its center are of a period marked by emergent efforts in Britain to develop practices for reflecting upon social structure, what we might call proto-sociology. In its earliest imaginings, this project began from the simple historical observation that sociology in its varied forms—scientific reflections upon the nature of society and the social bond—begins to take distinctive shape in a period that roughly overlaps with the height of realist literary form in the nineteenth century, while also noticing British proto-sociology's empiricist strain, its allergy to the theoretical work developing in Europe. By constellating literary works with a strand of sociology from the nineteenth and twentieth centuries that is especially interested in social form—ranging from Émile Durkheim and Georg Simmel to Erving Goffman and Pierre Bourdieu—I underscore how literature and sociology have converged to produce modern understandings of the shaping powers of the social. This book's historical claims are of a necessarily broad nature, less oriented toward the particular intellectual influence of, say, Herbert Spencer's sociological thought upon George Eliot. Instead, this study follows out the reverberations of a modern understanding of the social, which includes fantasies of lightening the social's force, as well as efforts to bend it to new articulations of collective life. As James's essay hints, the sociological imagination of these literary works is often joined at the hip to a wish to imagine means of relief from the social field they figure in such fine detail. Reflecting both the appeal and difficulty of escaping, if only momentarily, those closest to us, the comfort of strangers thus illuminates the proximity between Victorian impulses to negate social bonds and an effort to know them better.

The surprising investments in ephemeral communities, anonymity, and social distance within texts as diverse as *Middlemarch* and *The Importance of Being Earnest* illuminate a strain of sociality that is not imagined under J. S. Mill's description in *On Liberty* of society as a crowd whose "interference" and "encroachment" threatens the individual.[16] This sociality, while sensitive to the coercive powers of the social, is also attuned to the relational possibilities offered by the impersonal intimacy of life among those unknown, what I call, borrowing from the seminal sociological essay by Mark Granovetter, the power of weak social ties.[17] Studying social affiliations and labor networks, in particular, Granovetter shows the importance of thin social links—the acquaintances of acquaintances, say, or the seeming social isolates amidst a tight group—to the function of social networks, over and above those of denser, but more closed-off networks of intimates. While my interest here is not in excavating nineteenth-century precursors to contemporary network theory of the sort Granovetter develops, the thin social bonds at the heart of this study similarly underscore the ways in which weak forms of sociality, or even apparent antisociality, are hard to tell apart from the ties that bind.

This book steers clear, it should be said, of the project of contributing its own definitional history of the social. Instead, building upon a set of sociological accounts, it traces the effects of the "discovery" of the social as a phenomenon distinct from simple interpersonal relations in the nineteenth century through a series of exemplary literary works, pointing out the ways in which that discovery produces new challenges for traditional literary form. Like the strangers who are less thrilling (or terrifying) instantiations of the Other and simply a fact of everyday life, the force of the social's imprint within these works is often hard to detect for being so unremarkable, made nearly invisible by its ubiquity. Thus, apparent forms of social negation in these texts, the wish to get away from those closest by in order to more vividly sense the "unvisited London," often bear little of the drama of the sacrifices of self to the demands of the social that Christopher Lane discovers in Victorian misanthropy; or, though this project has learned much from his work, to the obliterating effects of desire in the name of psychological coherence in the realist novel that Leo Bersani has traced.[18] Instead, such escapes are effected at times by something as ordinary as a walk through the streets, or in the forms of reverie or absorption that Erving Goffman calls "awayness."[19] Less attuned to the violent encounter between desires and social and psychic structures that cannot tolerate them, this book instead turns to figurations and registrations, sometimes light, sometimes burdensome, of the felt pressure of the social as first described by Émile Durkheim: "ways of acting, thinking and feeling that present the remarkable property of existing outside the individual consciousness."[20]

In their interest in something as dimly perceptible and un-localizable as the social, however, the works in this study are often preoccupied with the problems of social attention—too much or too little each bearing perils—as well as properly attending to ambient social environments more generally, what Goffman calls the social "surround."[21] In turning to sociology, as I specify in more detail below as well as in my first chapter, I want to underscore the claim that sociology and literary form each take up this problem of social attentiveness in ways that overlap. We will see, for example, omniscient narration in the realist novel to be as concerned with how to properly apportion its attention among many characters as sociology is with the forms of attentiveness necessary to document the micro-dramas of everyday life. The forms of attentiveness to the social that are generated by sociology and aesthetic modes of disattending, such as reverie, turn out to be less opposed than they have been imagined to be. Instead, they are mutually constitutive of efforts to register the perceptual and figurative challenges posed by strangers and the expansive, anonymous social environments of the modern world.

In considering social evanescence and distanced forms of social intimacy as ways of getting some purchase on the emergent qualities of the social in the nineteenth century, I also mean to make the case for these literary authors as theorists of the social themselves. What is more, while theorists like Simmel describe and taxonomize the thin social bonds of modernity, in these literary works, stranger sociality often appears as an aspiration, a prescriptive ideal of social susceptibility or open-ended relationality. *The Comfort of Strangers* thus recovers quasi-utopic dimensions of what otherwise might resemble modern social alienation. That is, strangers not as alienating Other, but as spur to articulations of new forms of relationality.[22] Sociology's historical tendency to orient itself toward scales of social life broader than that of the individual, its interest in types and the nature of the social, for example, thus helps us to reconsider nineteenth-century realist literary form's presumptive orientation toward the valuation or production of inwardness and privacy in its protagonists. This book's largest argument is for a more expansive account of literary form's sociable effects and the centrality of unexpected modes of social detachment and yearnings toward collective social life sponsored by Victorian literature, from readerly reverie on the omnibus to epigrammatic evasiveness at a party. Marking the varied ways in which the unbound qualities of the modern socius, the society of strangers, are registered in these works brings to light forms of social affiliation that exceed, or fall short of, the kinds of social relations—lovers, family members, or friends—that are more forthrightly figured in realist form. The unexpected energies or affects borne by such ties, as well as the challenges they present to realist literary form, in turn help make the social into an object of reflective consideration.

In paying attention to what often would seem negligible about, or within, some of the works in this study—forms of attachment that are evanescent, singularly mild, or highly mediated—the insights this book pursues are themselves often sociological in nature. It looks to sociologists of social form, such as Georg Simmel and Erving Goffman, to evolve a critical approach supple enough to trace out the interrelations of literary form and social content in these works. It is this approach, combining sociological theory and literary critical methods of reading, which enables me to show how the sociological imagination of these works brings into high relief in their pages a sensitivity to the felt force of society in particularly intense or highly attenuated moments. This book's interest, however, is not only in the kinds of social experience the works in this study find emblematized in strangers. I am also interested in how literary form becomes a particular site of reflection upon, and in some cases the bearer of, impersonal social intimacy. A genre such as the realist novel often has been understood as a sort of training ground for social life, a way of learning forms of sociability and privacy that one then carries out and practices in the real world. By this book's lights, however, nineteenth-century literature is better understood as bearing a supplementary relation to the social, with literary form sponsoring the understanding of ways of being with other people that are otherwise impossible. In thinking about literary form's social effects, this study joins a set of recent critical works that have looked to the formal features of literature as not simply the reflection of social conditions, but as the place at which one can be hard pressed to tell literary form from social effects, and formal features from social concerns.[23] My hope here is to have developed an approach to reading that will allow us to attend not only to the social dimensions of aesthetic features of texts but also to the aesthetic effects of social forms.

This book has absorbed into its approach the thinking of a group of social theorists in order to set up a series of encounters between sociological thought and literary texts, encounters that in turn show how realist literary form itself becomes bound up with redefining notions of affiliation in the anonymous social settings of modern life. The realist novel has often been itself understood as semi-sociological, and certain forms of documentary sociology, in particular, have been seen as sharing the novel's interests (Dickens's novels on London appeared alongside parliamentary investigations into the health of the urban poor), even its modes of narrative presentation (particularly in naturalism's taxonomic representational strategies, for example).[24] This study, however, while taking up classical social theory's interest in the advent of "a society of strangers," and registering the reciprocity of the realist novel's subject matter and those of documentary sociology, argues that sociological thought and nineteenth-century literature find as well a shared terrain at the level of form. In keeping literary form in view throughout, we can better see the interrelation of literature's own formalizing activity, in the sense of turning experience into "significant form" for narrative, and the sense-making work of sociology, which dedicates itself to making something as vast and vague as society itself into a coherent subject of understanding.[25] And yet, in spite of these consonances, my readings of these works also show how under the pressure of its own sociological imagination, the literature of social density is careful to mark itself out from more official or avowedly scientific forms of reflection upon the social. As will become clear, the methods, interests, and even habits of attention in this project reflect having learned a great deal from the attention to social form paid by sociologists such as Goffman and Simmel. At the same time, however, the historical emergence of sociological thought and the relationship between literature and sociology is also one of its subjects, particularly in the opening chapter of this book, on Matthew Arnold, which takes up a more textured, specified version of the historical, sometimes frictive, relationship between literary works and the emergence of sociological thought in the nineteenth century.

Among the questions motivating this book: By what means do these works make both those who appear within their pages—characters in plays, novels, and dialogues, poetic speakers—and those reading them come alive to the reality of the force of the social? How is the everyday experience of being surrounded by strangers in urban landscapes (and not just urban landscapes, as we will see) mediated by, made sense of, or in productive conflict with realist literary form? Can strangers—unknown, anonymous, innumerable, the great subject of sociological theory—even have a story? Or, is their "charm," as Wilde put it, constituted in remaining unmet, and thus, in novelistic terms, remaining un-narrated, dwelling even outside of plot? Why does it feel so hard to get away from other people in these works, and what particular conditions of modernity might make doing so appealing? Finally, and most centrally, this book brings out a question that is asked indirectly, in different ways, by each of its works: what does modernity feel like?

Two quite different scenes will give some idea of what I am after here. Wilkie Collins's *The Woman in White* might be thought of as a long answer to the last question above. Collins's book is largely about the terrors of indistinct identity in modernity—a world in which a young woman might be swapped for another young woman who had been confined to a mental institution, without anyone noticing the difference. In its opening pages, the novel condenses a characteristic affective experience of modernity into an encounter with a stranger upon a lonely road. The novel's central character, Walter Hartright, is walking on the road from Hampstead toward London proper one night:

> In one moment, every drop of blood in my body was brought to a stop by the touch of a hand laid lightly and suddenly on my shoulder from behind me. . . . There, in the middle of the broad, bright high-road—there, as if it had that moment sprung out of the earth or dropped from the heaven—stood the figure of a solitary Woman, dressed from head to foot in white garments; her face bent in grave inquiry on mine, her hand pointing to the dark cloud over London.[26]

A stranger appearing as if out of nowhere, a hand lightly but unexpectedly on one's shoulder: this scene is exemplary of the nervous drama of the sensation novel, in which the slightest touch bears the capacity to shock one to the bone, even to the platelets. Collins's scene reads, indeed, as a Gothicized condensation of modernity: a pair of faces, and a woman's hand, are pointed toward London, epicenter of a *Gesellschaft* society bustling with strangers, the anonymous setting of modernity into which the woman in white will try to melt upon her arrival there. In her startling touch, however, the anonymizing powers of the city she seeks already inhabit her hand, with Hartright's identity momentarily dissolved, as if engulfed by London's stranger-filled streets without setting foot in the city ("It was like a dream. Was I Walter Hartright?" he asks). In stopping Hartright on a lonely road, the woman also makes vivid one of the central agreements of modernity by breaking it, the agreement for those unknown to indicate visibly that they are politely ignoring one another when passing by, what Erving Goffman calls in his studies of behavior in public places "civil inattention": "the eyes of the looker may pass over the other, but no 'recognition' is allowed. . . . By according another person in public civil inattention, the individual implies that he has no reason to suspect the intentions of others present" and they nothing to fear in him.[27]

In its scene of strangers encountering one another, this moment emblematizes a broad shift from a culture characterized by the predominance of kinship relations to the more contractual obligations associated with market subjectivity. In this new era, the dominance of a social sphere defined by kinship and familiarity gives way to one characterized by anonymity: "the ranks became increasingly like strangers to one another, both literally and figuratively," Elaine Hadley writes.[28] In the *Woman in White*, it is as if the contractual forms of social life of nineteenth-century modernity, the very definition of *Gesellschaft* society the novel identifies with London, have drifted beyond the city limits to Hampstead.[29] Tellingly, it is in the language of contract that the woman exacts a promise from Walter, who reassures her by ratifying their oral agreement: "you may trust me for any harmless purpose. . . . I have no right to ask you for any explanations."

> If you could show me where to get a fly—and if you will only promise not to interfere with me, and to let me leave you, when and how I please—I have a friend in London who will be glad to receive me—I want nothing else—will you promise me?[30]

In specifying the terms of a binding agreement between them, a promise not to interfere and to "let me leave you, when and how I please," the woman in white thus articulates in highly dramatic form the central agreement of nineteenth-century liberalism's notions of freedom and personal privacy, what would later be enshrined as the "right to be let alone."[31]

The woman's specification of the rules of public social interaction underscores the sensation novel's trademark Gothicization of what would otherwise be ordinary scenes. But, it also serves as reminder that the unconscious, unspoken rituals and rules of urban sociality were in the process of being elaborated across this period as urban multiplicity became a part of daily life. The woman in white's estranging specification and articulation of what should be tacit, in part, is a means of getting a handle on social rules of public life that are in flux. In Richard Sennett's account, the rule (or right) of civil inattention between strangers is one of the symptoms of the decline of the public realm in the nineteenth century. With the erosion of the eighteenth-century ideal of public life, Sennett argues, "the stranger himself [becomes] a threatening figure," and with that threat, city life turns quiet, the hubbub of its streets reduced to the hush of a library reading room: "Silence in public life became the only way one could experience public life, especially street life, without feeling overwhelmed."[32] Sennett's history is exemplary of much writing across the twentieth century, as well as contemporary accounts, in that it adduces strangers as a trope or figure of modernity, a condensation of the *Gesellschaft* forms of sociality that predominate in the wake of the loss of a more intimate premodern world. But Sennett's account is also exemplary in its understanding of the stranger as bearer of the alienating shock of the Other, one that has dominated a variety of accounts of modernity, from Walter Benjamin's account of trauma-philic types in his 1939 essay "On Some Motifs in Baudelaire" to Zygmunt Bauman's recent theorizations of ours as an era of "liquid modernity." Bauman accords strangers a central place in his periodization of this new era of "the liquid" in modernity, which is defined by transience, uncertainty, and the friability of social bonds—not as a stage on the way to securing a more stable order, but as a permanent condition. As the emblem of social transience, strangers thus incarnate locally the more global conditions of anxiety and insecurity under liquid modernity. In Bauman's understanding of the emptied-out nature of many public spaces under liquid modernity, cities become the site of "mixophobia," "an allergic, febrile sensitivity to strangers and the strange."[33]

The stranger as bearer of urban shock is a familiar trope in literature across the nineteenth century as well. To take just one well-known instance, Wordsworth's blind beggar in *The Prelude*:

> And once, far travelled in such mood, beyond
> The reach of common indications, lost
> Amid the moving pageant, 'twas my chance
> Abruptly to be smitten with the view
> Of a blind beggar. . . .
> My mind did at this spectacle turn round
> As with the might of waters.[34]

Encounters with strangers like the ones in Collins and Wordsworth register a nineteenth-century social sphere that is marked by anonymity and transience. Such encounters, Audrey Jaffe has argued, also served as the focal point for a range of anxieties that gathered around nineteenth-century representations of sympathy and identification between those of different classes. Building on understandings of Victorian life in public as increasingly emphasizing spectatorship, with strangers regarding one another silently in public rather than engaging, Jaffe suggests that the social field becomes a dominantly visual one in the nineteenth century. Strangers figure as circulating images, "alternative selves for the spectator," amidst a field of "confounded and interdependent projections of identity," and so produce a kind of Gothicized sympathetic response, a "(dread) fantasy of occupying another's social place."[35] By Jaffe's account of Victorian strangers and sympathy, the promises between Hartright and the woman in white would constitute an effort to halt the threat of one's identity being eroded by a sympathetic response to a stranger, substituting in place of a dangerous sympathy a prophylactic social contract to assist but ask no questions. The failure of that contract—Walter is dazed by this encounter, his sense of self upended, and the novel goes on to depict their intertwined fates—in turn energizes a frantic and compensatory rebuilding of a middle-class identity around its distinction from the lower classes.

The distance between Jaffe's account of strangers as inducing dread, anxiety, and a series of troubling identifications and Goffman's notion of the daily, barely noticeable acts of civil inattention, without which the thousands of small social claims of attention and interest of strangers upon one another would make city life "unbearably sticky," brings into focus this book's own account of strangers. If we take scenes of sympathy to be exemplary of a Victorian response to a social sphere seemingly more and more densely populated by strangers—a guilty conscience ready to be energized on every street corner, as it were—what is left out is the very quotidian quality of immersion in social fields saturated by those unknown. Jaffe shows how important public space and the experience of strangers became in the nineteenth century, correcting accounts that emphasize the production of privacy, withdrawal, and interiority in this period. But what gets overlooked in an account of strangers that emphasizes shock and spectacle is the social landscape of modernity in its most banal aspect, the very fact of public life lived routinely, if not always placidly, amidst strangers. To think about this form of what we might call "stranger intimacy" in literary representation is also to nudge us away from the sensational encounter depicted by Collins, as well as the destabilizing effects of the sympathetic imagination amidst a visual field that Jaffe illuminates, and toward the far less codified qualities and sensations I find not in the dread or the fear, but the comfort, or if not comfort, the neutrality, of strangers. Arrested by the sight of a stranger, Wordsworth's stunned, disoriented speaker here marks the gulf separating this passage's figuration of strangers from that of a smitten Henry James who falls for all of London. To bring George Eliot's best-known lines from *Middlemarch* to bear upon Richard Sennett's notion of a public realm defined by taciturnity: the strangers of this book figure "the roar on the other side of silence" in public. This is not to discount the place of sympathy, which a powerful critical history has shown to be crucial to varied ethical, philosophical, and representational projects in the nineteenth century. Rather, it is to mark the effects upon literary form of strangers as simultaneously ordinary and emblematic of an epochal transformation, as barely worth remarking upon and constituting the alluringly mysterious dark matter of the social universe, a facet of modern social life so fundamental and ubiquitous as to be barely discernible at all.

While "society" often has appeared to critics and readers as a means to an end in literature of this period—as the bearer of the ameliorative bonds of Victorian sympathy and community, for example—the works in this study figure and convey a sensitivity to the felt force of society, or appeals of sociability itself, apart from those more purposive forms of attachments that tend to be anchored in sentiment or ethics. The novel's cultivation of sympathy in its readers, modeled in part by the multiple perspectives and focalizations through different characters afforded by omniscient narration, has long been central to accounts of the nineteenth-century realist novel. In these accounts, readers might through their imaginative engagement with fictional characters, who themselves often engage in acts of sympathy within the novel, better imagine and sympathize with the lives of others in the world. Documenting the centrality of sympathy in diverse strands of Victorian thought, structuring ways of thinking about social reform, friendship, marriage, national bonds, ethics, relations between rich and poor, and more, has been one of the most productive critical projects of the past two decades, and sympathy has been one of the key terms in critical accounts of the novel's social effects and purpose.[36]

The signal place of sympathy in critical thinking about the Victorian period (in particular the novel), whether as a form of feeling, or in more recent work as an ambivalent structure of psychic identification and dis-identification, however, has eclipsed from view the forms of social relationality this book takes up, ones whose seeming negligible or ephemeral qualities place them outside sympathy's obvious purview. What the literature in this period discovers alongside sympathy, albeit in terms with little of the ethical purposiveness or psychic dramas of identification, is the power of thin social ties. Georg Simmel, an early theorist of weak social ties, writes of the bonds, thick and thin, that constitute social life:

> That people look at one another and are jealous of one another . . . that irrespective of all tangible interests they strike one another as pleasant or unpleasant . . . that gratitude for altruistic acts makes for inseparable union; that one asks another man for a certain street, and that people dress and adorn themselves for one another—the whole gamut of relations that play from one person to another and that may be momentary or permanent, conscious or unconscious, ephemeral or of grave consequence . . . all these incessantly tie men together. . . . They account for all the toughness and elasticity, all the color and consistency of social life, that is so striking and yet so mysterious.[37]

Simmel's nearly Dickensian narrative style here—the connections this passage traces between the grand (altruistic acts) and the trivial (asking for directions) are evocative of *Bleak House*'s famed opening, in which smoke, mud, soot, and fog make horses, dogs, and humans nearly indistinguishable from one another—emphasizes the clash of registers that make social life for Simmel "so striking and yet so mysterious." While a "general infection of ill temper" is what connects, and keeps aloof, "tens of thousands of foot passengers" on the muddy London street in the opening of *Bleak House*, Simmel locates the social bonds as much in the "momentary" and the "ephemeral" as he does in more enduring states, in tempers and looks singular or evanescent as much as general. *Bleak House*, of course, is frequently instanced as an example of the realist novel's own sociological ambitions, and it poses its own sociological question about the nature of affiliation, as well as about links between the grand and the ostensibly trivial: "What connexion can there have been between many people in the innumerable histories of this world who from opposite sides of great gulfs have, nevertheless, been very curiously brought together!"[38] *Bleak House* itself—its lengthy unfolding of its plot, and its vast set of characters who, by novel's end, have been revealed to be not simply a set, but a densely interconnected network of social affiliation—is the long answer to the book's own question about "connexion." What is significant here is the difference between Simmel's sociological account of the importance of weak, ephemeral social ties and Dickens's novelistic account of enduring "connexion," of ties that inevitably thicken. Pace Simmel, we would conclude from the lessons of sympathy, and of the novel as we have learned to read it under sympathy's guidance, is that no affiliation worth its name—or its narration—is merely ephemeral, simply the work of a moment and no more. To narrate, to tell any story at all in this account, is to trace out the mysterious yet enduring and consequential threads of "connexions" that constitute the novel.

A second scene, Omnibus from Dickens's early career work, *Sketches by Boz*. "Omnibus" affords a quite different scene of strangers than that of *The Woman in White*. In this sketch, Dickens's mouthpiece Boz is complaining about the forced long-term social intimacy of riding in a stagecoach, in which "the same people go all the way with you—there is no change, no variety" and "on smooth roads people frequently get prosy, and tell long stories."[39] Crammed into a tight space for a long period with strangers one will never see again, Boz here might be glad for the contracts—explicit and tacit—for leaving one another alone that are illuminated by Wilkie Collins and Erving Goffman. By contrast with the stagecoach, however, the more capacious omnibus with its shorter routes has "none of these afflictions." Being too loud to speak in and having a constantly changing cast of passengers, "sameness there can never be. The passengers change as often in the course of one journey as the figures in a kaleidoscope, and though not so glittering, are far more amusing."[40] The transient pleasures of the omnibus—a set of amusing and varied characters tumbling through a public transit kaleidoscope—are recognizably those of Dickensian narrative itself, though the image of a tumbling kaleidoscope emphasizes variety of character, rather than narrative momentum. Transience, however, renders even fictional character in these short sketches a murky category. A roving narrator amidst a changing scene ("sameness there can never be"): neither Boz nor the scene remain still long enough to let those who enter his field of vision to sediment into full-blown novelistic characters, with each remaining a passing fragment.

A number of people who ride the omnibus in this sketch appear to hover just on the outer edge of what we might call proper character-hood: "four or five of our party are regular passengers. We always take them up at the same places, and they generally occupy the same seats; they are always dressed in the same manner, and invariably discuss the same topics."[41] The unnamed, only semi-specified regulars (four or five) on the omnibus reliably resemble themselves day in and day out, as if by clockwork, repeating their dress, their choice of seat. But, they also resemble one another; their conversations are always the same, and they are not even differentiated from one another within Boz's narration. Viewed from the vantage of Dickens's later career as the novelist he would become, however, we can see that the barely outlined regulars in this sketch, who loiter on the outer edge of character-hood, will eventually be given stories, transformed into novelistic characters as Dickens becomes able to fold them into the long-form temporal structures and narrative arc of the novel. And yet, still bearing the traces of the habitual sameness that defines them as underspecified figures in the sketch, in the novels their repetitions on the omnibus will be not so much left behind as transformed into tics, unshakable habits of speech and gesture. Here in the sketches we find the embryonic form of those innumerable, flat, vibrating minor characters amidst whom Dickens will later place his novelistic protagonists.

While the piece begins with Boz's preference for the omnibus's kaleidoscopic variety and ceaseless change, what most interests the narrative as it goes on are the pleasures not of endless kaleidoscopic change, but the more modest ones of everyday familiarity. The good-humored satisfaction found in this scene is in the daily riders' reliable sameness, their "routines." Here, we might think of routines in the sense of daily habits but also in the theatrical sense of a regular performance on a social stage, like a comedy routine, with shows every weekday morning and evening.[42] When a regular rider does emerge as a more distinctive, which is to say quasi-novelistic, character, from this little daily scene of sameness—here "a little testy old man, with a powdered head"—even his distinguishing qualities are those of repetition: always sitting on the right-hand side of the bus, and "every morning" demanding of the driver, "'Now, what are you stopping for?'" the moment the bus begins to pull up at a corner.

Distinctive and yet regular: Dickens's man in the powdered wig instances an uncanny, and distinctly novelistic, play between particularity and representativeness. The scene bears the mark of a mode of novelistic narrative that Gerard Genette calls "the pseudo-iterative." Discussing Proust, Genette writes that the "pseudo-iterative" occurs in "scenes presented . . . as iterative (i.e. when the narrative recounts only once something that has happened repeatedly), whereas their richness and precision of detail ensure that no reader can seriously believe they occur and reoccur in that manner, several times, without any variation."[43] The pseudo-iterative is thus a narrative means of producing the illusion of repetitive everydayness, but by way of a scene that is descriptively exceptional, even impossibly singular: all the eccentricity of the man in the powdered wig, but set on "repeat." The richly textured and particularized rendition of what happens all the time—the everyday—is one of the realist novel's special talents, of course. And, to endow the everyday with coherence and meaning, to create what Franco Moretti calls "*a culture of everyday life*" (as against a world historical culture, or a critique of everyday life), is one of the novel's contributions to bourgeois ideology in the nineteenth century.[44] With the novel as the engine of the everyday, and in turn, the novel's remaking of the everyday into something narratively interesting, the pseudo-iterative aspect of narrative comes to look less like a somewhat esoteric narrative mode native to Proust, and more like the kernel of the novelistic itself. The modern stranger's own emergence in the nineteenth century as a phenomenon that is both singular and everyday suggests a particular historical relationship, then, to the emergence of the novelistic. The stranger is the bearer of a representativeness or generality that would seem to beg figuration within a literary genre, the realist novel, that is dedicated to depicting ordinary life as ordinary. At the same time, this constitutive generality or ordinariness is threatened by the specifying effects of narration, which necessarily obliterates the ordinariness of the ordinary by narrating those events as singular and meaningful, as unordinary. The stranger might be thought of as a sort of test case or productive problem for narration, then, one for which narrative mechanisms such as the pseudo-iterative evolve in order for the novel to be able to figure the particular texture—utterly ordinary, utterly new—of "a society of strangers."

The omnibus itself is recognizably a vehicle (as it were) for Dickens's incipient novelistic aspirations. It is a scale-model version of the highly evolved and large-scale forms of nearly endless variety and fascinating repetition that will later typify those vast numbers of minor characters who come to populate his novels. The contained qualities of the omnibus, however, with just enough passengers to discourage any conversations but those that are repeated every day, also keeps in check a multitudinous social scene that elsewhere in Dickens appears frequently as a profusion of people and of detail that nearly overwhelms its observer. Whatever the adequacy of the capacity of the omnibus to the actual number of passengers it would pick up on its route, it lends to the everyday a scale and scope precisely suited to Bozian narration.

In other moments in *Sketches by Boz*, the observer who strolls the streets of London, rather than riding along them in the "Omnibus" essay, registers the stress of bringing into semi-fictional representation the vast quantity of sensory observations presented by London's varied, crowded scenes, scenes that are always on the edge of engulfing him. So, "Greenwich Fair":

> The road to Greenwich during the whole of Easter Monday, is in a state of perpetual bustle and noise. Cabs, hackney-coaches, "shay" carts, coal-wagons, stages, omnibuses, sociables, gigs, donkey-chaises—all crammed with people (for the question is never, what the horse can draw, but what the vehicle will hold), roll along at their utmost speed; the dust flies in clouds, ginger beer corks go off in volleys, the balcony of every public house is crowded with people, smoking and drinking, half the private houses are turned into tea-shops, fiddles are in great request.[45]

The novels that follow *Sketches* and Dickens's other early work, *The Pickwick Papers*, develop a now-familiar set of fictional strategies for contending with the social and sensory multiplicity that nearly overwhelms the observer at Greenwich Fair, who can just barely keep up with what he sees, and who does so only by way of throwing his syntax and punctuation out the window.

London's vastness, its array and crowds of sites and people, as Alex Woloch has argued, is the social ground for the development in Dickens's novels of forms of characterization and narrative interest that can both encompass, and manage, this plurality. It is through the turns to the peculiar and the eccentric in characters and sights, Woloch suggests, that Dickens can focalize such scenes of sensory abundance, a narrator's interest in only the most singular people and things allowing him to encompass an overwhelming field of sensory data without being engulfed by it.[46] Dickens's style, his eye for something like the "typically" anomalous, and the large cast of eccentrics that populate his fiction, can be seen as representational strategies generated out of the too-much-ness of London's visual and sensory field, strategies aimed at better managing those fields into fiction.

What makes the omnibus sketch particularly interesting then, is its difference from the overwhelming sensory overload of "Greenwich Fair," as well as its difference from the attractions to eccentricity that enable the Dickens observer-narrator to focalize social fields that might otherwise prove too much to handle. With its "kaleidoscope of characters," the London omnibus is a vivid anticipatory emblem of the densely crowded novels Dickens would go on to write. This sense is reinforced by Boz who, after sketching out the numerous regulars who populate the bus daily, pauses to consider the bus's maximum capacity, as if contemplating Dickens's future talents for bringing throngs of characters into the novel. "We are not aware that it has ever been precisely ascertained, how many passengers our omnibus will contain."[47] However, unlike "Greenwich Fair," on one hand, and the stagecoach, on the other, the omnibus's social scene is neither a deluge of social activity that generates a compensatory condensation into vivid eccentricity, nor does it present the terrors of confinement and what we might call "uncivil attention" with only a few other passengers on a long road. While "Greenwich Fair" recognizably prefigures the thrills of being nearly engulfed, as well as the compensatory (and thrilling) attraction to eccentricity in narrative and characterization, without which we would not have novels to come like *Bleak House*, it is also worth noting that no such thrills and compensations are to be found in the "Omnibus." Instead, the omnibus, far from bursting at the seams of its unascertained capacity, seemingly carries exactly the number of people precisely suited to the representational capacities of the narrator-observer. The omnibus contains just enough people, just enough eccentricity (the testy old man with the powdered head), and characters lightly particularized enough to be handled without overwhelming either Boz or his narration. And, on the other side, it does not contain so few people as to generate an uncomfortable proximity to a stagecoach's eccentricity and suffocating social propinquity, nor does it carry numbers small enough to necessitate more distinctive characterization. More than a handful, but not so many that Boz could not recognize all the regulars with a quick glance.

This is another way of noticing that "Omnibus" presents, in a condensed urban form, a social and fictional field recognizable from that precursor to the realist novel, the picaresque: episodic narratives of characters who meet one another along some travels, then drift apart, only to meet again later on. The picaresque, placid and neutral with its "network of pleasant, unproblematic episodes," brings into being a historically new social space, what Franco Moretti has called with reference to the nation-state, the "new space of 'familiarity', where human beings recognize each other as members of the same wide group, serenely, and without tragedies."[48] Moretti refers here to the novel's relation to national space, its symbolic function of making the geographic boundaries of nations and cities imaginatively available to its readers. But "the space of familiarity" also usefully describes the semi-self-contained space and feel of "Omnibus," a recurring single episode of the picaresque that, if not quite placid and entirely unproblematic (the complaining man with the powdered hair), is nonetheless reliable and unchanging. Bearing just enough interest to gain some narrative traction through the regular complaints of the powder-headed man, it nevertheless does not present a multiplicity that would outstrip or pressure Boz's observations with a superabundance of detail or characters. Rather than passengers who get "prosy" in a stagecoach and so overtake Boz's own story, the omnibus's passengers repeat their same mild complaints about the bus, concurring in those complaints. Through their griping, they offer just enough attentiveness to one another to make it a space not overcrowded, but rather comfortably familiar.

In the picaresque's instantiation in "Omnibus," the space of the familiar is also characterized as necessarily made out of evanescence, out of social relations neither too brief or insubstantial to be unnoticed nor so durable or specified as to grow into prolonged intimacy. In Erving Goffman's words, it is the space of temporary social gatherings, which are "created by arrivals and killed by departures." But, on Boz's omnibus anyway, this space is also carefully calibrated as to just how many departures and arrivals can bend but not break this zone of familiarity. "It is rather remarkable, that the people already in an omnibus, always look at newcomers, as if they entertained some undefined idea that they have no business to come in at all."[49] Strictly regulated as to numbers, at least in this case, the familiar constitutes a social sphere both on the omnibus and of the picaresque. But the familiar also bears with it a sign of the made-to-measure fit between the number of people who inhabit that fictive space and its representation, neither too much nor too little, not only for the bus's regular riders who are there every day but also for the sketch's narration. What so suits Boz about the omnibus, and so suits Boz's narrative capacities, is the pitch-perfect number of people who make up its social sphere. The time it takes to ride an omnibus on the morning commute, its amusingly regular riders, the just-right proportion of mild conflict, the just-right number of people/characters: all of it is tailor-made for the sensibilities, the observational capacities, and the representational resources of a sketch by Boz.

In the allegory of Dickens's career I have suggested this passage encourages, however, the hostility of the omnibus's picaresque characters to newcomers suggests something like a small-scale resistance to their future: their transformation, over the course of Dickens's career, from inhabitants of the right-sized familiar space of the picaresque into citizen-characters of the far more geographically expansive and, importantly, far more heavily populated, narratives of Dickens's later multi-plot novels. As if fearful of the future bag of novelistic tricks by which the social plenitude of London will be squeezed by Dickens into narrative, the few characters who make up the carefully calibrated, familiar populace of the omnibus stare down newcomers, as if an increase in ridership might tip familiarity into something less unproblematic and pleasant—a story of unforeseen "connexion" for example. That is, into full-blown novelistic narrative itself, in which plot necessarily intertwines into consequential social relations those who in "Omnibus"—licensed by the pre-novelistic freedom granted by the picaresque—can remain endlessly civilly inattentive to one another, endlessly just shy of becoming familiars. While it is true that the episodic energies of the picaresque continue to find their way into Dickens's novels, even as those works are built around anti-picaresque, complex, enduring social networks, "Omnibus" shadows forth the appeals of narrative forms that are less staked to plot, less built around the almost ruthless inevitability of social convergence and consequential "connexion."

The space of familiarity constituted on and through "Omnibus," its minimal and just-right equilibrium of social engagement, scale, and narrative figuration, bears comparison to a condition Roland Barthes investigated in a late seminar as "the Neutral." Barthes's seminar is a meditation on in-between states or principles, experiential categories or conditions that "parry paradigms" as Barthes says, but decline to become systematic or affirmative. The Neutral finds expression in a multifarious set of sites ("twinklings" in Barthes's terms), ranging from values or practices such as benevolence, to activities such as tea ceremonies and sleep, to discourses such as fashion, as well as properties of discourse, above all "the neuter." Barthes's subject, as well as the organization of the seminar (e.g., "twinklings"), is languidly unsystematic, its ethos one of declining—declining to arrange, to systematize, to provide a rationale—but without negating.

Many versions of Barthes's Neutral find expression in specific modes of attention, as well as the affects and practices of social tact. Given how far apart they are in their disciplinary and philosophical orientations, however, Barthes's Neutral shows surprising overlaps with Erving Goffman's own interest in the neutral—both as a quality of his descriptivist methods, simply recording what he sees, as well as the neutralizing qualities of "civil inattention," and the evanescent encounters of groups. As if channeling Goffman's own field of the microsociology of public life, Barthes wonders at one point how "the Neutral" might find its expression within group social behavior in public. Not by keeping quiet, Barthes writes, since to do so would indicate one is *trying* to be silent in a pointed way, a firm sign of one's *refusing* to speak to others in public. Instead, Barthes suggests that as a form of sociality the Neutral might be practiced "by the minimal expenditure of a speech act meant to neutralize silence as a sign."[50] In Goffman's terms, such minimal forms of speech are "face work," the "tact" and "*savoir-faire*" by which those in public places signal appropriate levels of attention and a readiness to be engaged, neither too much nor too little, to the surrounding social group. While the forms of the Neutral are many, a number condense around affects or modes of sociality recognizably of a piece with the forms of stranger intimacy that are emblematic of modern life. The familiar as I have been discussing it here—as a social space, an affect, and even as a narrative mode—is allied with what Barthes describes as an "amorous state 'unhooked' from the desire-to-possess," a sociable desire he glosses as a "'familiarity singularly tinged with aloofness'."[51]

This state of unsocial sociability described by Barthes in the Neutral is one that becomes an important, if hard-to-place, feature of social experience and literary form in many of the works of the literature of social density in this study. This "familiarity singularly tinged with aloofness" usefully describes not just the space of "Omnibus," for example, but also Bozian narration's particular coordination of intimacy and detachment, its mixture of close-quartered curiosity and aloofness. More broadly in this study it also finds expression in the various urges to take one's leave of others, via civil inattention or the familiar's unsocial sociability, and in impulses to forms of intimacy at a distance, all of which are means of contending with the socially multitudinous landscapes of the modern world. By looking to an array of sociological thinkers, including Simmel and Goffman, for understandings of the comfort of strangers that are leagued with the Neutral, in uneven ways for certain, this book suggests that what Barthes describes transhistorically as the Neutral, has a particular historical ground in the social and literary forms of Victorian modernity. The forms of social evanescence or sociable antisociality Barthes associates with the Neutral are, like the sketch by Boz, a way of navigating the newly crowded social sphere of the nineteenth century.

What Barthes brings to the set of sociological thinkers I draw upon to think about these forms in literary texts is a more manifest sense of the felt qualities or affective dimensions of the thin social ties of the modern world. Part of my hope in this book is to make the case not only for the distinctiveness of the literature of social density as a discrete thread running through nineteenth-century literature, one found even in the works most associated with the ethos of sympathy with which it is at an oblique angel. It also is to make the case for both Simmel and Goffman as being especially attuned to the affective features of modern sociality and of social form itself, even to the pleasures afforded by the impersonal, transient, or thin social formations that emerge as a regular feature of modern life. As I discussed earlier, while society is usually in the nineteenth century valued only as a means to an end, such as sympathy, in the literature of social density, taking to the stranger-filled streets can be an end in itself, an autonomous social pleasure. It this pleasure that Georg Simmel ascribes to "sociability" in his description of it as the "play form of association," a "feeling for, . . . a satisfaction in, the very fact that one is associated with others." Sociability, a practice to which this work will have occasion to turn to frequently in the pages ahead, is thus a sociological version of the aloof familiarity Barthes finds figured by the Neutral.[52] In turning to social modes that are barely recognizable as such, it might seem this book is about a falling away of sociality proper, its diminishment under an increasingly "impersonal" world. Instead, the forms of social life I find in these works, at times fugitive or ephemeral, index a counter-movement to the privatizing and domestic trajectories of romantic and family plots. Moreover, in sociability we find something like sociality's autonomization, its emergence as its own ecology or "system." While most social interactions bear some consequential weight, however minimal, in sociability as Simmel describes it, one "plays" society. In the "game" of sociability, social interactions "lead their own lives; they are propelled exclusively by their own attraction." It is a sociality without issue.[53] Part of the story told in this book, then, is about the effects of this social autonomization upon literary form generally, and the novelistic in particular, especially upon the novel's structural orientation toward conscripting every social encounter into plot-producing ends, producing significant "connexion" out of the briefest of encounters.

The weapons-of-the-weak resistance put up by those who ride Dickens's "Omnibus," chaffing as if dimly aware of their future generic relocation from the sphere of the picaresque familiar into the more crowded, impersonal social climes of the triple-decker-novel, marks the familiar's awkward fit with the longer form narrative of the novel. To be transposed as a character from the omnibus of *Sketches by Boz* to say, *Bleak House*, is to leave behind the sketch's picaresque-style forms of friable social attachments, in which characters might meet, drift away, and then meet again "unproblematically." That is, it is to be introduced into novelistic narrative, novelistic characterization, the formal demand that every social interaction bear narrative significance: what George Eliot's *Middlemarch* describes as—a far cry from the unencumbered comings and goings of the riders of Dickens's "Omnibus"—"the stealthy convergence of human lots."

The familiar as I have sketched it here is a more affirmative condition or space than Barthes's Neutral. But Barthes's description of modes of experience, including social experience, that are in between, evanescent, or that decline to become fully articulated as a social experience underscore the ways in which sociality itself is transformed in the works I study. They instance, for example, social experiences that only appear as an effect of, or are realized through, literary form; or modes of social experience that fall just short of being properly a narratable subject. It is in this overlap between Goffman and Barthes—Goffman, the theorist of the Empire of the Little that constitutes the most minimal of social interactions, and Barthes, the theorist of the Empire of Signs—that this book wants to stake some of its territory. Bringing into view in-between experiences of the social, I show how literary forms such as the narrative technique of free indirect style, in the case of *Middlemarch* and Henry James, and the epigram in the case of Wilde, themselves become the site of an identification with, or yearning for, such social experiences that take their shape from or within literary form.

A third scene: not too far into the novel, Esther Summerson of Dickens's *Bleak House* finds herself in a coach not unlike the one so bitterly foresworn as socially claustrophobic by Boz. By the logic of the sketch, in Boz's complaint, the stagecoach's forced social propinquity with a prosy person threatens a kind of anti-picaresque: a stranger who will not freely, unproblematically drift away. Two can be a crowd, it seems. Esther, bound to Reading in a coach shared with a stranger, leaving Windsor for the first time to attend a school paid for by the mysterious, as yet unmet John Jarndyce: "There was a gentleman in the coach who sat on the opposite seat . . . but he sat gazing out the window and took no notice of me." Until, suddenly, "a voice in the coach gave me a terrible start. It said, 'What the devil are you crying for?'" Close enough to frighten, the stranger who speaks goes on to offer Esther cake, wipe her tears, and badger her with questions, until he then departs the coach at a milestone. Esther remarks, "I often walked past it afterwards, and never, for a long time, without thinking of him, and half expecting to meet him. But I never did; and so, as time went on, he passed out of my mind."[54]

Esther's ride seems to reiterate all of Boz's complaints about the stagecoach: trapped and frightened (rather than bored) with a stranger in the coach, Esther, like Boz's narratively shapeless "prosy" passenger, also identifies the stagecoach with a narrative dead end: "half expecting to meet him. But I never did." Two years on, however, Esther learns the lesson of the inevitability of social convergence that is taught by novelistic narrative: every social meeting becomes consequential, however minimally, for the plot or narrative. No one can remain a stranger long. And so, meeting her patron John Jarndyce for the first time, Esther feels she's met him before, finding herself recalled by his manner to "the gentleman in the stage-coach, six years ago. . . . I was certain it was he."[55] In the affiliative logic of novelistic narrative, strangers will always become intimates, the unknown turned into familiars. In Sharon Marcus's formulation, the novel is a machine that "turns strangers into kin."[56] The novel is often thought of as the literary form most suited to the figuration of the city, most able to accommodate the variety of discourses and complex plots, and most of all, the social multiplicity and density associated with urban spaces and the strangers that comprise them. It is startling, then, to recognize that as novelistic material, *strangers are reluctant to be narrated*. They are hard to enfold into a plot without making them known, transforming them into kin and character, and so immediately draining them of their anonymity. Draining them, that is to say, of the very socially under-conditioned qualities that make them strangers. The novelistic equivalent of a subatomic particle being displaced by its observation, strangers would seem to disappear the moment a novel takes notice of them. They are, paradoxically, at once an almost routine figure of modernity and the Heisenberg Uncertainty Principle of novelistic narrative. Even in the novel theory of Georg Lukács, for whom the realist novel is a kind of narrativized sociology, one singularly able to trace out the invisible, complex social networks and institutional histories that shape life in the modern era, novels that depict the "transient" relations of strangers, characters who "appear suddenly and just as suddenly disappear" are dismissed as "superficial."[57] Strangers, a privileged figure of analysis in the classical social theory of Simmel, mark a failure of the novel to be sociological for Lukács. In their dual instantiation of a social experience emblematic of modernity and their resistance to narration, strangers thus figure the outer edge of the novel's field of sociological vision in Lukács's theory.

Similarly, there would seem to be little place in novelistic logic for the familiar in the sense we have gleaned from Boz's "Omnibus" either, which itself depends upon a kind of cyclically minimalist narrative. Things happen in "Omnibus," but they are reiterations of what has happened before, and so bear less narrative interest than the charm of a social ceremony. Thus, plot and the familiar are interestingly at odds with one another. The unproblematic, neutral forms of attachment and letting go associated with this sketch by Boz and with the picaresque are pressed into the consequentiality, "significant form," and chronological movement, of narrative in the novel.

This set of works, none of them in any strict sense picaresque, nonetheless are exemplary in bearing a certain pre-novelistic yearning for "the familiar" that is brought into being and sustained by the picaresque, a mode largely eclipsed in the era of the multi-plot realist novel. In some respects, then, the kinds of social experience this book argues are central to emergent nineteenth-century understandings of the social have to be sought out in unlikely places within these works. While it is the case, for example, that the essays of Matthew Arnold's *Culture and Anarchy* are deeply concerned with the problems of social order and the threats posed by the anarchic energies of the crowd, if we turn to his poetry, we find figured forth a lyric intimacy that unexpectedly depends upon the presence of the collectivity of the crowd. Similarly, Oscar Wilde's antisocial sociability might be hard to recognize amidst the social vivacity of his characters, who never turn down an invitation to a good party. In the chapter on Wilde, then, I turn not to character or to narrative, but to

the epigram, Wilde's short and sharp rhetorical form, to show how social evanescence becomes the basis for Wildean freedom. To understand the felt force
of society in these works, to be able to find the forms of impersonal intimacy
loosely tied to the familiar and the neutral, I have taken approaches to reading
that at times might feel oblique or even perverse, though I hope productively
so, favoring moments when plot slows down amidst a narrative pause or disruption in a novel, for example; or reading *Middlemarch* as a novel that wants
us to lose interest in its protagonist. Such an approach is necessary precisely
because stranger sociality is frequently at odds with the very literary forms
in which it appears—strangers who resist their transformation into familiars,
within the novel, for example—their appearance often fugitive, visible only by
way of a passing glance or at an oblique angle.

One significant claim of this book is that the weak social ties instanced
by strangers also index an aspiration toward social knowledge in these
works: the unknown, detached stranger as emblem both of the modern
anonymous social sphere and of the possibility of a reflective, insightful relation to that sphere. In this sense, the stranger is not just a favored subject of
sociology, but an emblem of sociological thought and its own aspiration to
be both within society and to take society as its object of knowledge. This
book is thus engaged with a recent set of arguments about Victorian projects of disinterestedness—the varied efforts to gain some reflective purchase
on the social field through the elaboration of modes of limited or partial
participation—in critical works as diverse as Amanda Anderson's recupera-
tion of knowledge projects under liberalism in *The Powers of Distance*, James
Buzard's study of anthropology and the novel in *Disorienting Fictions*, and
Andrew Miller's recent *The Burdens of Perfection*, a work that thinks through
the Victorian ideal of self-improvement.[58] Although each takes up distinctive
terms and arguments, these works all meditate upon the wish to know the
world that characterizes a number of nineteenth-century projects defined by
partial detachment from that world. Anderson argues, for example, that the
cultivation of distance and detachment as a means of getting some purchase
on one's own barriers to understanding, in order to then try to move beyond
them, is a distinctive Victorian project.

> An ideal of critical distance, itself deriving from the project of the
> Enlightenment, lies behind many Victorian aesthetic and intellectual proj-
> ects, including the emergent human sciences and allied projects of social
> reform; various ideals of cosmopolitanism and disinterestedness; literary
> forms such as omniscient realism and dramatic monologue.[59]

The Comfort of Strangers is similarly interested in the forms of partial detachment or participation at a remove that Anderson's work has recently opened
up. The sociable forms of antisociality that I trace across a set of works are

particularly resonant sites of the "powers of distance." Where Anderson's work unfolds a more or less consciously undertaken set of projects and practices, or purposefully cultivated stances, of distance, however, I find less programmatic strains of distance, as well as ones that are more affectively felt than consciously cultivated. In related terms, Elaine Hadley's recent work on "cognitive detachment" and the lived experience and ambivalences of mid-Victorian liberalism, overlaps historically with the period this book focuses upon. "Disinterest, reserve, objectivity," Hadley writes, are the crucial terms under which Victorian subjects sought to develop reflective practices, but she traces in particular the wish "to mobilize them in the social world as modalities of embodied living." While Hadley emphasizes experience in ways consonant with my own interests, what she calls "the affect of rationality," her focus on the formalization of mental activity and rationality describes a far more programmatic and mental set of practices than the social affects and concerns I identify in these works, a difference reflected in our respective turns to political thought and sociology.[60] Distance, I show, takes some of its charge, finds its appeal in the Victorian world, not only in conscious ethical programs but also in its felt experience.[61] Distance and detachment may well carry their most powerful attractions, and their most powerful projects of knowing, when unanticipated—not cultivated but carried by the contingent relations of strangers. If the critical works just mentioned each give the systems-loving Victorians their due in reconstructing and articulating the "powers of distance" or cultivated detachment as projects, as at least plausibly consistent, even systematic approaches, the transient or collective forms of social life I find here necessarily fall to the side of such systemic understandings. Instead, they suggest such aspirations might also find complementary articulation or figuration in less codified, less recognizable or enduring, sites and moments.

Where some of the most compelling recent critical work in the field seeks to enfold literature within practices of nineteenth-century scientific discourses that promoted distanced views of the social, I show these works to be imprinted—thematically, but also formally—by the slow and uneven differentiation of literature and science from one another over the nineteenth century, a relation often characterized by productive friction as well as by continuity.[62] The story I tell here is also distinct from arguments that make claims about the demonstrable direct influence of individual sociological thinkers upon particular authors, as has been profitably undertaken by others who work in the nineteenth century.[63] Placing literary works in proximity to sociological thought—including the early forms of nineteenth-century sociology as I do in the chapter on Arnold—allows me to show how literary forms and other practices of social observation and representation mutually shaped one another. This helps bring into view Victorian literary texts' specification of their representational claims both alongside and against those of emergent sociological practices. My first chapter, on Matthew Arnold, is most explicitly engaged with how emergent sociological thought presents a challenge to the claims of literary culture to social explanation. But I also trace out more obliquely agonistic moments in George Eliot's *Middlemarch*, in which sociological ways of observing are disabling to individual characters, even as they are a constitutive aspect of realist narrative. When Mary Poovey writes that "the conventions of literature elevated individualizing narratives over the kind of aggregation used in government blue books" in the nineteenth century, she places the presumptively individuating effects of literary form in opposition to the abstractions of sociological thought.[64] Yet, literary form and sociology have a historically and intellectually complex and uneven relation both in the nineteenth century and beyond, one captured neither by complementarity nor friction alone, but by their interaction. Moreover, the appeals of or aspirations toward social experiences broader than the individual continue to energize literary genres that are historically allied with individualizing narratives, such as the novel. Instead of excavating from these works the varied traces or prefigurations of largely empiricist British proto-sociological practices—parliamentary blue books, narratives of social investigation, and the rise of social statistics, to name only a few—this book asks more broadly how literary form is shaped by the concerns that would eventually come to occupy and define social theory, marking resemblances between literature and theory as well as bringing out what is distinctive about these literary modes of social apprehension and affect.

The way this project thinks about literature and sociology together bears a passing resemblance to a narrative technique of the realist novel itself. Like the novel's narrative mode of free indirect style—moments when an omniscient narrator draws so impossibly close to a fictional character as to speak in that character's interior voice, momentarily thinning out, but ultimately leaving intact, the barrier separating narrator from character—I draw literature and social theory together so as to underscore both their mutuality and their apartness. In fact, free indirect style plays an unexpectedly central role in both this book's methodology and its account of attenuated forms of social experience or relations. I say unexpectedly in part because this book is not strictly a study of the novel, although its interests in the social analysis borne by literary form, the ways in which literary form and social experience are bound up together, even when thinking about, say, the essays of Henry James, are arguably novelistic. And unexpectedly because this book's attempt to give a historical account of sociology and literary form together is in the end one that has self-consciously thinned out those historical claims, not casting realism as sociology's more sensitive, more emotional twin in the nineteenth century, with the two developing and deforming one another hand in hand. This book instead takes up some of the concerns of a group of social theorists in order to stage a set of engagements with literary texts under the broad rubrics of modernity and the literature of social density. However, it does so with a sense both of how close literary form and sociology come, as well as their distinctiveness from one another, like the moments of attenuation and then separation between narrator and character in free indirect style.

Finally, free indirect style bears a particular relation to the concerns of this book because it is one of the nineteenth-century's most powerful technologies for combining social intimacy and distance. The close encounter between narrator and character in free indirect style, a narrative voice articulating the inward thoughts and experience of a character, is exemplary of a singularly novelistic social intimacy, as close as one could possibly be. Barred from ever truly crossing the barrier that divides them, narrator and speaker, story space and discourse space of the novel, in this narrative mode those who must remain apart are nonetheless brought together. They thus articulate, in what Ann Banfield calls free indirect style's "unspeakable sentences," social intimacies otherwise impossible in the worlds both within and outside the novel, intimacies that, in the end, often decline to actually become social. In this book's terms, they are also, in a sense, unlivable sentences.[65] In this way, free indirect discourse should also be understood as part of nineteenth-century considerations of properly calibrating distance and propinquity, social and mental intimacy, a key part of that century's liberal project as Amanda Anderson, Andrew Miller, and others have argued. As Adela Pinch suggests, with respect to a strain of nineteenth-century philosophy and literature that considers how the act of thinking about other people might actually produce effects, "one of the features of Victorian liberalism was a commitment to both the privacy *and* the sociability of mental life."[66]

While recent work in the field has tended to discover Victorian modernity in, say, commonalities between new technology such as the telegraph and omniscient novelistic narrative, this book argues that the very project of framing modernity—its social forms and structures—as a reflexive object of study and representation emerges in this period out of the interrelation between literary forms and sociological ways of knowing. Less abstractly, and in distinction from more materially historicist work, I bring together social theory and literary works in order to ask, as I said up front, what modernity feels like, to consider how the affective possibilities of modern stranger sociality shape, or strain, literary form. In my investment in a macroscopic set of governing terms (modernity, the social) taken from sociology, and in my interest in the relation of formal features of literary works to social complexity, I argue for a departure in Victorian studies from the superfine focus of more materialist approaches. By catching Victorian literary forms mid-stride, as it were, as they consider both their own relation to modern social life and the emergence of sociological thought that take this consideration as its own purview, I show that minor or transient forms of social affiliations point to these works' aspirations to social insight, as well as to ways in which literary form might be occasion and means for new articulations of social life, ways of speaking of the many rather than the one.

This book's first chapter, "Matthew Arnold's Crowd Management," traces out one early encounter between the claims of literary culture and emergent sociological thought. Its orientations are more historically specific than those of later chapters, which increasingly concern themselves with questions about social and literary form. What this first chapter endeavors to show, however, is how those historical encounters shape, or end up transmuted into allegory within, Arnold's poetry and his essays, not only in terms of subject matter but also formally. While eighteenth-century Britain had a famously vivid range of metaphors to hand for society—from Adam Smith's factory to Mandeville's bees to Hume's machine—Matthew Arnold's 1867 *Culture and Anarchy* narrows it to a single entity, the crowd, comprised of strangers *en masse*. Reading across genres, I show that in his poetry and essays Arnold elaborates a vision of the crowd as instancing not simply the terrifying dissolution of anarchy but also, in the proper managerial hands, an image and instrument of social order. Placing Arnold alongside Victorian debates about social science and literature in education, as well as early accounts of "the social," I show these practices' imprint upon Arnold's efforts to chart the manageability of modernity as it is embodied by the crowd. While early sociology identified the crowd as an instance of the aggregate social life that was its scientific object, culture alone, Arnold suggests, could speak to the "vast fermenting mind of the nation." Crowds drift across Arnold's poems—where the affect of anonymity offered by the crowd becomes the condition for intimacy between the lyric pair, an erotic of impersonality—and into his essays, appearing as both anarchic and as the site of culture's ameliorative effects. Importantly, it is as a singular site of public and impersonal sociality that the crowd underwrites Arnold's attempt to chart a middle ground for culture itself, one not liable to charges of mere inward aesthetic self-involvement, nor allied with the stultifying "machinery" of state institutions. Amidst emergent understandings of society as a "system," characterized by statistical regularities, the volatile energies of the anarchic crowd might be marshaled by culture into a re-enchanted social realm that escapes the enervation Arnold associates with rationalization.

This first chapter is the one most engaged with the historical relationship between early sociological thought and literature, and is intended to ground one early moment in an ongoing relation between literary form, literary criticism, and sociology. This account of the relation between criticism and sociological thought is bookended by my final chapter, which turns to an inaugural moment in the history of novel criticism in the work of Henry James, considering how social form becomes a preoccupation for literary critical practices. These two chapters, in particular, provide early coordinates for a range of recent sociologically inflected projects in literary study, ranging from practices such as "surface reading" that take their methods from Goffman's descriptive sociology, to contemporary work in the sociology of literature and literary institutions.[67]

My second chapter extends the opening chapter's concern with the literary form most appropriate to managing multitudes by turning to a novel of provincial life. "Losing Interest in George Eliot" takes up the implicitly sociological premise of the realist multi-plot novel: to transform social complexity into lucidity through fictional narratives of unlikely social convergences. Strangers, yes, but not for long, the novelistic plot promises. I show that *Middlemarch*, for all of its sociological specificity, is as much preoccupied with registering within its pages forms of social experience energized not by their specificity, their attachment to a single other person, but by their generality. This preoccupation becomes visible, among other sites, in its narration's effort to lose interest in its protagonist and attend to everyone who is not Dorothea. *Middlemarch*'s honorary status as historical sociology has underplayed a shaping tension for Eliot between sociological knowledge and novelistic narrative. Building my discussion around *Middlemarch*'s frequent narratorial pauses to reflect upon the interrelation of social and narrative structure—famously "the stealthy convergence of human lots"—I argue that Eliot's novel is shaped by a concern that novelistic plot might become indistinguishable from complex social structure.

Oscar Wilde marks the emergence of transient sociality as a full-fledged aesthetic project in the late nineteenth century and is the subject of my third chapter. Taking up the epigram, Wilde's miniature yet signal literary form, I show how what Wilde calls the "burden" of other people gives rise to innovative social and literary modes of deferring their claims. "All association must be quite voluntary," Wilde's edict goes, illuminating a wish to reconstitute society at the center of the responses to modernity I study. Although the epigram is often passed over even by Wilde's best critics as too slight or too embarrassingly catchy to bear critical weight, I show its function as a rhetorical crystallization of social transience, the means of inoculating the individual against the expansive forces of social determination Wilde's work registers so vividly. At the heart of the passing exchanges central to Wilde, the epigram is image and instrument of both engaging the social and evading the more enduring forms of social life, thus also offering an emblem of my book's intertwined formal and social concerns. Rather than dissolve social bonds altogether, however, Wilde's work posits forms of association drained of their obligatory dimensions. Wilde underscores aestheticism's affinity with what Georg Simmel terms "sociability," the "play form" of society and the epigram's unexpectedly socializing function. As socialphilic as it is socialphobic, the epigram renders artful and malleable a social imaginary otherwise crowded enough to elicit the remark that "other people are quite dreadful. The only possible society is oneself." By condensing social critique into a memorable one-liner, Wilde's epigrams are a retort to the maximalism of the Victorian novel, and vividly instantiate the aspiration to critical insight dwelling at the heart of Wildean social and formal promiscuity.

The book's final chapter finds Henry James once again smitten, sort of, this time not by London but by George Eliot, whose *Middlemarch* James memorably described in a review as "a treasure house of details but an indifferent whole," less a well-spun "web" than a "swarm" of characters. James's own novels often are read as a transitional node, a switch point between nineteenth-century realism's dramas of social convergence and the modernist novel's dramas of consciousness and phenomenology, one marking the ostensible waning of the novel's social imagination. This chapter, however, takes up James's essays on Eliot to bring out the sociable effects of realism's signature narrative technique, free indirect style, and its consequences for thinking about the novel in the century that follows. Where the preceding chapters examine the interrelation of aesthetic and social effects within a text, here I suggest that such effects might bleed into social relations conducted both through and alongside literary works. As a means of bringing close what can never touch—in a realist novel, the omniscient narrator and a character—the "impersonal intimacy" of free indirect style models for James a means of negotiating his relations with the novelist whose work he saw as rival to his own. James's silent, unmarked channeling of key vocabulary and syntax from *Middlemarch* within his review—a "free indirect critical style" that quietly assimilates Eliot's massive novel to the slim contours of his essay in the hope of reshaping it—also imagines the genre of the essay itself as a social space, a medium that is a site of collective authorship on a book already written but in need of "more form."

It is in his essays on Eliot that James begins to elaborate a vocabulary for novel criticism, one reliant upon the language of social form and manners to negotiate questions of aesthetic and social distance, the proper relation between critic and text, between intimacy and impersonality, immersive sympathy and critical coolness. "The way to become an acquaintance was first to become an intimate," a character remarks in James's *The Aspern Papers*—a story intensely concerned with the mediation of social relations by literary forms—unintentionally glossing James's two awkward, embarrassing visits to Eliot's home, visits after which James suggests the "sublimity" of his relation to Eliot increases the more it is conducted through her books. Fiction and writing about fiction become valued by James for the forms of social life and social distance they might sponsor, places of contact where the varieties of awkward social and novelistic mistakes might be given the coherence of the "social work of art" called sociability. In a brief Afterword, I consider in a more contemporary moment the afterlife of the comfort of strangers and the aesthetics of social maximalism, the wish to figure not just anyone but everyone.

While "society" is in Thomas Carlyle's 1831 proclamation "the standing wonder of our existence," with the invention of agoraphobia in the 1870s and the *fin de siècle* declaration by Oscar Wilde—"The only possible society is one-self"—things seem to have become a bit more crowded by century's end. That such declarations might not so much negate social relations as reconstitute them through transience itself, renovating sociality in the image of the flirtatious one-liners for which Wilde is so well-known, exemplifies the surprising social potentiality in the impersonal bonds of the comfort of strangers, bonds made newly legible by the literature and science of a crowded world. Put most succinctly, if paradoxically, this book argues that Oscar Wilde's room-clearing line is the beginning, not the end, of a beautiful relationship with others.

Matthew Arnold's Crowd Management

Through the length and breadth of our nation a sense,—vague and
obscure as yet,—of weariness with the old organisations . . . works
and grows. In the House of Commons the old organisations must
inevitably be most enduring and strongest, the transformation must
inevitably be longest in showing itself; and it may truly be averred,
therefore, that at the present juncture the centre of movement is
not in the House of Commons. It is in the fermenting mind of the
nation; and his is for the next twenty years the real influence who can
address himself to this.

—MATTHEW ARNOLD, *CULTURE AND ANARCHY* (1867-69)

The destinies of nations are elaborated at present in the heart of the
masses, and no longer in the councils of princes.

—GUSTAVE LE BON, *THE CROWD* (1896)

Gustave Le Bon declared in his 1896 text that the coming age was to be "The
Era of the Crowd." Matthew Arnold's own handbook to crowd control, *Culture
and Anarchy*, published in 1869, suggests however that Le Bon merely sensa-
tionalized elements already potent enough some thirty years earlier to occasion Arnold's polemic on behalf of culture. Energizing Arnold's claims that
through culture's opposition to and suppression of anarchy lies the way not
only to "perfection, but even to safety," "the era of the crowd" seems already
to have arrived by the 1860s. While Arnold's sloganeering on behalf of culture
produced such phrases as "the best that's been thought and said" and "sweetness and light," culture's presumptive antagonist, anarchy, has been a less
conspicuous part of Arnold's critical legacy. As the above passage indicates,
however, the power of the crowd figured by the mass "fermenting mind of the
nation" not only indicates some of the anxieties that might emerge around a
society of strangers, the crowd should rightfully be accorded a signal place in
reading *Culture and Anarchy*, a text whose own apocalyptic tones resonate in
the amplified echoes of Le Bon.[1]

The "monster procession" of the Reform League's demonstration for an
expanded franchise in July 1866, a demonstration that turned riotous after

police refused the league access to Hyde Park, inspired Arnold to revise the
initial title of his lecture, which was delivered a month prior to that demonstration, from "Culture and Its Enemies" to *Culture and Anarchy* upon
publication in book form in 1869.[2] Officially relegating the anarchic crowd
to a wound in the social body, Arnold insists that the "best self" of culture
enjoins us to set "our faces against" "whatever brings risk of tumult and disorder"—most egregiously, the "multitudinous processions in the streets of our
crowded towns" (*CA* 100). If these multitudinous meetings are to be put down,
as Arnold insists, by the soothing effects of "culture," however, the crowd duly
disperses, but does not quite disappear. Instead, in spite of a book intended to
castigate and expel it as anarchic, the crowd scatters, only to regroup. The collective character of the crowd is manifest not only in "monster processions,"
it also finds articulation in the men of culture who are "docile echoes of the
eternal voice, pliant organs of the infinite will," and our "best self" by which
"we are united, impersonal, at harmony" (*CA* 186, 99). Even as the crowd is
to be banished, Arnold acknowledges its governing power as a figure for the
social realm generally, the vast "fermenting mind" of the nation. Occupying
a "centre of movement" that cannot be ignored, the crowd's status as both
anarchy and the future of power for years to come impels in Arnold's work
figurative efflorescences of a social force that can be acknowledged officially
only in its suppression. While we will see the representational challenges and
opportunities that figuring the crowd presented for Arnold, the thickly populated Victorian social imaginary of a society of strangers appears in his work
initially and vividly as a political and social problem.

Arnold's well-known efforts to dispel the crowd in *Culture and Anarchy*,
however, also run the risk of eclipsing other, earlier crowd manifestations in
his work. While *Culture and Anarchy* is the site of the crowd's most infamous
gathering in Arnold's corpus, reading the poetry of the years prior to his critical writings reveals that Arnold's interest in crowds predates the Hyde Park
demonstrations, bearing a charge quite different from the anarchic multitudes
of his later essay. Although *Culture and Anarchy* is the site of Arnold's crowd
management in its official form, Arnold's poetry of the decades preceding his
critical work inaugurates an elaboration of an understanding of the crowd as
the manageable metonym of the social realm. The figurations of the crowd in
the poetry present a crucial alternative to the tumultuous social realm that
haunts *Culture and Anarchy*. Representing a vision of the crowd as other than
purely anarchic, these poems illuminate Arnold's earlier and ongoing negotiations with the challenges posed by the new social forces of modernity embodied by the crowd. The poems supplement by anticipating what I will argue
in this chapter is only a partial program for controlling the crowd's power
outlined in *Culture and Anarchy*. In other words, the rhetorical heights scaled
in that work reveal the urgency, but not the newness, of his project of crowd
management. Taken together, the different appearances and effects borne by

the crowd underscore the political, social, and representational challenges posed by new understandings of stranger society and social complexity. Men of culture, Arnold writes in his essay, must join in "repressing anarchy and disorder; because without order there can be no society, and without society there can be no perfection" (CA 181). Arnold enshrines culture in this text as the guardian of social order itself, a social order that is condensed by a chain of metonymic displacements into the figure of the managed crowd.[3]

Arnold was also only one of many in the mid-Victorian era seeking to develop critical practices aimed at managing a modern social order whose complexity took on fearsome aspects through such phenomena as the crowd. Arnold's proposals for crowd management, I will argue, should be read as being shaped by a variety of new mid-Victorian activities taking place under the general, emergent category of social science. These practices sought to develop a science for understanding, conceptualizing, and governing the structures of social order in the nineteenth century. Amidst a public sphere thought to no longer support the forms of sociability and rational debate that Jürgen Habermas famously identified in the eighteenth century, and in the drive to stake rival claims for the position of best guiding mid-Victorian society, of managing a modernity whose social complexity demanded an endless series of Blue Books, statistics, and government studies, Arnoldean criticism and proto-sociology both asserted respective ascendancy. The stranger-filled crowd, as Le Bon's and Arnold's texts indicate, served as one readily available figure for the challenges of social management to which social science and criticism were both responding.[4]

The curiously central place of the crowd in an essay written after the demise of the great English political movement identified with mass gatherings, Chartism, suggests that Arnoldean "crowd management" is responsive to more than the specific historical conditions of agitation for the mass franchise. If we understand the crowds of Culture and Anarchy within the conditions of a disciplinary contest between literary forms and nascent sociological practices, they can be seen to function in part as a placeholder for criticism's own quasi-social scientific aspirations. Reading Arnold's work with other nascent sociological efforts to understand and define the social realm as an object of inquiry and control will give some measure of the quasi-scientific work that non-scientific genres, such as poetry and the critical essay, aspired to in the mid-nineteenth century, and the arguments Arnold develops on their behalf. I turn to Arnold first in this book's discussion of the literature of social density then as the writer most consciously engaged with the emergence of proto-sociological thought in this period, particularly as it sought ways to specify and analyze the emergent domain of the social.

Claiming for the new "science of society" the power to both describe and prescribe how best to conduct life, sociologists such as Herbert Spencer and promoters of science in education such as T. H. Huxley explicitly took on

Arnold's claim of that status for the man of letters. In the drive to stake rival claims for the position of best guiding late Victorian society, literature and sociology both asserted respective ascendancy for "the man of letters" and the "man of science." But it was not only for the agents of culture and science that power was declared. Those agents also made claims of vast determining power for their respective objects, culture and "the social." By reading Arnold's crowds in the context of a nineteenth-century disciplinary contest between literature and sociology, we can see that "the age of the crowd" functions both as the acknowledgment of an expanding franchise and as a symptom of Arnold's effort to arrogate to the critical project of culture a power that was contemporaneously being ascribed to "the social" through a particular figure. This power, I will argue, is located not only by sociologists such as Durkheim and continental social psychologists but also by Arnold, in the common figure of the crowd. Traveling under the name of culture as well as anarchy in Arnold's work, I want to bring out a rhetorical slide with wider implications between the "multidinous" and "monster" "processions," the "forcible irruptions," that define the second term, and haunt the first, of the title of Arnold's *Culture and Anarchy*.

The consonance of the program of crowd control outlined in *Culture and Anarchy* and the crowd management of the poems suggests that they might be read together as unintended referents in Arnold's claim in his 1880 essay "The Study of Poetry," that "without poetry, our science will appear incomplete."[5] Arnold's claims for literature and criticism against the rising prestige of science and scientific thinking in the disciplinary developments of the nineteenth century are well-known, and his use of the word "science" frequently indicates simply objective, systematic study.[6] In this chapter, however, I want to read the "incomplete" science in Arnold's phrase specifically as an emergent nineteenth-century social science. Placing not only Arnold's critical work but also the poetry in the context of the burgeoning practices of social scientists in the nineteenth century shows that the boundaries of a disciplinary contest between criticism and nascent sociology extend beyond its most polemical sites in the essays and lectures by Arnold and various scientists. Such a contest takes place at the moment in which the disciplinary object of proto-sociological thinking, society, was only just beginning to be distinguished as a distinct subject of scientific inquiry. In addition, in Britain sociologist remains largely a "potential" role in the middle Victorian period, one tried on by a variety of disciplinary practices, including that of criticism, which sought to study and shape society. The early, incompletely differentiated state of the study of society thus set the stage for Arnold's contestation of this field of inquiry as he elaborates a new social role for criticism. A dream of social management coalesces in the figure of the crowd throughout Arnold's corpus, a dream that will be seen both to parallel and be shaped by English sociology's mid-century efforts to understand and guide the social sphere, and anticipate later continental theorists who took the crowd as their special object of study.[7]

Reading these efforts at social management together also revises some characterizations of British pre- or proto-sociology as largely uninterested in more theoretical questions of structure. Philip Abrams, for instance, argues that the incipient social science comprised in England by statistical research and ameliorist reform efforts, among other practices, lacked "any developed concept of a social system," or theorizations of social structure.[8] Similarly, Perry Anderson argues that while England developed a set of anthropological practices and discourses in the nineteenth century, because no political revolution ever impelled England to produce a "theory of its overall structure," it never produced a classical sociology of the sort that Durkheim and Weber developed.[9] And, seeking to understand the nature of social order and the phenomenon of social bonds through strict scientific methods, Herbert Spencer admits a faltering first epistemological challenge for scientists of the social realm: "the phenomena [to be examined by social science] are not of a directly-perceptible kind—cannot be noted by telescope and clock, like those of Astronomy."[10] The under-theorization of social structure and epistemological challenges of early British sociology, however, find a compensatory figuration in the manifestations of the crowd in Arnold's work as it takes on the metonymic function of representing a social totality amenable to the ministrations of culture.

Between the mid-1840s and the late 1860s, Arnold elaborates first in his poetry and then his prose a vision of the crowd as signifying not simply terrifying social dissolution, but also, in the proper hands, an image and instrument of social order—a society of strangers harmonized.[11] The metonymic chain by which society's dissolution is figured by the anarchic crowd in Culture and Anarchy is also reversible in the endless switchbacks and breathtaking turns of Arnold's prose style: the non-anarchic, pliable crowd also can function as a figure for a social realm amenable to the shaping powers of culture. Although the crowds in Culture and Anarchy have an actual, historical referent in the 1866 demonstrations of the Reform League, I trace here the modes by which the crowd in that text as well as the less historically specific crowds of the poems become figures, paradoxically, for both social order in general and its dissolution.[12] So, while much of Arnold's poetry was produced in the years around the 1848 revolutions across Europe, the crowds in the poems extend beyond any specific historical referents and become figures for a social sphere that is alternately repellant and alluring, chaotic and enervating. Through these poetic figurations, Arnold can suggest the transformative potential of the managed crowd, which the polemical critic of Culture and Anarchy must suppress as anarchic.

Arnold's later critical work also both continues and departs from the crowds of the poetry in developing the notion of culture, a structure that stands in opposition to the crowd, but also will be seen to be modeled by it.

The poetry's early figurations of the crowd complicate not only readings of *Culture and Anarchy*, which imagine the essay's two title terms as opposed, but also narratives that posit a sharp, clear turn from the personal to the public in Arnold's move away from writing poetry in the 1840s and 1850s to his critical prose of the 1860s and after. Instead, we can see the displacements and generic distinctions produced by Arnold's efforts to reformulate the crowds of his poems into the politically suspect crowds in his essays. In reading Arnold's poetry and critical essays with a proto-sociological background, I hope to show the mutual efforts of sociology and literary study in the mid-nineteenth century to chart the social complexity, and manageability, of modernity as it is embodied by the crowd. Only by reading the crowds of the poetry with both his critical prose and the work of early sociology can we begin to comprehend Arnold's contribution to the Victorian's incomplete efforts to conceptualize, study, and manage a social sphere that comes to seem at once binding and tenuous. At the same time, Arnold's own turn in his career away from the "private" poet to the "public" critic and schools inspector looks less like the story of a man shrugging off art for public duties. Instead, this turn from poetry to critical essay writing traces the migration of the private and intimate into the public sphere.

In Arnold's poems, we encounter versions of the crowd that are more oblique and less politically specific, as well as more openly alluring, than the eruptive Reform League demonstrators whose veiled appearance spurs the suppressive aspects of *Culture and Anarchy*. As one reads the crowd amid Arnold's poems and essays, its representational pliability becomes apparent. The crowd can one moment figure the site of anarchic social dissolution, the next an appealingly binding social order, a salve contained within the dispersive effects of modern life. As a figure for both social disorder and a spontaneously occurring harmony, anarchic explosiveness and a suffocating, enervating social realm, the crowd becomes a testing ground in Arnold for the power of culture to manage the challenges of social complexity in modernity. In the crowds of his poetry, we can then trace the effects that follow when elements of a "politically neutral" form like poetry, in Arnold's understanding, are carried over into the polemic of a more explicitly political form such as Arnold's essays. First, however, I want to make clearer both the crowd's availability as a figure for the Victorian social realm, and the conditions under which Arnold's work was affected by adjacent debates about the role of social scientific thinking.

Crowd Publics

While Arnold's *Culture and Anarchy* takes as its explicit mission the quelling of "doing as one likes" in favor of culture's "best self," by which we are "impersonal" and "at harmony," it does so under an explicit pressure from claims by social scientists and scientific advocates that culture is merely *belles-lettres* and incapable of guiding society. The figure of the crowd precipitates a certain parallel blurring between culture and anarchy, an anarchy that is allied with "the social," for reasons I will argue below. This blurring occurs in Arnold's work as a result of this disciplinary pressure, a blurring that I want to argue is less intentional than necessary, a sliding of figurative language, but importantly, an unacknowledged disciplinary deformation. My argument then allies itself neither with those accounts of Arnold which see his essay as positing culture as a complete rejection of the social, and in turn, of social transformation, such as Catherine Gallagher's in *The Industrial Reformation of English Fiction*, nor with those readings that discover in Arnold's culture an over-investment in the social benefits of the critical project, such as Christopher Baldick's *The Social Mission of English Criticism*.[13] Rather, I want to trace through the figure of the crowd the contradictory impulses toward privacy and publicity, the "inward operation" upon individuals and the public social mission, that Arnold tries to negotiate for culture in his work. What I would like to suggest is that it is through, rather than in opposition to, the crowd that Arnold can, if only imaginatively, achieve the mutual incorporation of inward growth and public benefit that he envisions for culture. The contradictory powers of a crowd that seems both to negate individual social relations altogether as anarchy, and instance a coercive power that comes to be called "the social," impel Arnold into the crowd even as he attempts to banish it.[14]

In negotiating a space for the effects of culture that is neither allied simply with individual *bildung* and privacy nor is beholden to the "machinery" of public politics proper, Arnold's aspirations are recognizably of a piece with some aspects of mid-nineteenth-century liberal political thought as it had been recently understood. In Elaine Hadley's reassessment of "lived liberalism," amidst a steadily increasing franchise the lived practice of liberalism attempted to formulate modes of government and thought that were less laissez-faire than a form of "engaged disengagement."[15] In her account of the mid-Victorian practices of abstraction and detachment she calls "liberal cognition," Hadley stresses the ambivalences of a liberalism that sought to preserve normative order amidst its valuation of individual eccentricity and play. "Liberal cognition" thus describes a region for thought somewhere in between the public and the purely personal. In Hadley's argument, such cognition carves out a space apart from a "fractious" public sphere, and thus is private but not domestic—a mental space of Arnoldian "free play" that also enables the movement of thought and feeling from the private to the public domain of lived experience.[16] Hadley's emphasis on lived experience and the "engaged disengagement" of liberalism resonates with the neutral or thinned out forms of unsocial sociability, forms of detachment within public spaces I ally with stranger intimacy in this book, though such forms are far less programmatic than the ideals of lived liberalism. However, in distinction from

Hadley's emphasis on individuation and cognitive practices amidst a tumultuous liberal public sphere both generally and in her account of Matthew Arnold's aesthetic liberalism specifically, I stress Arnold's submerged but ongoing investment in the collective and collectivizing powers of the crowd.

To read Arnold's crowds as anything but monstrous is to go against the grain not only of most understandings of Arnold but also of understandings of the public sphere in the nineteenth century. Generally depicted as either a nostalgic invocation of an unrealized eighteenth-century era of pure, rational conversation, or visible only through the withdrawal of affective investment from it or negative valences placed on it, the nineteenth-century public sphere would seem to be notable mostly for its absence.[17] Recent work on the public sphere, however, suggests an expansion beyond Habermas's eighteenth-century bourgeois public sphere of "rational critical debate" to include many types of cultural, political, and social forms that seek to make claims in public, including forms of protest in the nineteenth century.[18] Reading the crowd in the context of Arnold's claims of social efficacy on behalf of culture, a critical effort that imagines a public realm as the site for its effects, suggests that the crowd is a necessary if ambivalent figure in Arnold's project. The power accorded the mass mind by Arnold is in part an acknowledgment of a political ground shifting toward extra-parliamentary forms of power in the 1870s as a result of an expanding franchise. The crowd, as Eric Hobsbawm's work on the development of mass traditions such as large spectator sporting events indicates, was a rising political force to be reckoned with in the latter part of the nineteenth century, a force that required new modes of accounting for and harnessing its power.[19] As the embodiment of the movement of political power to extra-parliamentary forms in the late nineteenth century, the crowd crucially structures Arnold's argument for the centrality of culture, itself posited as an extra-parliamentary form of power that must appeal to the "fermenting mind."[20]

Any discussion of "the public," however, brings with it some attendant epistemological difficulties. By definition not locatable or reducible to any specific relationship or site, "the public" itself could be read as merely catachresis, a formation brought into being only as an imaginary point of reference rather than an empirical entity. The crowd, in its embodied and all-too-present anarchy, might then be thought of as the antithesis of "the public," and any effort to read them together as perverse. However, as shown by the nineteenth-century work on crowds by Le Bon along with other influential European theorists such as Hippolyte Taine and Gabriel Tarde, work that allies entities as various as parliament, juries, and riots with the crowd, the public and the crowd were not entirely distinct conceptual entities in this period. While not arguing for an identical relation between the crowd and the public, this chapter hopes to illuminate their congruity in theories of the public and the crowd in the nineteenth century and beyond.[21]

Arnold's crowds emerge as stand-in for a public unavailable to direct representation, a metonymic figuration of the social. For Arnold, those unknown, the strangers of a stranger, have to collectivize into the crowd as bearers of a social sphere at once violent and potentially revisable into the bearer of culture's effects, "the group as bearer of ideas."[22] Rather than recasting the social formation "the crowd" as "merely" figurative language, however, I want to maintain the contradictory nature of the crowd in this period, a contradictory nature that locates its dynamic in both anarchy and culture, sequestration and engagement, self-extension and self-extinction, social form and rhetorical figure. The unavailability of "the public" to representation—its phantasmagoric properties—and its resultant metonymization in the form of the crowd impels the inflection of "the public" as potentially dangerous, famously in Arnold's words, "meeting where it likes, bawling what it likes, breaking what it likes."[23] The crowd finds itself enlisted as a metonym for the public in Arnold's work as a means of announcing the dangerous tendency that public has toward anarchy, an excoriation of the public life too involved in "machinery" to be allowed the agent of culture. But the crowd is also deployed by Arnold as the necessary medium through which the positive effects of culture will be realized, the "fermenting mind of the nation," an instance of what Hadley calls the Victorian effort to embody liberal abstraction. While the man of culture's sole allotment of political activity is to stand against the "monster procession" and violent "irruptions" of the crowd in Arnold's essay, it regroups in a suffusion of his language of culture with its collective structure, uneasily figuring the public orientation of criticism's project.

Literature and Science

Arnold raised the issue of how culture could offer a prescriptive, as well as descriptive, function in society at precisely the moment that the incipient science of sociology was competing for that same role. Addressing the issue of criticism's social effects in his two essays, "The Function of Criticism at the Present Time" (1864) and "Literature and Science" (1882), Arnold seeks to defend the study of literature against the movement to install the "science of society" as the predominant guiding discipline for the nation. We can trace in some historical detail the mutual borrowings between sociology and literary study from the time of sociology's disciplinary formation in the latter half of the nineteenth century.[24] Arnold took part in what was a vigorous debate between himself and promoters of natural and social science such as T. H. Huxley and Herbert Spencer over the role of literature and sciences in education. Huxley began the debate in earnest with his 1880 lecture "Science and Culture." Using Arnold's own description of poetry as a "criticism of life," Huxley allocated that role instead to science, with nature, not taste or opinion, as its authority: "Moreover this scientific 'criticism of life' presents itself to us with different credentials from any other. It appeals not to authority, nor to what anybody may have thought or said, but to nature."[25] Spencer claims primacy for science in training students to deal with life, and dismisses literature as *belles-lettres*: "As they occupy the leisure part of life, so should they occupy the leisure part of education."[26] Arnold for his part mocked the man of science's "notorious" revolt against the "tyranny of letters" in his essay "Literature and Dogma." He countered the arguments of the men of science by admitting the power of science in gathering knowledge, but argued that relating knowledge to conduct would be the special task of culture. Arnold sought to trump these claims on behalf of science by declaring literature not just the realm of *belles-lettres*, but an expanse so broad that it had no horizon: "By literature I mean anything written with letters or printed in a book" (*CPW* 10:58). In his 1880 essay "The Study of Poetry," Arnold prophesizes a future in which the world would turn away from religion and science and toward poetry: "More and more mankind will discover that we have to turn to poetry to interpret life for us, to console us, to sustain us. Without poetry, our science will appear incomplete; and most of what now passes with us for religion and philosophy will be replaced by poetry" (*CPW* 9:161–62). Arnold's description of poetry as "a criticism of life" should be seen then in this broader scope of a general contention between sociology and literature to perform that function, as well as an effort by Arnold to position literature as a form of anti-science.

It was precisely as a criticism of life, as posing and exploring this same question of "how we ought to live," however, that sociology positioned itself. Huxley's lectures promoting the primacy of science in education, as well as the ensuing debates with Spencer, defined the trajectory of social efficaciousness for literary criticism that Arnold argued for in his essays on criticism and science. The rising status of science in debates about education impels Arnold toward vast claims for culture and criticism to perform the function of both describing the ills of the social realm, and for prescribing its cure. Arnold's literary criticism, due to his best efforts to demonstrate the social superiority of literary education to that of a purely scientific one, in the words of Wolf Lepenies, thus becomes a "concealed sociology."[27]

The crowd, however, as a companion figuration of the public's "fermenting mind" that Arnold wants to address, pushes this analysis in the direction of the more general question of culture's private affect and public effect. Arnold's installment of culture as having a public beneficence raises time and again the question of its empirical effects, a question that Arnold steadfastly refuses to answer:

> But then, *how* do [literature and poetry] exercise [their power] so as to affect man's sense for conduct, his sense for beauty? . . . But how, finally, are

poetry and eloquence to exercise the power of relating the modern results
of natural science to man's instinct for conduct, his instinct for beauty?
And here again I answer that I do not know *how* they will exercise it, but
that they can and will exercise it I am sure. *(CPW 10:68)*

Culture, as Arnold repeats throughout his essays, is "an inward operation,"
but it is precisely this inward status that troubles his efforts to claim social
efficacy on behalf of culture. "It will be said that it is a very subtle and indirect action which I am thus prescribing for criticism. . . . Slow and obscure it
may be, but it is the only proper work of criticism" *(CPW 3:274)*. It is precisely
the crowd's boundary-dissolving capacities, the blurring of interior states
and exterior social conditions, that impel its figurative efflorescence in his
work. Through the crowd, the divide between "inward operation" and social
power that culture takes as a problem can be dissolved.

Crowds and Social Facts

Arnold's work can also be read within a framework of European sociology
and social psychology oriented somewhat differently from the one outlined
by Lepenies, one that took the crowd as its exemplary object in the science
of society. Social scientific and proto-sociological thought sought a place in
nineteenth-century education by offering itself as a guide to the rapid social
transformations brought about by industrial expansion, one buttressed by
the rise of statistical thinking, with statistical regularity taking on the quality of "laws" rival to those of the natural world, a development nurtured by
the necessities of governing modern industrial society in the nineteenth
century.[28] Distinct from the psychological study of individuals, sociology
was, in Huxley's words, "a higher division of science still, which considers living beings as aggregates." As Ian Hacking puts it, in the nineteenth
century "society became statistical."[29] It was through the study of group
behavior, the study of individuals in aggregate, that sociology distilled its
basic unit of analysis: "the social." From the general study of society to the
study of an abstract but verifiable basic structure, "the social" is described
by the French sociologist Émile Durkheim later in the century as "ways of
acting, thinking, and feeling that present the remarkable property of existing outside the individual consciousness," ways, moreover, that have "an
imperative and coercive power, by virtue of which they impose themselves
upon him, independent of his individual will."[30] The social, in Durkheim's
formulation of one of the building blocks of early sociological theory, has
an existence outside the individual, but is nevertheless felt by the individual
as obligatory or compulsory in character.

In 1895 Durkheim takes the crowd as the paradigmatic empirical instance of the fact, the external and verifiable character, of the social:

> Thus in a public gathering the great waves of enthusiasm, indignation, and pity that are produced have their seat in no one individual consciousness. They come to each one of us from outside and can sweep us along in spite of ourselves. . . . I may not be conscious of the pressure they are exerting on me, but that pressure makes its presence felt immediately [if] I attempt to struggle against them.[31]

The crowd offers a paradigm for the way the power of the social operates: at once supra-individual and yet felt as obligatory by the individual. "The social" thus troubles any division between the social environment and the autonomous subject, any construction of the individual as supremely independent.

Durkheim's example of the crowd as an instance of the social finds numerous correlatives across myriad, more and less reactionary, works of social psychology on the phenomenon of crowds in the latter part of the nineteenth century. Gustave Le Bon's *The Crowd*, cited in the epigraph to this chapter, declared the age to be "the era of the crowd," a time whose principle social characteristic is the "substitution of the unconscious action of crowds for the conscious activity of individuals" (xiii, v). His work describes a world terrorized by an imminent expanding franchise and the rising power of mass politics. Le Bon's fascination and fear of the crowd, however, was the popularization of an earlier strain of writing by European social psychologists on the crowd that began in the 1870s, an interest spurred by the threat of the Paris Commune, and the development of mass politics in Europe.[32] Social psychologists Hippolyte Taine and Gabriel Tarde, as well as Victor Albert-Espinas, who was called by Durkheim the first academic sociologist of the Third Republic, developed theories of the crowd that associated mass gatherings with anarchism and alcoholism.[33]

The sociological achievement of Durkheim in taking the crowd as an instance of the social was to translate these primarily negative theories of the crowd into a theory that took the crowd as the paradigm for the way social facts operated in general. Rather than instancing a psychology unique to groups, the crowd is only the most spectacular version of the various forms of social rules, obligations, or compulsions—often as light as air, until we resist them—that define the social world that nascent sociology began to take as its special object of inquiry. That is, crowds could and did certainly threaten violence and social disorder, but the obligatory or coercive aspect of the power of the crowd was an instance of the way sociological theories such as those of Durkheim viewed the social realm as functioning at all times. The identification of the social as a force drew upon the various forms of social research that had elevated statistical information about society, the astonishing regularity of diverse, individual events such

as birth, death, and marriage rates, to the status of "laws" governing society. The crowd offered the ur-empirical instance of Durkheim's "ways of
acting, thinking, and feeling" that exist outside the individual consciousness, and that have "an imperative and coercive power" upon the individual. The crowd is adduced by not just sociologists such as Durkheim, but
also the literary critic Arnold, as the social's paradigmatic manifestations.
Society could not only be described by these statistical regularities, but
social order itself could be explained by a force detectable in the regularities identified by these studies. The power that might become terrifying in
an anarchic crowd is a general rather than an aberrant condition: one version of the force newly identified by sociologists as enabling social cohesion and order more generally.

The objectifying power of sociology, however, was not sufficiently strong
to keep political theorists' opinions of the mass public from bearing traces
of the negative treatments at the hands of fellow European social theorists. John Stuart Mill's 1859 "On Liberty" suggests the degree to which the
continental work on crowd psychology represents a current of thinking
about the crowd at work in English political theory as well. Mill's essay on
the nature of political government and popular opinion portrays the individual as suffering under the mass of his fellow creatures who appear as
an "impediment," and "interference," as a "compelling" threatening entity
against which the individual is in need of protection.[34] The power of the
crowd to induce behavior and forms of thinking is reflected in Mill's general conception of the coercive and dangerous power of society at large,
a conception of the social over which the language of the crowd hovers.
Society, in the form of the crowd, is here explicitly construed as threatening
the liberty of the individual in Mill's essay. I will take up this understanding of the social as a form of "interference" by an overly crowded world
in more detail in my reading of *Culture and Anarchy*, which in important
ways both coheres with and revises Mill's terms. A very different representation of the social, however, can be discovered if we turn from political
theory to the crowd poetry of Arnold, one that will be useful in illuminating his later essays where Arnold takes up the problem of how to socialize
the inward effects of culture, how to bring its effects to bear upon the lived
experience of the social world.

Crowd Poems

The various congregations of people that appear in Arnold's poems—"The
armies of the homeless and unfed" in "To a Republican Friend" (1848), "the
mortal millions" who live *"alone"* in "To Marguerite—Continued" (1849), and
the "swarms of men" in "Stanzas in Memory of the Author of 'Obermann'"

(1849), to cite a few invocations of the many—have been described by Isobel Armstrong as "depersonalised crowds." These crowds include not only the working class but also a creeping influx of strangers from beyond Britain, all of whom exert a "terrible pressure" on Arnold's poetry.[35] And it is difficult *not* to read the heart of a conflicted agoraphobe into Arnold's complaint of a world divided between living either in tormented solitude or suffering infection by "unavoidable contact with millions of small [natures]."[36] As the rhetorical doubling of the offhandedly enumerated collective "mortal millions" and an individual solitude that is no less general evinces, however, the distinction between the crowd and the isolated subject is not always so clear in Arnold. Reading the depersonalized, less politically insurgent crowds of the poetry with the Reform League demonstrators of *Culture and Anarchy* introduces a more variegated sense of Arnold's crowds than is encompassed by usual understandings of the term "impersonal." This reading of poetry and prose together illuminates the crowd's contradictory status as a figure not only of an alienated world, but also the site of an obliquely pleasurable form of sociation in his work, as well as its emerging status as a figure for both social order and dissolution in English discourse.

The year preceding the publication of Arnold's first book of poetry in 1849 saw the last of the large-scale Chartist demonstrations in England, a peaceful gathering in 1848 on Kennington Common which Arnold attended. But it also was the year of a series of revolutionary movements across Europe in France, Italy, Germany, and Hungary. The events of 1848, in particular, the revolutionary activity in France and the temporary installation of the poet Lamartine as the new French leader, spurred excitement in Arnold, as well as concern over the undirected violence that England's "masses" were likely to fall into in imitating their French counterparts. Arnold writes in a letter, "If the new state of things succeeds in France, social changes are *inevitable* here and elsewhere." But the state of England's working class is such that "their movements now *can* only be brutal plundering and destroying." In the opposition Arnold goes on to draw between the "*intelligence* of the idea-moved masses" of France and the "*insensible masses* of England," the outlines of a taxonomy of collective forms comes into view, one that Arnold will later elaborate in *Culture and Anarchy* by both distinguishing and allying anarchy—the nation's "fermenting mind"—and culture.[37] The contrast of "intelligence" and "idea" to describe the French with the "insensible" English, as well as Arnold's stated fears of English plundering, suggest "insensible" ought to be read as signifying a lack of intelligence or irrationality: the crowd for Arnold is a kind of excitable, overcharged entity, worryingly given over to eruptions of violence.

In an instance of the characteristic reversibility of meanings that can be assigned to the crowd, however, a contradictory sense clings to Arnold's description of the English "masses" as "insensible": the quality of being unaffected, or indifferent. This quality of indifference or dullness shadows the crowds of the poetry as well as the criticism, evoking not the spectacularly violent public realm of 1866, but a social sphere at times characterized as "action's dizzying eddy," at times as the site of indifference. An indifferent, or to use a term I will return to, disenchanted, social sphere is allied asymmetrically to those more typically Arnoldean judgments of the social realm as the site of "sick hurry," the "strange disease of modern life" as his poem "The Scholar Gipsy" phrases it.

"Resignation" (1849) introduces one of Arnold's recurrent poetic themes: a self-sustaining self-repression that the poet-speaker, in describing an ideal poetic consciousness to his sister and us as readers, proclaims as an alternative to a life of unsatisfying activity amidst the "something that infects this world" (l. 278).[38] Loosely following the narrative scheme of Wordsworth's "Tintern Abbey," "Resignation" tells of a return to the Lake Country by a matured poet-speaker and his sister. Occasioning a discourse by the poet-speaker on the nature of the poetic soul, this longed-for ideal is figured in the descriptions of a poet within the poem. Rejecting a romantic consonance between nature and the soul, the poet is described as stoically resigned to a world indifferent to the lives that pass through, an enervated "eternal mundane spectacle" (l. 228). The poet-speaker devotes considerable energy to elaborating upon a poetic "resign'd" consciousness (l. 243), an elaboration carried out largely through a series of oppositions between the poet and the social realm.

The poet-speaker describes the figure of the poet as one who, by virtue of having been granted not "joy," but rather the compensatory "sad lucidity of soul" of a poet, nonetheless claims difference from the world of work, those "whom labours, self-ordain'd, enthrall" (ll. 198, 14). In a quick extension of the theory of labor under capitalism as self-estrangement, in this line even work freely undertaken "enthralls" in the sense of making one a slave. Thus, even the poem we are reading is a product of a less successful navigation of stoicism than that accomplished by the poet being described, whose signal poetic "production" is a poetic consciousness. The poet-speaker describes the poetic consciousness that is, whether through "schooling of stubborn mind" or "birth," among those "freed from passions, and the state / Of struggle these necessitate" (ll. 24–27). In a poem so desiccated of desire, the only "crav[ing]" is for a form of self-negation, to live the "life of plants, and stones, and rain" who themselves seem "to bear rather than rejoice" in life (ll. 195, 270). The poem's complicated engagement of self-negation as self-preservation is imagined as a withdrawal from the social realm, but this withdrawal is accomplished, crucially, without a corresponding sense of alienation.

Such assertions of detachment, however, may seem like empty boasts, and the poem enlists the test case of the crowd in order to exemplify the poet's passionlessness. The power possessed by the poet is in the maintenance of a subdued self which understands the lives of others, but remains free from an identification with those lives which might draw him into their activity.

> The poet, to whose mighty heart
> Heaven doth a quicker pulse impart,
> Subdues that energy to scan
> Not his own course, but that of man. (ll. 144–47)

The poet rests on a "high station" (l. 164) observing a town from above at the end of the workday:

> At sunset, on a populous town;
> Surveys each happy group, which fleets,
> Toils ended, through the shining streets,
> Each with some errand of its own—
> And does not say: *I am alone.* (ll. 165–69)

The scene regarded, significantly, is not described as that of a crowd, but rather a cluster of "group[s]," acquaintances together carrying out "some errand," that lighter, sociable version of labor that follows upon "toils." This scene of pleasurable sociability is not taken up by the poet who is content to "survey" rather than engage the groups, and the remote location of the poet gazing upon this happy idyll fails to engender any expected sense of disabling isolation: "And does not say: *I am alone.*" Detachment, a value and term central to Arnold's corpus, is here valued unreservedly as both the safeguard, and the enabling condition, of a poetic consciousness that is securely distanced but not nihilistic. The lines preceding this idyll of happy groups elaborate detachment as a practice in the midst of a more crowded scene. Here, the poet

> sees, in some great-historied land
> A ruler of the people stand,
> Sees his strong thought in fiery flood
> Roll through the heaving multitude;
> Exults—yet for no moment's space
> Envies the all-regarded place.
> Beautiful eyes meet his—and he
> Bears to admire uncravingly;
> They pass—he, mingled with the crowd,
> Is in their far-off triumphs proud. (ll. 154–63)

Two versions of the crowd as well as two distinct forms of its management appear in these lines as a measure of the poet's powers of detachment. The ruler's amplification of his thoughts through the medium of the "heaving multitude" describes a Le Bon-esque, apocalyptic ("fiery flood") version of crowd control, from which the poet maintains an admiring, but not envying, distance. Possessing no thoughts of their own, the "heaving multitude" is an image of the crowd controlled through demagoguery.

By contrast, the crowd management practiced by the poet is of a piece with erotic self-management, a form of the unsocial unsociability, a "familiarity singularly tinged with aloofness" that Roland Barthes allies with the category he calls The Neutral.[39] "Beautiful eyes meet his—and he / Bears to admire uncravingly; / They pass—he, mingled with the crowd." Here, admiring without desiring, the poet enacts a version of aesthetic disinterestedness as social practice in "mingl[ing] with the crowd" "uncravingly." Thus highlighting his own power to move within the multitude, the poet is both singled out and singles out others—in his recognition by, and judgment of, "beautiful eyes"—while remaining untouched physically and affectively. The erotic potential in the passing glances of the beautiful eyes which is deflected by the "uncraving" poet, however, is also an erotic *of* potential. In failing to be fulfilled, it also fails to locate itself, to find an end, in any single individual. Endlessly potential, the serial erotic of the poet in the crowd is recouped as further evidence of a consciousness-securing disinterest defined as social management: a freedom *from*, purchased by being *within* ("mingled with the crowd"), the modern social world. The poet's detachment allows him to move in a sociable realm whose crowd character nevertheless licenses an erotics of neutrality, an erotic purified of "craving," an energy that can be conserved for the maintenance of a self all the stronger for being subdued. But such detachment also is the condition for freedom from any individual social obligation, all the while remaining in pleasurable "contact" with a generalized social sphere in the image of the crowd, a form of intimacy in public.[40] In these lines, circulating within the crowd exemplifies for Arnold a form of public affect, but one purified of obligation to any particular individual.

Arnold's efforts to carve out a zone of autonomy amidst the crowd take a more specific locale in the hybrid pastoral-urban space of the 1852 "Lines Written in Kensington Gardens" (*PW* 248–49). Arnold's poem revises a romantic landscape, transferring the "air-stirr'd forest" of a bucolic Lake Country scene to an "open glade" of a London park, a refuge encircled by the "girdling city's hum." In this ersatz forest, the buzzing multitude of people in the populous city that surround the speaker as he lies in the park are placed at a double remove. They first are flattened into mere background noise, a "hum," which is then attributed to the city itself rather than any human presence. Against the peopled world which has been generalized to noise, is a natural world all the more able succinctly to individuate itself: "Birds here make song, each bird has his, / Across the city's girdling hum" (ll. 5-6). The lyric opposition between self and world becomes here an opposition between noise and individuating music or meaning. Both the bird's songs and the speaker's thoughts come into focus only against the contrasting world of the "hum." A child occasionally crosses the glade, but even this human presence is (temporarily) elided by the speaker's gently self-mocking engrossment in the miniaturized country idyll. "Here at my feet what wonders pass, / What endless, active life is here! / What blowing daisies, fragrant grass!" while "the huge world, which roars hard by" engrosses the multitude outside the glade (ll. 13–15, 21).

Arnold's lyric negotiation of the self's relation to the world both reduces the crowd to a hum and structures its own claims to meaningfulness against this necessary noise. This negotiation is seen to be only momentarily sustainable as the speaker's reverie is broken off by direct supplications for peace toward the end of the poem. Abandoning the elaboration of the trope of an ersatz, depopulated, sylvan retreat, the speaker cries:

> Calm soul of all things! make it mine
> to feel, amid the city's jar,
> That there abides a peace of thine,
> Man did not make, and cannot mar. (ll. 37–40)

The abrupt move into direct address breaks the lyric mode, a fragmenting not untypical of Arnold. But the lyric condition of a self both constituted by its remove from the world, and yet painfully longing for contact with that world, remains.[41] Reversing the earlier translation of the people of London into a mere noise, sympathy is now enlisted to compensate for an unsustainable peace: "The power to feel with others give! / Calm, calm me more! nor let me die / Before I have begun to live" (ll. 42–44). The speaker both desiring to feel and not feel, to know and not know, the generalized social world that began as a crowd's hum here is vainly called back into individualized, sympathy-ready form in order to reclaim his peace.

Arnold's lyric mode of securing the self, albeit only momentarily, by opposition to or difference from a more crowded world also bears with it a counter-possibility of alienation, a self not secured, but enervated by its difference. "In the deserted, moon-blanch'd street, / How lonely rings the echo of my feet!" begins "A Summer Night" (*PW* 242–44). Complaining of the "the old unquiet breast" "Never by passion quite possess'd / and never quite benumb'd by the world's sway," dispassion is less a satisfactory mode of poetic consciousness, as it was in "Resignation," than a feature of an insufficiently energized social realm.

While the crowd has been the problem against, or the medium within, which a poetic subjectivity might be secured in the above poems, I want to turn finally to a poem in which the crowd might also be read as the solution for the ambivalent negations of the social sphere brought on by this self-securing Arnoldean subjectivity. If the crowd does not precisely show its face in "The Buried Life" (1852), its force is registered as all the more powerful for its dispersion in the text as the governing presence of "the world's most crowded streets," a line that might serve as shorthand for the social landscape of a society of strangers (*PW* 245–47). The allure of these streets, I will argue, renders the lyric binary of lovers at a pleasurable remove from the social world ambiguous. "The Buried Life" enacts an Arnoldean ideal of social management by staking out a middle territory between the self and the crowd through a plunge into the "world's most crowded streets," and in doing so, momentarily achieves the type of reconciliation precluded elsewhere.

"The Buried Life" invokes a characteristic gesture of withdrawal in its lyric scene of lovers residing in a space of intimacy sheltered from all other social relations: "Give me thy hand, and hush awhile, / And turn those limpid eyes on mine" (ll. 9–10). Even this scene of pleasurable isolation, however, may be dangerously consonant with a troubling self-alienation that characterizes modernity: "long we try in vain to speak and act / Our hidden self," "But hardly have we, for one little hour, / Been on our own line, have we been ourselves" (ll. 64–65, 59–60). With the silencing of the beloved, the pleasurable exile of the lyric pair shades into, and is doubled by, the complaint of the speaker's own intrapsychic exile. The "light words" and "gay smiles" of the beloved bring "no rest," "no anodyne" to a nameless sadness within. The complaint of a love that can speak only its occlusion—"Are even lovers powerless to reveal / To one another what indeed they feel?"—occasions a turn inward to "a something in this breast," a turn ostensibly propelled by the exquisite pain of the erotic pair's love beyond words (ll. 14–15, 6).

The turn inward, however, is more precisely the precipitant of a turn away from the zone of erotic sequestration and into the stranger-filled streets of men. The exquisite pain of unspeakable feelings that first places the speaker-beloved pair in pleasurable isolation is in the next stanza generalized to the common lot of men:

> I knew the mass of men conceal'd
> Their thoughts, for fear that if reveal'd
> They would by other men be met
> With blank indifference, or with blame reproved. (ll. 16–19)

The particularity of the speaker-beloved pair with which the poem opens is mitigated by the increasing investment of the narrative energies of the poem instead in the "mass of men." The intimate scene of lover and beloved first presented as the spur to the inward turn, the yearning for perfect knowledge, "let me read there, love! thy inmost soul," is shadowed by what would appear to be opposed to the private space of the lovers, the urban crowd:

> But often, in the world's most crowded streets,
> But often, in the din of strife,
> There rises an unspeakable desire
> After the knowledge of our buried life. (ll. 45–48)

The overall movement of the scenes of the poem, from private pair to public streets and back again in the final stanzas, forecasts a trajectory in which the din of public life is merely a foil to the deeper pleasures of the sequestered erotic pair. This movement, however, is complicated both by the centrality of the crowd experience to the mining of the "hidden self," and by the vastly greater rhetorical energy of the desires that arise in the crowd in comparison to the uninflected "a something in this breast" of the erotic pair.

The opening invocation of the socially dense space of the crowd in the sixth stanza locates the public, urban anonymity of the crowd as the experiential ground that produces the most energized turn, "an unspeakable desire," toward the hidden self. It is not just the buried self that is inaccessible even to a lover's language, as is argued in the opening of the poem: the desires induced by the crowd are themselves unspeakable. Unspeakability, then, might be less symptomatic of self-alienation than of the lyric poem's necessary disavowal of its investment in the power of the "the world's most crowded streets" over that of the lyric pair. After all, what kind of nineteenth-century English love lyric would take "the streets of men" as the site of a desire stronger than that of the speaker for the beloved? This desire is "unspeakable" in part because it is unrepresentable, a desire predicated on an absence that recedes from any but figural representation; it is specified only by the generalized scene of its production: "the world's most crowded streets." "The world's most crowded streets" produce a desire that is both self-constituting and self-dissolving, a desire for something described with equal force as the self and the social; or, in other words, the kind of desire induced by a crowd. The public, urban anonymity of the crowd in this poem drives the strongest desire to know the hidden self, thus suggesting that the desire for identity itself, the desire to discover one's "buried life" may be stronger than any erotic desire for the beloved, and that such a buried self is already a public formation. And it is only by immersion in the tumultuous "mass of men," rather than simply in detached retirement, that "the buried life" can be known.[42]

The poem's return from the scene of crowded streets to the sequestered lyric couple in the final stanzas is a return to a realm that has been transformed. The social sphere of the crowd's "din of strife" rezones the intimate space of the lyric couple into a public one.

> Only—but this is rare—
> When a beloved hand is laid in ours,
> When jaded with the rush and glare
> Of the interminable hours,
> Our eyes can in another's eyes read clear,
> When our world-deafen'd ear
> Is by the tones of a loved voice caress'd—

A bolt is shot back somewhere in our breast,
And a lost pulse of feeling stirs again. (ll. 77–84)

The first-person address of the opening stanza, "Give me thy hand and hush awhile," changes here to a third-person narration of exempla, mitigating its immediacy: "When a beloved hand is laid in ours," "A bolt is shot back somewhere in our breast / And a lost pulse of feeling stirs again." The transformation that enables the release of the buried self takes place not in the first-person present tense of dramatic address; rather, it is in the generality of example. At the moment of claiming love's power to redress the alienation of the buried life—the speaker's invocation of "a beloved" in which "Our eyes can in another's eyes read clear"—the specific beloved addressed in the first stanza vanishes (ll. 78, 81). Installing the anonymity of a case ("*A* beloved," "*another's* eyes") in place of the particular lyric pair, the poem despecifies the agent that unlocks the bolt in the breast, as if the individuality-annulling spirit of the crowd has descended upon the formerly private couple, who appear now less as the lyric's traditional erotic pair than as intimate strangers.

With the transformative power of the specific erotic pair's love mooted by generality, we can read the social world's effects—"the rush and glare / Of the interminable hours," "our world-deafn'd ear"—not as the wearied defeat by, or noisy interference of, the social realm. Instead, these conditions are the necessary and crucial inflection of the "tones of a loved voice." The specific erotic pair's dispersion into generalities is not the frustration but the *expansion* of the paradise of pure communication from the lyric pair to a fantasized generality of society. Not in spite of, but rather due to, "the rush and glare of interminable hours," can the speaker enter into the field of pure communication: "what we mean, we say, and what we would, we know" (l. 87). The collective deliverance, which takes "we" rather than "I" as its point of reference, annuls the specificity of the individual speaker by dispersing him into the plurality of an expansive social realm.[43] The poem's incorporation of the encounter with the crowd as a condition for the revelation of what is less a deep privacy than a collective communion blurs the lines of division between the crowd and the erotic pair that the poem seems to set out to amplify. Relieving the burdens of subjectivity imposed by "the buried life," the "crowded streets" drives a social fantasy of generalized linguistic communion and transparency. The crowd appears obliquely in these lines in its productive, managed form, an image of a social realm unburdened by separation and alienation.[44]

Such lyric expansiveness, however, can be sustained only momentarily. The final lines return us to the singular pronoun, "And then he thinks he knows / The hills where his life rose, / And the sea where it goes," as well as to a less assured condition of communication—"he *thinks* he knows" (ll. 96–98, my emphasis). While maintaining the generality of the exemplum of "*a* man" who "becomes aware of his life's flow," these lines qualify this field of pure communication, suggesting that the effects of the crowded stranger-filled streets might be, like the crowd on those streets, only passing.

Culture and Anarchy

Arnold's turn to critical prose and increasing neglect of poetry in the late 1850s and after was not a turn away from the concerns that had occupied his verse, as is often thought of the man who turned from the writing of poetry to the more public writing life as social critic. The change in genre, however, did entail a crucial reconfiguration of the figure of the crowd in his work. Such a reconfiguration, we shall see, remains incomplete in ways with significant effects. The rhetorical energy Arnold devotes to the crowd in his conceptualization of culture as the steward of English social order in his prose can be seen in part as an attempt to overcome these earlier crowds of the poetry. As the more general crowds of the poems give way to the specific Reform League crowd castigated in *Culture and Anarchy*, Arnold continues to elaborate an understanding of the social realm against the background of nascent sociology's efforts to do the same. While sociology identified the crowd as an instance of the aggregate behavior that was its scientific object, culture alone, Arnold would seem to claim in critical prose aimed at quelling mass eruptions, could speak its language. In its various transformations, begun in the poetry, from anarchic figure to an image of the social order upon which culture will act, the crowd is thus recast as the proper object of control for the literary critic rather than the sociologist. A more efficacious manager of crowd sentiment than science or politics, culture alone claims to be capable of addressing and controlling the anarchic crowd, of speaking to the vast "fermenting mind" of the nation.

The crowd can be seen here to underwrite Arnold's attempts to chart a role for culture that places it neither as mere inward aesthetic self-involvement, nor as allied with the stultifying "machinery" of public life. Arnold's aesthetic and political program of detachment, in which culture must remain aloof from the "fetish" of activism, enlists the coercive, public power of the crowd in an effort to resolve the contradictory elaboration of culture as both an "inward condition" and the shaping force of a social sphere. Arnold's claims for criticism's powerful social mission, a social mission that would not only quell anarchy, but would assign to poetry the power to both complete science and religion, drive his arguments on behalf of culture toward elaborate rhetorical strategies for representing its socially beneficent effects.

Arnold invokes the anarchic crowd of the 1866 Hyde Park riots in *Culture and Anarchy* in order to array culture against what he famously calls "doing as one likes." Culture will be a palliative and constraining force on the "strong individualism" so prevalent in modern society, a mode of shaping the "unrestrained swing of the individual's personality" (*CA* 63). In the essay "Democracy," Arnold warns of the singular individual as dangerously inchoate, being possessed by an incompleteness that threatens violence unless the individual is molded by the shaping, forming effects of culture: "character without culture ... is something raw, blind, and dangerous" (*CPW* 2:24). In *Culture and Anarchy*, culture is not only the sum of great aesthetic and scientific works, the "best that's been thought and said," but a power enlisted to shape the "unrestrained swing" of the individual, a social force with all the coercive and imperative potency ascribed to the crowd by later sociologists. In phrases that invert the terms of Mill's concern for the protection of the individual from the mass in "On Liberty," in which society at large is an "impediment" to individual freedom, it is the individual's freedom here that poses the threat to society. "Then we have got a practical benefit out of culture ... a principle of authority; to counteract the tendency to anarchy which seems to be threatening us" (*CA* 89). Rewriting Mill's argument, the individual in Arnold risks if not dissolution, then a grotesque arrest in growth if he ignores the collective world in which he exists. And it is not only the men of culture, those "docile echoes of the eternal voice, pliant organs of the infinite will," who are strangely allied with collective structures (*CA* 186). "Men are all members of one great whole," he writes, and culture dictates that "the individual is required, under pain of being stunted and enfeebled in his own development if he disobeys, to carry others along with him in his march toward perfection" (*CA* 62). The relation between the individual and the social sphere more generally, in Mill's essay exemplified by hostile "interference" and "impediments" posed to the individual by society, is here in Arnold a mutually sustaining contradiction. The individual subject is both under duress from the vividly described power of "one great whole," which "requires" "under pain" that he "obey" its commands, and gains sustenance, perhaps even the possibility of social existence from that "one great whole."

The individualism that culture will restrain, however, itself looks paradoxically like collectivism later in Arnold's essay. Echoing Mill again, in the chapter entitled "Doing as One Likes" Arnold argues that a blind faith in freedom leads directly to anarchy:

> This and that man, and this and that body of men, all over the country, are beginning to assert and put in practice an Englishman's right to do what he likes; his right to march where he likes, meet where he likes, enter where he likes, hoot as he likes, threaten as he likes, smash as he likes. *(CA 85)*

Presenting a continuum between rampant individualism and the coercive collectivism of a mass riot, "doing as one likes" inverts the poles between the individual and the crowd. Dangerous individual freedom appears not as a cause but an effect of anarchic crowd behavior in this passage. Arnold moves without remarking from the singular "this and that man" to the plural "this and that body of men." The "unrestrained swing of the individual" becomes a crowd "march[ing] where he likes," "meet[ing] where he likes." Arnold's syntactical maneuvers in utilizing the singular pronoun "he" with verbs, "meeting" and "marching," associated with collective behavior underscore the degree to which it is in fact the collective that sets the terms for his pillorying of individualism. Arnold raises the question of whether the individual is ever capable of being distinguished from the crowd at all, and thus perhaps puts Mill's fear of the mass as "interference" in even stronger terms. The rampant individualism and selfishness that seemed at first glance to be Arnold's target and worst enemy is seen to be an individualism that is more accurately an effect, rather than a cause, of anarchic collectivism. "Doing as one likes" could be more accurately phrased as "doing as the crowd likes."

Indeed, the crowd is general: it manifests itself not just in moments of excitation in Hyde Park, but dwells in the heart of everyone. In Arnold's taxonomy of social and cultural class identity in this essay, even the citizens of the upper two classes, the Barbarians and the Philistines, are not safe from impulses toward mass behavior that he more generally associates with the lowest class, the Populace. Every time "we long to crush an adversary" or "add our voice to swell a blind clamour . . . every time we trample savagely on the fallen,— he has found in his own bosom the eternal spirit of the Populace, and . . . there needs only a little help from circumstances to make it triumph in him untamably" (CA 109). Eliding the gap between the collective "our voice" and the individual "his own bosom," Arnold makes an implicit identification between crowds and the mass of the population explicit, as well as promotes a view of the population acting in concert, no matter what the cause, as a dangerous anarchism. All types of collective demonstrations in public are subject to the same iron law: "monster-processions in the streets and forcible irruptions into the parks, even in professed support of . . . good design, ought to be unflinchingly forbidden and repressed" (CA 181).

More than that, however, the "untamable" self-dissolving crowd activity of the populace threatens every individual, regardless of class. The individual in Arnold's world teeters on the edge of the collective mania of the crowd in an account that shares much with Le Bon's forecast of the "age of the crowd." Arnold posits that with "only a little help from circumstances" anyone may join with an anarchic crowd. In describing the danger that social conditions themselves seem to pose, Arnold also seems to join with the reactionary work of students of the crowd such as Le Bon who warned of the volatility of all forms of mass congregation. With only a "little help from circumstances," Arnold writes, a member of any class could find himself meeting, marching, and smashing as one likes. The crowd thus instances, and is the occasion for, describing a relationship between the individual subject and social conditions dangerous enough to help give rise to myriad practices and methods of inquiry that sought to study and control it. Sociologists were beginning to take this field as their object, but Arnold, seeking to elaborate a relationship between the social and the individual that is at once more free (the "flexibility" that culture encourages), and more constraining (culture's governing powers), must take it as a problem. If all that is required for an outbreak of anarchic behavior in the upper-class Barbarian to find in himself the mass spirit of "the Populace" is "a little help from circumstances," then Arnold's culture must address all the more urgently the conjunction between the individual and the social that the crowd instances, a conjunction that is named by Arnold "anarchy."

Alongside its indictment of individualism as "doing as one likes," *Culture and Anarchy* also insists that the apostles of culture refrain from directly intervening in the public sphere. In abjuring any concrete activity, the men of culture for whom "public life and direct political action" are not "much permitted," "must keep out of the region of immediate practice" (*CA* 183–84; *CPW* 3:275). The temporary retreat of the Arnoldean apostle-critic is a withdrawal to safety from a violent public sphere dominated by "tumult and disorder," "multitudinous processions in the streets of our crowded towns" (*CA* 100). The violence of the social sphere is one force that drives the critic's retreat from the public realm; such a retreat, however, is the condition for the man of culture being all the more able to apply the "fresh stream" of critical thought to the public realm. Invoking a word with a complex array of meanings in his vocabulary, Arnold insists the man of culture withdraw from the realm of social action and instead practice a detachment he names "disinterest."[45]

Arnold's effort to establish a realm of social autonomy is doubled into a subjective autonomy by his pointed placement of culture's effect *inside* an individual. Culture, as he repeats throughout his essay, is "above all, an inward operation" (*CA* 190). The effects of culture are primarily those of *bildung*, or self-development, as many of Arnold's commentators have remarked. Self-development, Arnold is careful to stress, however, is always oriented toward a more general ideal, a point ignored by many of his critics: not a withdrawn *aesthete*, but a "best self." Culture produces a desire to "augment the being of our nature," and while like religion, it looks to improve an "internal condition," it is also characterized by its "social" desires, the will to improve the world (*CA* 59, 61). It is this combination of inward orientation and withdrawal from the social sphere, however, that troubles Arnold's claims of culture's social beneficence.[46] The "cultivated inaction" of the man of culture appears to Arnold's critics as less a contribution to the social good than a form of anemic self-involvement, characterized by an "effeminate horror" of political reform (*CA* 162).[47]

If a violent social sphere is one precipitant of criticism's spatial and subjective retreat, however, another is something like its very opposite: a social sphere characterized not by chaotic tumult, but by an enervating, constrictive "bondage to machinery," and unthinking attachment to the "fetish" of politics and freedom (*CA* 83). This characterization of the current social realm both accompanies and opposes its more tumultuous timbre as we have come to know it through Arnold's excoriation of the crowd. A modern social world described as mere "external and mechanical rule" creates the need for culture, however, as much as its agitated counterpart the crowd does in Arnold's polemic. Such "mechanical rule" calls into action a culture that will impart "flexibility" in our thinking, thus allowing the cultured person to turn a "fresh stream" and "free play of thought" upon stock notions and habits (*CA* 128, 167).

The particular concept and social role of culture is elaborated by Arnold partially as a more limber understanding and response to the complexities of a social world than that of official branches of a British science of society interested largely in statistical averages and direct, legislative instruments of reform. As part of an increasing rationalization of the state and the roles of individuals within it in the nineteenth century, statistical analyses of society could provide a measure of social conditions. Such statistical social data, however, could also take on an air of determinism for those individuals within this state. The apparent social forces governing life, and death, manifest, for example, in Émile Durkheim's analysis of the predictability of the number of suicides in a given society, would in later years provoke terror.[48]

Such an understanding of the social realm in the modern era inspired new strategies for securing a sense of self-determinism. Frances Ferguson has described a romantic "aesthetics of individuation" that emerges under a more and more rationalized social realm which takes on a systemic, deterministic aspect to those living in it: "with the notion of system emerged an antitype to the notion of society as a collection of individuals."[49] While culture's aesthetic self-development might be one version of individuation, Ferguson's formulation of society as system also suggests some of what is at stake in Arnold's vocabulary of "machinery" and "fetish" in describing the current social sphere.

As a characteristic feature of a nineteenth-century society experiencing the growth of government agencies and scientific techniques for charting and controlling the social realm, rationalization is allied with what Max Weber calls the "disenchantment" characteristic of a rational, scientific world's self-understanding.[50] Scientific understanding banishes the supernatural forces that seemed once to rule society from this disenchanted world of modernity, a world that the science of society is instrumental in both illuminating and constructing. As the quasi-mystical descriptions of the binding powers of social statistics in Durkheim, and Arnold's own appropriation of mystical tones in describing the powers of culture, suggest, however, the banishing of enchantment is always an incomplete project. A social realm characterized by "machinery," a realm studied for the purpose of governing—through scores of statistical analyses of social conditions and government agencies that accumulate them—are for Arnold all features of a disenchanted world. Society as a system, with the suggestion in "system" of structural intractability, threatens not just the autonomy of the individual, but also the malleability of a social realm that Arnold argues culture will shape in guiding England's future. Society as a crowd, however, suggests a solution to the problem of this modernity. Culture's role of crowd management allows Arnold to describe a public, non-bureaucratic, non-parliamentary sphere for its effects, a sphere of the crowd that escapes the enervation attending social rationalization.

In the crucial substitution by Arnold of the crowd for the social more generally lies a powerful vision of the tractability of the social realm—a fantasy all the more potent for a new understanding of society, generated by incipient social scientific practices, as governed by immutable laws. The volatile energies of the anarchic crowd might be marshaled, not by social science, but by Arnoldean culture, into an image of a re-enchanted social realm freed from the machinery of modern bureaucracy and politics. In Arnold's extensive program for governing the crowd, culture displays all the coercive powers of the social, but none of its recalcitrance or obduracy as system. This re-enchanted social realm, purified of anarchy but retaining the alluring potency and energy of the crowd, will be managed by a culture which is thus granted in Arnold's scheme "the future of powers for years to come."

Theodore Adorno's analysis of lyric poetry's doomed utopian urges describes the dream and nightmare of the relations figured by the crowd: a world of people "between whom the barriers have fallen."[51] It is this fantasy of an unmediated but manageable relationship to the social order for the agents of culture that pushes Arnold toward the crowd. Perhaps more *flâneur* than Carlylean prophet, Arnold, impelled by sociology, performs a negotiation of the opposing poles of engagement and autonomy, social actor and "inwardness" for the critical agent of culture on the terrain of the crowd. Unlike the *flâneur*, however, Arnold must manage rather than simply bathe in the crowd, shaping it from anarchy into the vehicle for culture. Enabling a sustaining fantasy of social order, the crowd in Arnold's texts is a power that is everywhere, so diffusive that it is difficult to pin down. At once "anarchy," "the centre of movement," the mass mind, and the fantasized pliant addressee of culture, the collective figurations of the crowd in Arnold can only be managed.

Losing Interest in George Eliot

Introduction: Losing Interest

"—but why always Dorothea?" Somewhere around a third of the way into *Middlemarch* the novel's narrator stops mid-sentence, nerves and narration slightly frayed by its heroine, Dorothea Brooke, absorbing all the attention. It is a startling moment, a narrative break that confesses the enthralling power of a handful of individual fictional lives—usually those of the young, the beautiful—upon readers and narrators both. Such lives, Eliot's narrator reminds us, can be absorbing enough to blot out nearly everyone else in a fictional social universe, our interest in Dorothea leaving us only vaguely attending to the array of other characters dwelling dimly in the background. Earlier in the novel, the narrator had reflected upon the pleasantly busy fullness of its responsibilities, with "so much to do in unraveling certain human lots, and seeing how they were woven and interwoven."[1] By the time we arrive at the line quoted above, however, those pleasant duties seem to have become a burden, a superabundance of characters and plotlines vying for a now harried narrator's attention.

The narrator's interruption is well known to readers of *Middlemarch*, thrilling for the abruptness with which it brings a chapter only just begun to a dead stop in its first sentence. Still, the tone of exasperation that has crept into the narrator's voice is a little hard to place. Is it directed toward us, the readers, and our Dorothea-enthralled selves? Or, maybe this is a moment of self-castigation over the narrator's tendency toward over-absorption, lingering on a single character when so many other stories need telling? Whether we feel implicated in or impatient with this moment, the force of the interruption—stopping both *Middlemarch*'s plot and narration in its tracks—radiates out toward a more general consideration of the realist novel form itself. In posing the question of Dorothea, this moment underscores the limited resources of attention that are available to any third-person narrator, even to one who is, like *Middlemarch*'s own narrator, nearly superhumanly mindful of a bustling fictional world.

In the narrator's exasperation we are reminded that the nineteenth-century novel is nothing if not crowded. With scores of characters both major and minor jamming its pages, teeming with the extras who, while often not given speaking roles or even acquiring the legibility of being recognizable as characters, nonetheless constitute the ambient social environment of a densely peopled world within its pages, there is one thing we know about the realist novel in Britain: it has a Big Tent policy of representational inclusiveness. And, for all the novel's dedication to delineating the warp and weft of individual consciousness, the nineteenth-century novel's talent for social description is continuous with its talent for making even three characters feel, if not exactly or always like a crowd, at least like a fully populated world.

George Eliot's novels are unusually sensitive to the thickly settled quality of their fictional social landscapes, with representational resources devoted even to characters far removed from the foreground of the novel's story. Intent on prying us and narration away from our rapt attention to Dorothea, the narrator's interjection gives a sense, however, of the effort involved in sustaining focus on the novel's protagonists even while apportioning attention amongst other characters who, though not central to the story, nonetheless elicit mindful attention. Alongside a novel as populous as Charles Dickens's *Bleak House*, with its fifty or so main-ish characters crowding its pages, *Middlemarch* might seem relatively manageable, a populous but hardly overwhelming fictional social world. But the strain of trying to grant every character, no matter how peripheral to the plot, some measure of narrative attention endows Eliot's socius with an ambient sense of social density out of proportion to its actual number of characters. Not surprisingly then, one of the signal effects remarked upon by early readers of *Middlemarch* is a sense of strenuousness produced by the combination of its length, breadth, and carefully wrought qualities: "the elaborate care given to the separate parts, leaves in the mind a sense of something like strain, and makes it hard to look at the work as a whole."[2] The narrator's impatient interjection about Dorothea, then, might also be a moment of sympathy with a reader's own sense of wearying cognitive strain.

Eliot's scrupulous narrative mindfulness has been allied customarily with a salutary capacity for readers and narrators both to imagine the lives of others. However, *Middlemarch* here underscores a countervailing principle within its pages. Marked by the novel's narrator at this moment is less an effort to renew the energies of narratorial attentiveness than the need to let that attention flag a bit, to force itself to let go of those it holds so dear. With so many to attend to, among them some fascinating enough to eclipse interest in anyone else, Eliot's narrator here musters not attentiveness, but detachment, an effort to disattend.

To think of narration as working to loosen a character's hold on its interest may feel strange, in part because *Middlemarch*'s narration is distinctive precisely in being carefully attuned to the ethical and perceptual effort involved in being attentive to other people. But for the literature of social density, with so many lives to attend to, just such techniques of disattending and detachment become central. "The primitive art of losing interest in things or people," Adam Phillips suggests, is among the childhood practices of promiscuity that are left behind in adulthood, with adulthood's expectations of more focused, monogamous modes of interest and desire.[3] While "mature" is the signature feature of Eliot's narrator in *Middlemarch*—a tempered voice teaching us the hard, adult lessons of compromise, disappointment, and accommodation—this narrative interruption in fact seems pitched against the narrator's own mature habits of focus. Pitched against, because those habits might shade from careful attentiveness to individual lives into something like the opposite. Rapt by Dorothea, a narrator's purposeful attention and sensitivity become hard to tell cleanly apart from unthinking absorption or reverie, a form of inattentiveness that is paradoxically produced by absorption.[4]

The art of losing interest: the realist novel, we have been told, and Eliot's realist novel, in particular, is all about interest and immersion in the particularity of lives and historical contexts. And, any reader of *Middlemarch* cannot help but be awed by the scale at which this novel knits together characters' lives, depicted at a granular level of detail, with the broad sweep of an historical "study of provincial life," as the novel's subtitle goes. But what if we tried to find an Eliot beyond, or maybe below, the almost superhuman qualities of observation and synthesis demonstrated by her novels and narrators?

Picking up on the narrator's suggestion, this chapter will bring out a *Middlemarch* as interested in prying us away from the particularities of individual lives and social contexts as it is in asking us to immerse ourselves in them. I suggest that *Middlemarch* is concerned not just with the realist specification of complex historical social worlds and their navigation by individual characters, or with how characters interconnect through intricate networks of social affiliation—two of our usual ways of thinking about this novel's scope. Instead, we find a *Middlemarch* preoccupied with forms of social experience that are energized not by their specificity, but by their generality or expansiveness. Opening onto extensive social fields, often felt as moments of surprise or break—as when the narrator suddenly turns away from Dorothea—*Middlemarch* considers how the novel makes us, and its characters, come alive to the reality of the force of the social itself. It is this concern that drives the novel's preoccupation with attentiveness—too much or too little—to ambient social environments, what Erving Goffman calls the social "surround."[5] In the most general terms—and generality is one of the features of both the novel and its figurations of the social I hope to illuminate—this chapter suggests that among *Middlemarch*'s central preoccupations, for all of its dedication to granular-level realist specificity and historical texture, is the far more diffuse sense of what modernity feels like.

To bring this out will entail what may seem an elliptical way of approaching *Middlemarch*, hewing at times to moments found nearly in passing—vaguely delineated or gestural social experiences—as well as transitions in the novel, moments of narrative dis- and reorientation. What this approach brings into view are forms of social experience that are less narratable, or even immediately discernible, than the figurations of social interactions between characters that is the usual business of the novel, but that are no less powerfully felt for their vagueness. To think of *Middlemarch* in this way is thus to retexture the importance of character in a novel so careful of its characters as *Middlemarch*. At the risk of pithiness, the central question of this chapter is: How might a novel make good on a wish to tell a story about everyone who is not Dorothea? *Middlemarch*'s engagement with the aesthetics of social density and forms of social neutrality—which I have been arguing throughout this book are condensed in the stranger—present a particular challenge for a novel whose narrative scope aspires to an expansiveness broad enough to include everyone who is not Dorothea. Paying attention to the novel's figurations of expansive social experiences, we can mark *Middlemarch*'s attunement to the social multiplicity of modernity as well as that multiplicity's effect upon realist form.

Through *Middlemarch* this chapter will bring into focus forms of social relationality made imaginable or possible by the novel, but that have been hard to discern due to criticism's focus on sympathy as a singularly valorized form of social attachment in Eliot: the art of letting go, for example, in which detachment is not a means of escaping the world, but of opening one's self to attachments that might not be tied to any single person. In thinking beyond, or to the side of, sympathy between individuals, the appearance in *Middlemarch* of the more neutral or detached social modes that characterize modern sociality open up to critical view. Like the narrator in a harried state of attentiveness to everybody, being with one other person is often shadowed by the prospect of more collective forms of social experience in *Middlemarch*. These massified forms of sociality are more central to Eliot's account of modern social experience than a focus on sympathy, with its ethos of compassionating individuals, allows us to see. However, because these forms are so frequently indirect, merely passing, or oriented toward collectivities too amorphous to bear a label, such forms of sociality are hard to figure or detect. As a result, such forms present challenges to the realist novel's commitment to the codification of social relations through plot and character. In marking these unexpected relational modes or instances within *Middlemarch*, my case for reading this book's divergences from the usual understanding of a novelistic commitment to psychological inwardness and singularity might be put most directly as a rewriting of its subtitle: *Middlemarch: A Novel of Collective Life*.

A second aim of this chapter is to show the "art of letting go" to be part of the case the novel makes for its own capacities to figure or evoke "the social" over those of contemporaneous sociological thought. While critics of many stripes have brought attention to the power of her novels' sociological imagination, Eliot pitches the realist novel and its sympathy-generating powers in contradistinction to the abstractions and statistical compilations of early sociology. At the same time, by finding unexpected resonances between Eliot's evocations of those many unknown, the not-Dorotheas, and early sociology's own efforts to conceptualize and study populaces on a large scale—whether in blue books, statistical analyses, or chronicles—I mark the friction between *Middlemarch*'s own sociological imagination and the realist novel's dedication to those well-known. That is, its dedication to the careful figuration and making known, both psychologically and socially, of individuated characters. That *Middlemarch* might be as much about those we do not know as it is about those we come to know so well in its pages is to take seriously the narrator's question: "Why always Dorothea?"

That question is ultimately an Eliotic version of the question posed by any realist novel intent on broad social description. How to calibrate what we might think of as the sociological arm of the realist novel—its tireless and theoretically inexhaustible description of complex fictional social landscapes—with the codifying impulses of plot and characterization, impulses that dial down the sprawling reach of the sociological by transforming it into plots of courtship, mysteries of family lineage, and their attendant resolution? The particular form this tension takes in *Middlemarch* is magnified, we will see, by its wish to figure social life on a maximal scale. The novel's tendency to become arrested, if only temporarily, by social experiences that are themselves incomplete, open-ended or uncodified, moments that cannot quite square with the coherence-bestowing effects of plot or narration, reflect the unresolved qualities of this tension. Like static in the novel that can be reduced but not quite tuned out, this is one of the varied facets of *Middlemarch* that this chapter takes up and amplifies—the social or informational "noise" that is produced by the novel's expansiveness and complexity. In turn, the varied meanings of "noise" in its auditory, social, and informational senses will help bring into view the novel's surprisingly frictional relationship to more avowedly sociological modes of figuring the social.

Here Comes Everybody: *Middlemarch* and Social Extensivity

Middlemarch is in no small part a novel about expanding our sense of the claims of other people, the difficulty of overcoming self-absorption to recognize the independence of what the novel calls the "equivalent centre of self" within even those closest to us.[6] But given our interest in its protagonist, the narrator's questioning of Dorothea's nearly gravitational pull on narrative attention feels something like a global reassessment of the very notion of character centrality itself, which is a surprise in a novel frequently taken as a touchstone for classical realist form. Such a radical leveling of the field of characters, however, might seem less radical if we recognize it as an intensification of a flattening readers long have tended to find in Eliot's novels. Henry James on *Felix Holt*: "There is no person in the book who attains to triumphant vitality; but there is not a single figure, of however little importance, that has not caught from without a certain reflection of life."[7] James's account of Eliot's de-stratified set of characters underscores her meticulous narrative concern for everyone within the novel, as well as a narrative principle of neutrality or impartiality that manifests itself as a reluctance to privilege any of its characters. The author of *Felix Holt*, by James's lights, sacrifices the singular energy of a few central characters rendered vividly for the more dispersive, equitably apportioned "certain reflection of life."

What distinguishes "Why always Dorothea?" from James's faint praise of Eliot's even-handedness, however, is the fact that the narrator does not here ask "What about Casaubon?" (Dorothea's new husband to whom the narrator eventually turns). Rather than directing attention toward a particular other character, the novel asks us to consider the vast range of implied, unspecified others who are not Dorothea. A mark of Eliot's democratizing practices of narration and characterization, the narrator's question conjures a *Middlemarch* of only protagonists, its characters placed on furlough from the hierarchies of central protagonists and subordinated minor characters that render some mere background to Dorothea and Co.

In the *Middlemarch* briefly opened up by this question no fictional life would be beneath the full sensitivity and care bestowed by an Eliot narrator, each as vivid and as intelligently attended to as any Dorothea. Bursting at its (imagined) bindings, this impossible *Middlemarch* is Eliot's novel as a Director's Cut version of itself as broad as the globe. Invited to consider a novel with a nearly unbounded fictional field of characters—all those who are not Dorothea—a fictional social sublime comes fleetingly into view, a vast shadow *Middlemarch* that hovers alongside the one in our hands. This brief gesture toward a populace of novelistic characters vast beyond a reader's ken brings the reader of *Middlemarch* into close quarters with a novel teeming with centrality, no consciousness left undetailed. If part of an Eliot novel's appeal for her earliest readers was the experience of social multiplicity (a point I take up below), this moment in *Middlemarch* flirts with a novel populous enough to escape any fictional head count.

The narrator's gesture here toward an open-ended fictional socius extensive enough to escape apprehension might be seen as a technique by which the novel bestows coherence upon, and solidifies our attachment to, the bounded social landscape we are reading about, what *Middlemarch* calls "this particular web." Indeed, Eliot's novels often call conspicuous attention to the delimited qualities of their fictional worlds—"a novel of provincial life," "this particular web"—and for all of Eliot's evocations of sympathetic relations across class lines and various forms of social distance, they often ultimately affirm social proximity and local communities, the claims of those closest to us.

This aspect of Eliot has been given historical specificity by James Buzard's account of the British realist novel's auto-ethnographic features. Amidst the increasing dispersion of British citizens and institutions across the globe under imperial projects in the nineteenth century, the novel sought to endow British culture with an ethnographic specificity that would enable it to be understood as naming a clearly demarcated and locatable space. Under the realist novel's efforts, the argument goes, British culture acquires coherence and meaning via a realist narration that brings a proto-ethnographic stance, developed first in the imperial periphery, to bear upon Britain itself. In the fictional world of the novel but not of it, the narrator gains the detached, anthropological perspective from which the nearly infinitely varied social practices of a people can be seen as possessing the coherence of a "culture."[8] I share this sense that *Middlemarch*, and the novel more generally, is concerned with the relation between detachment and the aspiration to achieve some purchase upon social knowledge, and that nineteenth-century literary form is shaped by the contiguous practices of early social sciences like anthropology and sociology. However, accounts by Buzard as well as others of the novel's particular contributions to, or anticipations of, ethnographic or anthropological practices and the constitution of cultural integrity foreground the effects of codification that produce culture as "integral." As a result, they tend to overlook the more gestural, transient, or nearly directionless forms of sociality that appear unexpectedly alongside the more familiarly, novelistically codified ones—friends, lovers, kin—in *Middlemarch*.[9] By being attentive to moments when the novel imagines characters or its readers coming in close range to social plenitude—episodes or fleeting instances when the ambient texture of sociality itself is intensely felt—we can see that our understanding of *Middlemarch* as a novel dedicated to the affirmation of sympathetic understanding, ethical commitments, and social attachments that are local and embodied, takes shape alongside highly charged figurations of open-endedness, forms of sociality without cleanly demarcated objects or borders.

The horizonless social multitude evoked by "Why always Dorothea?" would be, by necessity, barred from the plot of the novel itself. In essence, it would signal the obliteration of plot. A realist novel devouring itself in the name of social inclusiveness, a *Middlemarch* fully realized would be its own cancellation. However, brought into something just shy of existence through implication, the failure of the novel to make good on this sublime experience of generalized character centrality—a gesture foreclosed by the narrator's relatively quick return to Dorothea a few paragraphs later—retains rather than dispenses with it. Beyond figuration, this possible *Middlemarch* is equally hard to put out of a reader's mind once evoked and so lingers as part of the novel's counterfactual texture.[10] Floating alongside our reading of the novel as a potential event, this moment's virtual social sublime remains at the edge of our imagination.

Eliot's novels concentrate in particularly interesting ways the general sense of the nineteenth-century realist novel as overflowing with fictional life, and the populousness of Eliot's fiction is part of her distinctiveness in historical accounts of the development of the realist novel. Extending the representational franchise of the novel well beyond her British predecessors, in Eliot, we find that characters who used to be minor, mere background, "are no longer a colorful picture gallery to be gazed at from a distance, but are active forces which must be interacted with in the plot itself."[11] In an exhilarating expansion upon this insight, Alex Woloch has recently argued that over the first part of the nineteenth century the novel's expansion to include fictional characters from more heterogeneous social classes impelled a tendency to take on more characters in general, a burgeoning democratization in fiction alongside the political expansion of the franchise in Britain to more voters in the period. Illuminating the novel's formal transformation by this population boom, Woloch shows realist narration and characterization to be constituted through a defining tension: the novel's delineation of the consciousnesses of its protagonist versus the myriad lives vying for narrative attention within the book, those who constitute the social field amidst which the singular protagonist is situated.[12] Endowed with enough humanness to make us aware of their constricted position in narrative and their stunted characterization, the minor character is not just background leaping into foreground; instead, the minor character's minorness is itself foregrounded.

In this, however, minor characters also bear a melancholy freedom: through a reader's sense of their palpable boundedness, selves forced into the cramped space of minorness, such characters imply stories beyond the role scripted for them by the novel, a space opening between the character and the story in which they appear.[13] Similarly, Andrew Miller identifies the urge to consider alternate paths for novelistic characters, "lives unled," as one of prose narrative's central ethical operations, a counter-fictional way of imagining that is built into the novel.[14] For all the almost overwhelming complexly interrelated plotlines it contains, then, the realist novel nonetheless impels a sense of still more, alternate stories that might have been narrated, but are not. With eyes adjusted to the light shed by these accounts, we can better glimpse the alternate lives suggested by minor characters, and in doing so recognize the nineteenth-century novel as being even more densely peopled than it already had seemed.

If we press beyond the characterological orientation of each of these studies, however, we also see that such impulses are powerful enough to exceed even character and narration themselves, impelling a concern not only for individual lives unled but also for the vast numbers of even those we might call "un-narrated." In the narrator's challenge to Dorothea's hold on us, our attention turns not simply to this or that life not lived, but more broadly to an aggregate shadow populace of the un-narrated and un-characterized. To Woloch's observation that any human being who enters the fictional world of the novel inevitably disrupts narrative attention, we can add that Eliot's case implies an even more radical axiom: even those who don't enter the narrative world, at least not in any way that would render them legible as characters, shapes narration in *Middlemarch*.[15] Even the most fully populated of Eliot's novels, no matter how abundant with fictional life, is concerned to nudge our attention in the direction of those many others—stories or lives—that have not found voice or figuration within its pages. By sensitizing us to how characters might have led lives other than the one scripted for them—whether through what Miller calls the optative or through the thwarted qualities of minorness—these two accounts seek to renovate the status of character itself in novel studies. These renovations, however, while attuning us to lives led, and those contemplated but not led, should also attune us to lives that decline to eventuate even into proper characters, and to the more gestural forms of social experience that cannot precisely locate or limit themselves within the contours of face-to-face contact between individual characters.

By these lights, if one were inclined to take the measure of the breadth and scope of Eliot's social environments, it would not be enough to compile a catalogue of her characters (a favorite pastime of her earliest readers, as we will see). Rather, we should extend the possibility of lives unled to narrative as well, understanding a narrator's wish to expand the novel's purview to include everyone who is not Dorothea as both implied by the novel and an "unacted possibility."[16] This gesture toward the unacted, impossible experience of a novel that figures social populousness itself, one without specific, individualized characters is analogue to our heightened awareness of "lives unled" in the novel, but one better phrased as "lives unread" because unwritten.

That we could give weight to such an impossible experience, what we might call a near or virtual event in the novel, seems less improbable than it otherwise might because *Middlemarch* has already brought us into proximity with such an experience earlier in the book.[17] In a well-known passage, the narrator concedes that the disheartened state of Dorothea Brooke on her honeymoon in Rome with her new husband Casaubon is hardly unusual. Dorothea's early marital disappointment is so common, so widespread amongst the young and newly wed that it would not be likely to strike a reader as tragic. However:

> That element of tragedy which lies in the very fact of frequency, has not yet wrought itself in the coarse emotion of mankind; and perhaps our frames could hardly bear much of it. If we had a keen vision and feeling of all

ordinary human life, it would be like hearing the grass grow and the squirrel's heart beat, and we should die of that roar which lies on the other side
of silence. (194)

Along with the narrator's self-interrogation about Dorothea, these lines are
among the most frequently cited passages from *Middlemarch*. Linked by
their mutual appeal to sympathetic imagination, they suggest that to read
and draw the lessons of *Middlemarch* is to become aware of the claims of the
many quiet, ordinary lives lived around us. Together they dramatize the formal bind of the novel, caught between attending to "all ordinary life," which
would overwhelm and shatter us if it were not muted into silence, and the
representational pull of specific individual protagonists, the handful of ordinary lives right nearby.

What makes these passages especially resonant with each other, however, is
that each fixes upon events that are evoked for the reader without quite taking
place. In essence, these events are brought before us as not quite taking place.
Whether by description or implication, they point to intense experiences that
are most powerful for not actually being experienced by anybody in particular
and are even outside the limits of what is recognizable as experience. To have
such a "keen vision and feeling" would at first seem to be to move from being
a reader of the novel to its narrator, to possessing the unbounded perspicacity
of omniscient narration.[18] And yet, as we have found, even *Middlemarch*'s narrator can only evoke, rather than figure, the immensity of a socius comprised
by "all ordinary human life." What "has not yet wrought itself in the coarse
emotion of mankind" here is both unfelt and unavailable to us, a sensitivity to
the vast range of life that *Middlemarch* suggests lies not only "on the other side
of silence" but also on the other side of "Why always Dorothea?"

Drawing these lines even closer to the implied shadow populace of
Middlemarch is that each passage takes a close encounter with a social vista
on a massive new scale as their occasion, a momentary scaling up of social
awareness or sensitivity. Possessing a "keen vision and feeling of all ordinary
human life" is what the novel itself might offer us ostensibly as readers, an
expanded sensitivity to the everyday but invisible suffering that surrounds
us. But such vision and feeling would also give us something like the knowledge and feeling of typicality itself: a "feeling of all *ordinary* human life."
This feeling is quotidian in its orientation to unfamous, ordinary people; but,
it is also quotidian in the sense of being utterly general, so ordinary as to
encompass the entirety of the human world: "*all* ordinary human life." This
"keen feeling" thus attunes us not only to the personal story of Dorothea
but also suggests an experience of the social as ubiquitous, as not locatable
within any single person, or even in a massive collation of specific people. The
social's all-encompassing non-personal character is here part and parcel of its
apprehension.

While "the fact of frequency" most immediately refers us to the regular and recurrent nature of such small tragedies, the aural sense of "frequency" as sound also burbles up as the passage continues. Converting social commonality into sonic intensity, the passage imagines a sensitivity to the social whole as the unbearable waves of sound on the "other side of silence," which like the "grass grow[ing]" or "a squirrel's heartbeat," are unheard by human ears.[19] But it is worth remarking too that the amplificatory social effects of "frequency" are not just heard (or unheard), they are also felt in this passage.

Among the surprisingly varied meanings of "frequency" this passage solicits, the *O.E.D*'s definition as the "condition of being crowded" is maybe least familiar and most useful in getting a handle on the passage's call to sympathetically imagine all ordinary life.[20] "The fact of frequency" in the sense of crowdedness would best be read then as the experience of social density itself. This sense of the self *en masse* bring us back to the understanding of typicality evoked by "all ordinary human life," in which typicality becomes the experience or apprehension of oneself as part of a crowd or collectivity, like Durkheim's instance of the social as "great waves of enthusiasm, indignation, and pity" that can occur in "a public gathering."[21] Because this passage articulates so finely Eliot's ethos of sympathetic imagination and its implicitly individuating effects, even keen readers, however, might not notice that it diverts us away from particular experiences and persons—experiences of psychic interiority and suffering—and instead into social particularity's inverse: a social generality known only by its imaged impossibility, even its unbearability. Likewise, readers have tended to overlook the sociological texture of a stance that grants one a "vision and feeling of all ordinary human life," a sociological texture underscored by the new meaning of "frequency" within a nascent nineteenth-century statistical idiom of intervals and measurement.[22] Eliot's ordinariness here evokes novel modes of social experience that emerged amidst the rise of statistical accounts of society, a transformation that Audrey Jaffe traces in her recent account of the stock market and the nineteenth-century novel's figurations of collective feeling, what she calls "affective life of the average man." A felt condition, the "fact of frequency" not only posits the ordinariness of marital disappointment but also the highly charged, felt qualities of a ramped-up sensitivity to social commonality, of the sociological imagination. Character in Eliot, as Jaffe puts a point that I would here underscore, "emerges distinctly as a felt relation to the collective."[23]

Eliot had begun to think about the novel in relation to early forms of sociology in her 1856 essay "The Natural History of German Life," in which she praises W. H. Riehl's proto-sociological study of German peasantry for making the "images that are habitually associated with abstract or collective terms," like "peasantry" much more accurate and concrete. However, Eliot argues in the essay that the novel is superior to emergent sociology in the knowledge it can produce about the social world and the uses to which that knowledge can be put. Lacking the sympathy-generating powers of the novel, Eliot writes, social science leaves us affectively untouched: "appeals founded on generalizations and statistics . . . require a sympathy ready made." But great art like the novel "surprises even the trivial and selfish into that attention to what is apart from themselves."[24] In Eliot's essay, sociological knowledge, gained through new Victorian social scientific tools such as statistics, fails to produce any emotional effect. However, in the passage from *Middlemarch* we just looked at, sociological knowledge itself is the source of unexpectedly powerful affective responses, turning the representations of collective or average life, like those found in statistical tables, into a felt condition. To encounter social extensivity in this passage is as much affective and bodily as it is cognitive.[25] In the novel's formal coherence and its conventions for telling the story of society, it might appear to be just as Eliot's essay understands it: a countertype to the vast, unruly amounts of information about society, the great semi-digested masses of statistical studies, chronicles, and parliamentary Blue Book investigations that began to be produced in the early decades of the century.[26] But the overwhelming nature of sociological awareness and the social's felt qualities here in *Middlemarch* make vivid instead the opposite point, the surprising *continuities* between social statistics and the realist novel's own sociological imagination.

The amplified *Middlemarch* of "Why always Dorothea?" imagines the extension of narrative attention to more and more characters, expanding the energies of narrative individuation to every character in the novel, however marginal. In linking this moment with the "keen vision and feeling of all ordinary human life," we can better recognize that narrative interruption as an iteration of "hearing the squirrel's heart beat." The fictional social sublime conjured by a narrator whose touch might turn every character into a protagonist suggests that for a reader of *Middlemarch*, the experience of a multitude of characters' overwhelming centrality is a sensation courted though never fully realized, an impossible experience whose potential or threat is nonetheless part of the thrill of readerly immersion within such a multitudinous fictional world.[27] To hear the roar on the other side of silence would be akin to reading *Middlemarch*, amplified.

With this impossible *Middlemarch* in mind, we might take the force of the narrator's interruption to be less about extending narrative attention to an ever-increasing number of specific characters—a novel, but bigger—and more about extensionality or social amplitude itself. The overwhelming, possibly lethal thrills of the characterological sublime implied by the narrator's interruption, and whose potentiality helps makes *Middlemarch* seem more fully peopled than it is, also might direct us toward affects of the novel that, while by no means dispensing with characters altogether, are less frequently attended to in readings of Eliot or the novel more generally. These affects and orientations are more corporate in nature, made up less of the intimacy with a singular character than the impersonal intimacy of the ambient landscape constituted by immersion in numerous fictional lives, as well as the combinatory powers of plot, the networks of affiliation that draw far-flung characters into relation to one another. As the great novelist of reminding us of the simple but difficult fact that other people exist, George Eliot might appear an improbable candidate for the appeals of system over character, of ambient social density over singular selves. However, *Middlemarch* enables us to recognize that a reader would not need a heart of stone to thrill to a novel less for its finely detailed depictions of individual lives than for the totality of those lives, the overall system or set of characters themselves and the varied networks that link them together across the novel, or even an intimacy with everyone who is not Dorothea.

From one angle then, *Middlemarch*'s signal quality as a novel might itself be understood as an aspiration toward hyper-expansiveness: its hope to narrate and interconnect the lives of an immense number of central characters, drawn from a wide-ranging social scale, but also its wish to integrate vast swathes of contemporary scientific and historical knowledge, as well as philosophical thought, into its narration. Much of this novel's substantial and oft-remarked engagement with contemporary developments in science has to do with modernity's ambitions to render more and more of the world the subject of inquiry. But it also has to do with the problems of scale that beset such expansiveness.[28] This includes Casaubon's doomed—because both methodologically outdated and outlandishly vast—project of discovering a "Key to All Mythologies," as well as contemporary scientific research projects organized by problems of scale, such as Lydgate's medical research into the "primitive tissue," the microscopically small structure he believes (wrongly, it turns out) to constitute the elemental substance of the human body. But it also includes the narrator's own oscillations, zooming in to the extraordinarily miniscule in one moment, drawing back to take in the breathtakingly far-reaching in another; or, translating the sublime into the minute, with a vast social field of "ordinary life" figured by the tininess of a squirrel's beating heart, a variability of narrative scale underscored by the recurrent use of telescopes and microscopes as figures for the narrator's zoom effects. Likewise, the scale of social life presents its own problems for the novel's usual processes of empathetic identification, which would necessarily be transformed as its social field exceeds physical or even psychic proximity. But it also presents challenges for the number of characters a realist novel might contain before their very populousness undoes them, the point at which they cease to be characters in any recognizable sense.

In its interest in the scale of social experience in *Middlemarch*, as well as the breadth of the realist novel's sociological imagination, this chapter swings into the outer orbit of recent work focused on distance and scale as methodological issues for literary study. Part of a broader interest in "the new sociology of literature," this work has various iterations, but some of the most powerful are intent on diverting literary study away from its traditional analysis of individual literary works.[29] Seeking to upend an ongoing commitment in literary critics to textual intimacy—the careful, close reading of a small canon of literary texts—Franco Moretti has begun to outline arguments for macroscopic, data-driven techniques of "distant reading." Bringing into view not individual texts to be more and more carefully read, but data in the form of literary systems, "distant reading" "allows you to focus on units that are much smaller or much larger than the text: devices, themes, tropes—or genres and systems." In doing so, new objects of knowledge emerge: networks or systems, evolutionary branches of micro-genres. By this account, the single novel appears as just the wrong size for analysis. In his own methodological version of hearing the squirrel's heart beat, Moretti argues that one consequence of our bias toward close reading and the individual text is we have little chance of understanding literary productivity on a large scale: "thirty thousand nineteenth-century British novels out there, forty, fifty, sixty thousand—no one really knows, no one has read them, and no one ever will."[30] Vast beyond even the most dedicated of reader's reach, the totality of nineteenth-century British novels puts in doubt an approach that takes the reading of individual novels as its basic procedure. In other words, Moretti is asking something like: Why always *Middlemarch*?

However, we should also see the techniques of distant reading of the novel as bearing a strong affinity with the *Middlemarch* I have been bringing to light. Each is interested in figuring out ways to be responsive to the problems and questions posed by what we might call the novel on a grand scale, albeit on different axes: a vast number of novels for Moretti, a single vast novel for *Middlemarch* and its narrator. *Middlemarch*'s own interest in diverting us away from its protagonist, its conjecture of a novel extensive enough to include "all ordinary human life," should remind us that Moretti's effort to wean us away from our absorption in a small number of Victorian novels and our intensive practices of close reading have their analogue and precursor in the realist novel itself. *Middlemarch*'s preoccupation with generality, extensiveness, and commonness suggests an alternative to the stark choice Moretti presents between reading and data collection, close and distanced reading.[31] In other words, a reflexive critical tendency to ally close reading with the novel form itself, to think of close reading as a critical method bearing the imprint of the novel's own immersive particularity, fails to account for the ways in which the novel has a preoccupation with generality written into it.

In this sense, the project of distant reading is itself more novelistic than some critics, who detect a kind of science envy in the project's social scientific aspirations, or likely Moretti himself, would contend. That a contemporary project of social scientific data-driven "distant reading" would find its interest in large-scale formations anticipated by the novel itself has a satisfyingly recursive quality to it, placing novelistic form as the invisible structure behind a literary critical project aimed at moving us away from individual novels. No doubt, in its concern with a single author and a single text, this chapter's data set is far too small for any project of "distant reading." But by turning to ways in which the novel, and even its readers, engage questions of generality, distance, and knowledge—the scale, complexity, and the ways of knowing broad social formations in both *Middlemarch* and Middlemarch—we can see how much the novel thematizes and makes over into a formal concern both the socially intimate appeal of intensive engagement and the promises of social extensiveness indexed by strangers.

Large-Scale Eliot: Strangers and *Middlemarch*'s Sociological Imagination

To be a reader of Eliot is to be overwhelmed by a super-abundance of fictional life on intimate terms. So, at least, one early reviewer suggests: "It is not natural to most men to know so much of their fellow-creatures as George Eliot shows them . . . to watch . . . the tangled course of intermingled lives. . . . [A] feeling of even painful bewilderment in its contemplation is not entirely unbecoming."[32] That Eliot's first readers were equal parts delighted and oppressed by the social intimacy on the large scale afforded by her novels might account for the slightly manic catalogue of characters that regularly appeared in reviews of her work, such as this one:

> Dorothea with her generous ardour and ideal cravings; Mr. Brooke with his good-natured viewy incoherency and self-complacence; Celia with her narrow worldly sense seasoned by affectionateness; Chettham with his honourable prejudices; Ladislaw with his dispersed ambitions . . . Casaubon with his learning which is lumber . . . Lydgate with his solid ambitions which fail and his hollow which succeed; Rosamond . . . [with] all the faults which can underlie skin-deep graces . . . the Garth household, the Farebrother household, the Vincys, the country bankers and country tradesmen, the rival practitioners, the horse-dealer.[33]

In the face of the "painful bewilderment" of mass intimacy, producing a character population overview in list form might make Eliot's formidable populations feel more manageable; a populace catalogued would become less bewildering. And, as a miniaturized stand-in for the novel itself, a list of Eliot's characters offers the cognitive consolation of abbreviated scale, a shorthand way of taking in the novel's whole populace (one otherwise so vast as to nearly exceed apprehension) with a quick glance, a *Middlemarch* in little.

Like "Why always Dorothea?," these lists index the challenges of contending with Eliot's social expansiveness. A jury-rigged effort to convey a novel's
social range in a short review, a list of characters also draws the appeals of
multiplicity and systematicity together with the more familiar ones of novelistic singularity. If Eliot in list form casts another light on the structural
tension between individual characters and vast social fields, that tension also
generates its own attractions, the pleasures of cataloguing and counting.
Tabulating Eliot's novelistic populations enables readers to take the measure
of the novel's scope person by person, generating a serial social aesthetic that
underscores the attractions of both seriality and systems alongside the more
traditional pleasures of novelistic narrative.[34]

Arranging characters into new social configurations within a list is at
odds, of course, with *Middlemarch's* own carefully plotted articulation of the
social interconnections formed by familial networks, gossip, marriage, and
sympathy among its characters. Pried apart from the novel's textured, tightly
integrated fictional social environments—"this particular web"—lists recon-
stellate characters into social proximities not dreamed of within the novel's
own plot: a horse breeder dwelling closer to Rosamond Vincy than either the
novel, or Rosamond herself, could imagine. Strangers to one another in the
novel's plot, paths never crossing, they nevertheless are brought into contigu-
ity within the list. The very expansiveness of Eliot's fictional social fields—so
large as to generate the need for proxy means of apprehending them—enable
occasions for unlikely juxtapositions among characters otherwise unintroduced to one another.

As byproduct of the novel's expansive set of characters, the lists echo
Middlemarch's notable habit of offering its reader shorthand versions of its
own plot or social field. Scale-model *Middlemarch's*, these abbreviations of
itself—of which the narrator's description of its locus of interest in the novel as
"this particular web" is only the most famous instance—distil a socially complex fictional world into something seemingly more graspable. Considered
as compensatory responses to the formal and cognitive challenges of the
novel's social extensiveness, these shorthands are inverted forms of "Why
always Dorothea?" Where that question about a single character opens onto
an unbounded socius, the list transistorizes a vast social field into manageable form. This toggling between miniaturized and amplified versions of itself
thus indicates how *Middlemarch* is shaped stylistically by the pressures of its
own social expansiveness, as well as the effect of extensivity upon the novel's
early reception. Moreover, this toggling underscores the elusiveness of the
social itself to figuration in *Middlemarch*, its resistance to being brought into
view as anything but a necessarily limited set of particularized and accretive
instances of people coming together, or as being evoked only gesturally, by
dramatic breaks away from its narrative absorption in a single character.

In rendering a complex social field into an object of knowledge—the list as a census of the novel's sprawling populace—the character tabulations of *Middlemarch* echo the forms of sociological understanding with which Eliot's fiction has long been leagued. Herbert Spencer's exception for Eliot to the London Library's rule of not including fiction within its collection, on the grounds that her novels were a form of fictional historical sociology, is only one of the earlier instances of seeing Eliot's fiction as closely allied with emergent nineteenth-century sociological thought.[35] The shared terrain of the novel and sociological thought—their mutual efforts to make the abstraction known as "society" into the subject of representation—becomes, however, a preoccupation for *Middlemarch* itself. The figuration of expansive social environments, as well as the figuration of the understanding or registration of those environments, becomes a concern not only for the novel's narration but also for the characters within it.

In this next section, rather than marking out Eliot's own well-known engagements with early sociologically minded thinkers, such as Herbert Spencer or Auguste Comte, I will show how sociological mindsets or stances are not just mutual partner to the novel, but also perceived antagonist. Allied with sociological knowledge in its representational aims, *Middlemarch* nevertheless is concerned to differentiate itself as an aesthetic form from such alliances, uneasy about the erosion of the distinctiveness of the novel alongside other forms of social explanation. If the novel is understood as the bearer of sociological insight, and *Middlemarch* is driven by the aspiration to bear such insight, Eliot's novel is also shaped by a counter-effort to differentiate itself from "mere" sociological insight. As concerned as *Middlemarch* is to bring before us individuals in their particularity, its countervailing evocations of large-scale social formations—social fields nearly unbound—structure a tension between the novelistic and the sociological that shapes *Middlemarch* in important ways.

> Certainly nothing at present could seem much less important to Lydgate than the turn of Miss Brooke's mind, or to Miss Brooke than the qualities of a woman who had attracted this young surgeon. But any one watching keenly the stealthy convergence of human lots, sees a slow preparation of effect from one life on another, which tells like a calculated irony on the indifference or the frozen stare with which we look at our unintroduced neighbour. Destiny stands by sarcastic with our *dramatis personae* folded in her hand. (95)

Another moment of stock-taking in *Middlemarch*: the novel's narrator again pauses, with the apparent inattention of characters to one another ("nothing at present could seem much less important to Lydgate") now the occasion to consider the proper calibration of narrative attentiveness amidst a fictional social field awash with characters. Coming as this passage does—the novel is completing the introduction of its central characters and shifting its narrative attention dramatically away from its presumptive protagonist—a reader might be forgiven for wondering where this is all headed, a concern that the phrase "stealthy convergence" promises to allay. And, in fact, a great deal of information—many characters, many plotlines, many historical, medical, and philosophical excurses—has accumulated in the novel's early pages. As if upon the precipice of narrative overload, the novel pauses to consider its future, giving both readers and itself a moment to catch their respective breath.

Read with an eye toward the sociological imagination of the realist novel, this passage suggests a rhyme between omniscient narration and the macroscopic, detached viewpoints being elaborated in nascent nineteenth-century sociological practices such as social statistics. In this light, the "convergence of human lots" might read as an especially lyrical description of sociology's general object, social life, and this passage an exemplary instance of the novel offering an overview of its own fictional social field—as if to remind us we are reading a study of provincial life. Sweeping its gaze across the future meetings of some of its central characters, *Middlemarch* considers an ironic future of social convergence for the "unintroduced."

This moment, however, is not just an example of the novel's sociological imagination; it also illuminates a tension between the novelistic and the sociological. In pausing, the novel produces what could be called a sociological account of its plot: abstracting from the specificity of its individual characters' soon-to-be-intertwined lives, it gives an account of those meetings not as particularized plot, but as social fields—the "convergence of human lots." In this moment Dorothea and Lydgate, otherwise particularized and narratively central characters, are eroded into near indistinction. Transformed into strangers with "frozen stares" toward their "unintroduced neighbors," these protagonists are demoted temporarily into *anonyma* within their own novel, cast as de-specified sociological figures for the general stealth of social convergence. While elsewhere in *Middlemarch* any character might potentially become central under the plenitude of its narrative attentiveness, here we find the inverse. Character is dissolved into a social existence too thin even to bear characterhood, "sociologized" out of distinctiveness, as if to reassert strangerhood as a necessary step on the way to becoming familiars.

A recognizably modern social scene of strangers, with its vivid mix of social aloofness and propinquity, the passage thus departs from Eliot's usual go-to figure for social complexity in *Middlemarch*, the woven web. Like a city dweller who cannot quite relax on a weekend in the provinces, it is as if Eliot's narrator temporarily overlays the novel's provincial setting with an urban template.[36] In this moment, *Middlemarch* underscores what Anthony Giddens calls the "abstract" character of modernity, the unknowable qualities of a modern social realm constituted largely by a world outside one's immediate personal experience, one permeated by the networks and forms of knowledge beyond our ken. The condition of large-scale social structures, a world beyond the scope of everyday personal interaction, however, is in this passage far from abstract. Instead, it takes on all the affective immediacy, and familiarity, of a cold stare.[37] Oddly, for a novel famously concerned with provincial life and with nurturing a capacity for sympathy, the "frozen stare" here reminds us of nothing so much as the urban strategy of achieving isolation amidst social propinquity, familiar to anyone who has ever ridden the subway and quickly learned the first rule of city living: never make eye contact.

"Civil inattention," Erving Goffman calls this, a modern and ordinary practice of "awayness" in the polite aversion of one's eyes when in close quarters in public. As sensitive to the minute calibrations of social attentiveness as Goffman, Eliot nevertheless here underscores not the everyday necessity of social absorption in public, but its perils.[38] The quaint phrase for the stranger whose indifferent stare reflects the habit of big-city modernity—the as-yet "unintroduced neighbour"—imagines something like awayness's opposite: an unforeseen, and uninvited, intimacy with those unknown. The faint *film noir* tone of the passage suggests the modern world's fearsomeness does not lie in being unknown and alone, surrounded by strangers in the indifferent city. Instead, the anxiety of modernity lies equally in the possibility of suddenly being known to the strangers one had comfortably tuned out by staring right past.[39]

In its attention to attentiveness, this passage also distinguishes between those perspicacious enough to attend to the social world by means of "watching keenly" and those whose vision is arrested in the unknowing "indifference" and "frozen stare" of strangers in close quarters. In a novel that calls us to the sympathetic imagination of the lives of others, it is notable when it dwells on waning interest or indifference. The indifference of strangers here highlights two forms of disattending, one in, and the other to, the novel. In the novel: the stare of strangers here underscores social short-sightedness as a basic feature of the modern world, a kind of cognitive myopia that keeps us from getting much purchase on the complex interrelations constituting the social sphere in modernity. It is not just that we need our personal space on the omnibus. Rather, the casual aversion of one's eyes in order to preserve privacy in public—the civil inattention without which the millions of small social claims in any densely peopled environment would make life "unbearably sticky" as Goffman puts it—makes a virtue out of the complex and crowded social condition of modernity. To the novel: the passage reassures potentially weary readers that a broad cast of characters—some inhabiting entirely different plotlines, chapters, and parts of town, and whose paths have not much crossed at this point—not only will be brought together by the novel's plot, but will be so surprisingly—stealthily. The "Destiny" who "stands by, sarcastic, with our *dramatis personae* folded in her hands" is in part a promise that the novel's disparate storylines really are going to come together eventually, an image of convergence within Destiny's folded hands.

If we bring this set of observations together, we can see that the passage reads paradoxically: as both a condensed image of social convergence and attachment and as an emblem of specifically modern indifference or social detachment. In this, it marks not just a continuity between the projects of sociology and the novel. It also makes vivid a tension between the sociological and realist narrative, one that is threaded throughout Eliot's novel. The novel's imagination of social amplitude or extensivity, figured here through strangers, is at odds with consequential, plot-furthering social relations, the genre's imperative to specify and codify social affiliations by conferring legibility and meaning on them through plot. As I noted in the Introduction, the genre of the novel itself might be thought of as a machine for producing tight social affiliations, transforming "strangers into kin," as Sharon Marcus puts it, through the convergence of human lots. Novelistic plot converts an initial set of "weak ties" among characters who are far-flung, unknown, or distant to one another at the novel's start, into the densely interwoven set of relations that typify novel endings: friends united, weddings celebrated, relatives long-lost brought home at last.[40]

To think of the novel in these terms, however, is also to hew closely to a traditional understanding of plot as the singular site, and organizing structure, of social experience in the novel. What Marcus's account helps us see is the novel's imperative to specify and make social affiliations meaningful both within and by means of its plot—to turn strangers into familiars—is also an imperative to drain the modern socius of the very conditions of anonymity that constitute it. Strangers cannot have a story, the novel tells us; to give them one is to make them no longer strangers. In turn, to thin out the specificity and "plottedness" of novelistic characters, as this passage does by turning them momentarily into strangers, is to untether them from the novel's diegetic structure, to unbind them from the demands of realist, particularized characterization and the social convergences necessitated by plot. Doing so enables a brief figuration of the multiplicity and populousness of the modern socius, a socius whose breadth and "unplottedness" is otherwise counter to the novel genre's specifying and codifying imperatives. Like "Why always Dorothea?" and the lists of characters, which mine a countercurrent to the novel's carefully constructed tight social affiliations, this passage marks a sociological imagination at odds with the realist novel's own codifying structures of plot and social convergence.

Eliot's emblematic strangers should remind us that inaugural theorists of society such as Georg Simmel took "the stranger" as an unofficial ur-figure for modernity's conjunction of impersonality and intimacy in everyday life. Early theorists turned to the city as an exemplary site of new forms of consciousness and sensory experience brought on by social agglomeration. For Simmel, life amidst strangers in the city produces the characteristic "blasé attitude" and "reserve" of urban inhabitants.[41] This newly quotidian experience of being amidst strangers, Simmel observes some decades before Goffman, gives rise to new forms of disattending to others in public, even while remaining nonetheless attuned to one's social surroundings.

More broadly, the conditions under which strangers and the neutral social forms they instance become an ordinary part of everyday life are also the enabling condition for the science of modernity, sociology. In Simmel's early strain of social theory, strangers on the bus are not figures of social negation. Instead, they are the crystallization of a society understood to be constituted by social evanescence: the unremarkable, transient relations of those unknown to one another in a public space. For all our sense of the overlapping projects of the novel and sociology, and for all the sociological inflection of *Middlemarch*'s reflection on social convergences, what is notable here is how Simmel's strangers mark an important difference between the novel and sociology. The novelistic drama and deep irony of Eliot's "Destiny" and "stealthy convergence" have no place in Simmel's society, which is comprised by social neutrality and transience.

> Thus, two people who for a moment look at one another or who collide in front of a ticket window . . . even here, where interaction is so superficial and momentary, one could speak, with some justification, of sociation. One has only to remember that interactions of this sort merely need become more frequent and intensive and join other similar ones to deserve properly the name of sociation. It is only a superficial attachment to linguistic usage (a usage quite inadequate for daily practice) which makes us want to reserve the term "society" for permanent interactions only.[42]

Even granting Simmel's novelistic taste for the micro-dramas of everyday life, next to *Middlemarch* his sociology neglects all the texture and specificity of social life on which novels thrive. But for Simmel, such "neglect" is just another name for an enabling abstraction, what allows him to generalize the thing called "society" out of innumerable specific social interactions.

Eliot's and Simmel's strangers thus operate in radically distinct ways. Figures of stupidity and indifference in Eliot, these zoned-out strangers remind us of the ironies of plot and the opaque, "stealthy" qualities of the modern socius. In Simmel strangers are instead the bearers not of stupidity but of knowledge, the site of sociology's diffuse object—society—in its lustrated, graspable form, the atomic units of sociality in its most neutral, minimal mode, what Goffman later calls "unfocused interaction." Their non-specificity in effect enables social theory to take society as an object of study.[43] Eliot's strangers, by contrast, carry an anxiety that the crowdedness of the modern world might not give rise to connection, "the effect from one life on another," nor to a "keen vision" of such effects. Instead, for *Middlemarch* the dilatory qualities of social evanescence or asociality render strangers resistant to narration's demand that even the briefest of social interactions become specified and produce plot-furthering meaning. Asociality, not knowing one's "unintroduced neighbor," is precisely what narration is poised explicitly to *overcome*, what is to be repaired through the novel's "stealthy convergence of human lots." Strangers yes, but not for long, the novel promises.

Strangerhood is thus a kind of productive threat to plot and narration in *Middlemarch*, as well as to the novel's ethos of sympathetic relations, one to be healed by stealthy social convergence. Thinking in these terms underscores the unlikely relation of sympathy to the modern social scene of strangers within Eliot. Sympathy is not only a crucial ethical practice in Eliot, by which particular characters come to bear upon one another's lives. It also parallels novelistic plot's own impetus toward social convergence, another means by which strangers become familiars. Sympathy in *Middlemarch* tends to take place under conditions of unlikely sociality, meetings whose exceptional character, outside everyday social life, are crucial to the exercise of sympathy they occasion.[44] Strangers turn into familiars through unexpected encounters with others, "stealthy" forms of affiliation otherwise improbable in a particular social field—meeting someone either from, or in, the wrong side of town, say—thus, a Rosamond Vincy and a Dorothea Brooke in this passage, who come from such different social classes they effectively inhabit separate worlds. Such convergences, with their mix of surprise and predictability are, of course, part of what we expect from a novel: the unlikely (though not too unlikely) bringing together of characters.

In this account, to break free of everyday social roles, to act as if one were momentarily unbound by barriers such as class or gender, as well as unbound by Victorian liberal society's first right, later codified as the right to be let alone, is a condition for entry into sympathy in Eliot's books. Such unlikely affiliations between people, we should notice, are redolent precisely of the contingent interactions of strangers, the very forms of social evanescence and detachment that are sympathy's presumed antitype. Relationships that occasion the exercise of sympathy in Eliot's books are thrilling in part for their very disruption of the routines and social barriers of everyday life depicted in the novel. But, that thrill also comes from the unlikeliness and improbability of such encounters even within the logic of the plot, making sympathy into equal parts ethical imperative and engine of narrative. In a reversal of our usual understanding of sympathy in Eliot as the site of comity, identification, and understanding between people—turning strangers into kin—sympathy here depends upon the unpredictability, the imperfect knowledge of others identified with strangers and the modern urban socius. Social distance is not simply what sympathy heals; it is sympathy's enabling and necessary condition. It takes one not to know one for sympathy to do its narrative and ethical work in Eliot.

The tone of suspenseful hesitation in this passage reads as if Eliot were momentarily channeling the unlikeliest of fellow novelists, Wilkie Collins, whose fiction we have already seen is no stranger to the unlikely and melodramatic convergences of strangers. "Certainly nothing at present could seem much less important to Lydgate than the turn of Miss Brooke's mind." In the turn from its promise to deliver thrillingly unlikely meetings between characters to the general claim about calculated irony, the passage lingers for a moment over the narrative and social potentiality of any brief encounter between strangers. Eliot, the great attender to each and all, allows narration a moment of "unfocused interaction," propelled not by forward movement but dilating laterally out into counter-plot energies of social potentiality and expansiveness, a momentary appearance of the social space of "the familiar," as I discussed in the Introduction.

Like the briefest meeting of eyes on the train, however, moments like this in Eliot cannot last, with even the barest figuration of asociality not permitted to loiter in her pages. In the logic of plot-driven social convergence, no character can remain socially indistinct for long. Likewise, in a rhyme between the imperatives of realist form and *Middlemarch*'s own plot, a stranger cannot remain so for long in Middlemarch either. "A stranger was absolutely essential to Rosamond's social romance" (118), we are told upon the newcomer Doctor Tertius Lydgate's arrival in provincial Middlemarch, signaling his part in a story already written by Rosamond Vincy herself, a socially ambitious young woman intent on not marrying locally. From the point of view of narrative structure, strangers represent a purely functional asociality. Like Lydgate in Rosamond's social romance, they exist only in order to be brought together by the "stealthy convergence" of human lots. Like a slightly too eager hostess at a cocktail party, Eliot cannot bear for anyone to remain unintroduced. Instead, the "unintroduced" become, in this passage's logic of inevitable narrative convergence, members of a strange, distinctively Eliotic social category: the pre-introduced.

In bringing narration to a pause so as to get a better grip on the novel's own already considerable complexity, *Middlemarch* here teeters at the edge of an overload of what information theory calls "noise." The presence of excessive information in a channel of communication, noise, is what we hear as static in the message.[45] The "noisiness" generated by the intricate social interconnections of a novel with ten or so central characters, along with those many others whose possible centrality is never far from the narrator's consciousness—a complex information system to be sure—is first underscored and heightened by Eliot's grafting of the urban onto (or into) provincial life. *Middlemarch*'s "social noise" here—condensed into the figure of socially indistinct strangers—will then be reduced through plots of sympathy and social convergence across the novel's remaining pages.

The social noise of the novel, and its anticipated reduction into manageable narrative and social proportions, picks up on the various registers of noisiness and amplification that accumulate around the "frequency" of "all ordinary human life." Rather than this static needing to be refined out of *Middlemarch* entirely, however, it instead here acts as the background hum against which the social relations figured within the plot appear, by contrast, more coherent and legible. As I suggested earlier, if this passage is not literally crowded with a multitude of people, the social pressure produced by the opening chapters' accumulated characters permeates it. In this passage's glance ahead to the courtship plot of Lydgate and Rosamond, and Dorothea's later sympathetic acts toward them ("Certainly nothing at present could seem much less important to Lydgate than the turn of Miss Brooke's mind, or to Miss Brooke than the qualities of a woman who had attracted this young surgeon.") the narrative shrinks a scene imbued with an almost overwhelming social plenitude, promising to thin it out into the story of just three people.

Even in a genre given to allegorizing its own effects, the diorama of plot laid out by this passage is a particularly strange piece of novelistic reflexivity. It is as if a miniature version of *Middlemarch* appears within its own pages, a ship in a bottle, rendering this expansively scaled novel graspable with a glance. The novel's recurrent figurations and acknowledgments of its own expansiveness here, however, are not just a means of reflecting on the representational challenges of social complexity, as with "Why always Dorothea?," but a means of resolving them. As if impatient with the unfolding of its own plot, the novel does not even wait for that promised meeting. With their "stealthy convergence" to occur only many hundreds of pages later in the novel's story, these strangers are in some sense nonetheless already gathered together by and within the space of narrative, "*dramatis personae*" folded within the hands of "Destiny." In this sense, narration's promise of future social convergences within the plot is not just a promissory note. Instead, it is more like a body double for it, preempting plotlessness by generating affiliations even between characters who have not yet met. While meaningful social affiliation is the usual product of novelistic plot, which "turns strangers into kin," here affiliation is constituted through narration, relocated from the diegetic world of plot to the discourse space of narration. A salve for the indifference and anonymity of modern social life, narrative space here becomes a refuge from the novel's noisiness, the plethora of plots, characters, and information, a site of lustrated sociality that is at once of the novel and outside its plot.

The sociality figured in this moment is mediated in an extreme sense, anchored not in the face-to-face meeting of the novel's story world, but within the discourse space of narrative. A social intimacy paradoxically constituted through its apartness from the social world proper of the novel, this intimacy is also—like the "keen feeling for all ordinary human life"—an experience not actually had by anyone within the story of the novel. It is a purified or asocial sociality because it is thoroughly mediated out of the novel's bustling, messy fictional social world and into the space of discourse, as well as being a strangely unexperienced experience for its characters.[46]

"The stealthy convergence of human lots": With the novel unable to sustain plotlessness for more than a moment, strangers do not stand much chance of remaining in their socially indistinct state for long in *Middlemarch*. However, the ways in which social convergence happens seem to matter to Eliot, and the novel makes a point of differentiating between two ways of making strangers into familiars. We might read Eliot's passage and ask of such convergences: "'Stealthy,' sure, as opposed to what?" As if in response, the novel sharpens its linking of sympathy with unforeseen social encounters by contrasting them with forms of social life that are characterized not by surprise, but by utter predictability. These un-stealthy convergences, forms of social life that emerge inevitably and unthinkingly, unsurprisingly, from the complex social structures of Middlemarch itself, earn a remarkable disdain from the novel.

The valuing of contingent, exceptional forms of social convergence might simply be read as the bread and butter of the realist novel, of course, the means, long fascinating to its lovers and endlessly annoying to its detractors, by which the novel keeps readers turning the pages in a game of waiting and deferral. Narrative suspense in the realist novel did its part in contributing to a broader project of reshaping doubt in the nineteenth century, Caroline Levine has recently suggested. By making the act of stopping to doubt our most entrenched beliefs about the world pleasurable, the suspenseful novel taught its readers to enjoy the wait for the world to reveal its surprises, making reading fiction into a kind of Humean pleasure principle. The pleasurable instruction in skepticism by narrative suspense in this account depends upon the expectation of at least the possibility of not getting what you came for, of decent odds of having one's expectations defied.[47]

If we flip this coin of contingency and get its other face, however, we might also wonder if Eliot's narrative practice only can value social worlds that feature sizable doses of unpredictability. By this light, the extent to which social structures might be made the object of predictive knowledge, or that effects within the social field might be known or anticipated with some accuracy—as a rough description of sociological thought's aspirations might have it—such a world presents an antitype to narrative suspense, and in turn to the ethics and pleasure Eliot associates with it.

The complexity and interconnectedness of social life in *Middlemarch* is, of course, one of its most well-known aspects, the subject of much remark by both its readers and its narrator, as we have seen. And complex social structures are one powerful way of both building suspense into novelistic narrative and introducing contingency, a means of differently interrelating numerous characters, but also of diffusing and diverting the effects of actions and conversations. As Fredric Jameson discusses in relation to Providential narrative in the nineteenth-century novel, any particular well-intentioned action can be transformed as it travels across the complex circuits of "this particular web" in Middlemarch, with acts intended benevolently giving rise to ill, and vice versa.[48] But as anyone who has spent more than a day in a small town knows, the densely interconnected but acutely observed social structures of provincial life also might turn out to make a social field all too predictable. And, as Eliot suggests in "The Natural History of German Life" with reference to statistics being unable to generate the surprise necessary for sympathy, too much predictability would be a risk not only to the pleasures of suspense but also to the novel's ethos of vicarious sympathy.

Meeting the Vincys in Style

That Eliot's sympathy is occasioned by the unexpected, the "stealth" of social convergence, underscores its dependence upon an ethic of not knowing, I have suggested. That ethic in turn rests upon an understanding of the social realm as both ubiquitous and "noisy," as characteristically unknowable and unpredictable to those who inhabit it. But, what of those who think otherwise? The sociologist, for example, who would seek to study and better understand social structure; but more close to home for this novel, a doctor who moves to the provinces from the city for what he thinks are country folk's more easily ducked social claims. And his future wife, Rosamond Vincy, who even before the first encounter, in which their "eyes met with that peculiar meeting which is never arrived at by effort," already "had woven a little future, of which something like this scene was the necessary beginning" (117). Here is a convergence less stealthy and more a foregone conclusion, at least as Rosamond has imagined it.

In the final two sections of this chapter, the ways and means of navigating social density, emblematized as a narrative concern in "Why always Dorothea?," bring a particular interest to bear on the characters most beset and exasperated by Middlemarch's own dense, surprisingly complex social environment, Rosamond Vincy and Tertius Lydgate. Lydgate the cosmopolitan doctor and Rosamond the local beauty, each in their own way, emphasize the knowable or manageable nature of the Middlemarch social field over its noisiness. While differing in their techniques—those of social confidence and supercilious indifference, respectively—each is blithely convinced of his or her ability to remain apart from enmeshment in the "particular web" of Middlemarch's own set of densely interconnected social networks and the social forms they occasion. Rosamond has tended to be neglected (or treated) by critics as one of the novel's least likeable characters, and Lydgate fails in his dreams of scientific greatness in part because of his taste for "the flower of Middlemarch." But, it is just their socially vitiated qualities that connects the challenges of narrative attention in *Middlemarch* to characters in a provincial town, one whose very peopled-ness, at least for Lydgate, comes as something of a surprise. In shifting focus from narration to character, we will see how the challenges of social extensivity for narration are recast at the level of character as the problem of navigating the dense and complex social fields of Middlemarch.

In turning to Rosamond and Lydgate's courtship, a different version of social convergence comes into view, one that transpires amidst and emerges from a social field drained of much of the stealth and noise I have suggested is central to *Middlemarch*. The most attractive man and woman in town by the Middlemarcher's lights anyway, the inevitability of their coupling is phrased by the novel as having all the surprise and depth of the high school prom king and queen dating one another. Which is to say, no surprise at all, given that their prom-like coronation depends upon their acceptance of the structures with which the social system has already made a match between them inevitable. It is in contrast to such mechanistically inevitable social convergences within the plot that narrative space can come to seem a harbor of relative social freedom, but also, as we will see, the bearer of a social intimacy otherwise impossible within the novel's fictional world.

The one character more at home in the city than the country, Lydgate has thrown off his taste for European capitals in order to pursue his medical career more single-mindedly in the provinces, planning to remain uninvolved with the local amusements of the Vincy house, where Middlemarchers go for "gossip, protracted good cheer, whist-playing, and general futility" (349). Not just a big city character's snobbish disdain for country fun, Lydgate's plan is symptomatic of his belief that it is possible to remain outside the central nervous system of social connection in Middlemarch. Avoiding such entertainment at the Vincy's within *Middlemarch*, however, is pretty much like trying to avoid being within the plot of the novel altogether. And in the story of Lydgate and Rosamond's courtship, plot itself takes on an almost uncanny life of its own, allied with a mechanistic determinism that emerges from the social organization of Middlemarch. In this storyline, the complex of social relations that constitute the communal structures of Middlemarch itself becomes the engine of plot development, a plot-generating social reflex whose bland automatism is counterpoised to social convergences that are more properly "stealthy."

"A study of provincial life": so Eliot's subtitle for her novel reads. And any reader with a taste for the precision and analysis promised in the scientific ring of "study" will not be disappointed by the precision and analytic qualities of the narration within *Middlemarch*, which become as compelling as the story itself. Yet, Eliot herself seems to be disappointed at times, at least when her book's characters begin to comport themselves as if they were the too-cooperative subjects of a scientific experiment instead of characters in a novel. As we have seen, some lives in *Middlemarch* converge with enough stealthy high drama to cast the nonetheless inevitable character of their social affiliations in the light of sympathy's secular grace or Destiny's sarcastic smile. At other times, inevitability is short on such rhetorical drama; short, in fact, on both rhetoric and drama. Rosamond's likelihood of meeting the handsome new doctor in town is phrased instead in the language of common sense.

> Lydgate could not be long in Middlemarch without having that agreeable vision [of Rosamond] or even without making the acquaintance of the Vincy family. . . . For who of any consequence in Middlemarch was not connected or at least acquainted with the Vincys? They were old manufacturers, and had kept a good house for three generations, in which there had naturally been much intermarrying with neighbours more or less decidedly genteel. (96)

Who indeed, at least in the opinion of those with whose voice the narrator briefly speaks? The unimpeachable certitude and self-affirming logic of the collective voice of Middlemarchers are heard here in the narrator's brief, ironic channeling of its mindset.

"For who of any consequence . . . ?" Eliot's book is dedicated to refuting such narrow social views in the name of a democratic expansiveness ("Why always Dorothea?"), to mocking and exposing the casually invidious social distinctions on display here in this passage. Even the very form of free indirect style, in which narration temporarily takes on the idiom and perspective of a character (or here, community), might be said to support the inclusive ethos of a novel that would mitigate these kinds of social distinctions, lending its narrative voice to all comers. But, at its most democratic, Eliot's free indirect style gives voice even to the anti-democratic, to those pitched against any expansion of the in-crowd, lending voice even to the mindset of social distinction itself. Catching the ironic effect of this particular moment of free indirect style, however, should not keep us from noticing that ironizing such a mindset can equally be a means of confirming rather than negating that mindset's conclusions, if not the habits of thought that arrive at them.

Free indirect style's rise has been central to the story told by a number of recent studies of nineteenth-century realism, and *Middlemarch* makes liberal use of this narrative technique. Effecting a compromise between the novel's narrator and a character by momentarily thinning out the barrier between discourse space and story space that normally separates them, free indirect style is a "technique for rendering a character's thought in his own idiom while maintaining the third-person reference and the basic tense of narration."[49] Narration in free indirect style thus conveys to readers a sense of unmediated access to a character by speaking as nearly as possible in, and with, the voice and thoughts of that character. But it does so, crucially, without either overwhelming a character's point of view through direct address, as with more didactic eighteenth-century narrators, or simply dissolving itself into that character's voice. Conversely, a character momentarily can be availed the narrator's perspective and voice, but stops short of staging a raid upon the narrator's authority. A middle territory between narrator and narrated, free indirect style might be thought of more broadly as a compromise between the energies of individual freedom and social stability, a tension central to the realist novel, particularly in its *bildungsroman* form: free indirect style, Franco Moretti writes, "leaves the individual voice a certain amount of freedom . . . while coloring individual emotions with the supra-personal idiom of the narrator." The voice we hear in free indirect style is neither exactly that of the character, nor that of the author. Instead, "it is a *third voice*, intermediate and almost neutral: the slightly abstract, thoroughly socialized voice of the achieved social contract."[50]

"Intermediate, almost neutral": The neutrality and transience of stranger sociality, its expansive lateral qualities, are counter to the plot's forward momentum, I have said. Counter to plot, it is nonetheless essential to the texture of modern life that the realist novel takes as its subject: this is the central tension we have been exploring. Here I want to suggest that, uneasily housed in plot, such a strangery social mode finds expression instead in the novel by migrating from plot into narration. Stranger sociality, the central experience of modern urban life, is transmuted into a free indirect style that stranger-like—transiently, semi-neutrally—inhabits a multitude of characters' perspectives, and vice versa. In being endowed with a particular voice, the "well-socialized individual" is also endowed with the social legibility and coherence we recognize as novelistic "character." As with the plot's inevitable transformation of unknown (which is to say unplotted) strangers into well-met characters and kin, however, free indirect style too ultimately transforms strangers into familiars for readers, which is to say into characters. And yet, free indirect style's combination of social propinquity and detachment, its affordance of what D. A. Miller calls "impersonal intimacy," threads together familiarity and detachment, interior and exterior in ways that plot, "a machine for turning strangers into kin," cannot. Closer to a character, and yet more neutral, free indirect style "grants us at one and the same time the experience of a character's inner life as she herself lives it, and an experience of the same inner life as she never could."[51] The narrative style of social neutrality, free indirect style thus transmutes novelistic "noisiness," the abstract or indistinct qualities of strangers and their awkward fit with the socially codifying impulses of plot, into the central narrative innovation of the nineteenth-century novel.[52]

In tying this form of narration to an impersonal intimacy or the well-socialized self, it is nevertheless important to observe that what free indirect style instances is a pointedly unsocial form of intimacy. It is, in fact, an intimacy predicted on the impossibility of anything like actual social contact between its participants. The third-person narrator and character of the realist novel can meet only (and can only "meet") in the "unspeakable sentences" of free indirect style, a phrase Ann Banfield uses to underscores that such sentences occurs only in fictional narrative, never in dialogue or ordinary speech. Put in the terms of the point I am arguing here, its socialization is predicated on a social life with another that is grammatical rather than actual, viable only as a narrative technique and form of experience that are the exclusive properties of neither the character nor the narrator.[53] With character and narrator barred from ever crossing over into one another's separate worlds in the novel—those of story space and discourse space—free indirect style nonetheless brings together those who must remain apart, articulating social convergences that, in the end, decline to actually become social. That is, only articulating such relations, in the sense of rendering them through or within narrative discourse, rather than giving those relations solidity and weight within the depicted world of the novel.[54]

It is just this hypothetical quality, however, the purely grammatical social intimacy granted by free indirect style that suggests *Middlemarch's* narrative form does not simply underwrite or replicate the forms of sociality depicted within the novel's story. Instead, narrative discourse itself comes to house social relationalities that are unsustainable within the plot, or even able to be experienced by a fictional character, forms outside the "stealthy convergences" plot demands. Expressible only within and as a narrative technique, the neutral sociality of free indirect style thus remains free from the world of events within the novel itself. So too can it maintain distance from the imperatives toward social legibility within realist plots, by which intimacy is necessarily personal, strangers inevitably and irresistibly drawn into codified relationships as familiars or kin, friends or lovers. Narrative space might provide some refuge or relief from the codifying demands of plot, expressing forms of impersonal intimacy otherwise impossible.[55]

"The well socialized individual": in Eliot's thinking, maybe too well, if socialization means, as Dorothea complains "call[ing] everything by the same name that all the people about me [do]" (537). Her sister Celia, to Dorothea: "You always see what nobody else sees; it is impossible to satisfy you; yet you never see what is quite plain" (36). Frustrating as it is to Celia, Dorothea's "seeing what nobody else sees" is a central quality of the *bildungsroman's* protagonist, a singular point of view set against a world, with whose forces nonetheless she must eventually reconcile her autonomy. For Celia, seeing anything else is something both more and less than an epistemological error; it is a lapse in social form, a falling away from social correctness. And one means by which readers are encouraged to dislike Rosamond Vincy from the start is because of her socially attuned consciousness, her abiding sensitivity to social forms cast by the novel as the effect of a too-accomplished socialization. If accounts of free indirect style as ideological instrument cast it as the novelistic technique of modern socialization, perfectly suited in its neutral tones to the novel's generic inclinations toward the middle ground between individual freedom and societal stability, it is worth noting how frequently it is the Middlemarcher's own too-eager socialization imperatives that are voiced and ironized by Eliot's free indirect style. Drawing near to the socially correct, narration establishes and intensifies its difference from bare social conformity—a conformity that would include only seeing what is "quite plain"—by bringing itself within close range of it.[56]

"For who of any consequence . . .?" In *Middlemarch*'s whispered rewriting of the opening sentence of *Pride and Prejudice*, the certainty of this voice indicates that the romantic convergence of Rosamond and Lydgate is both a foregone conclusion, a truth universally acknowledged, and a natural emanation of the social structures of Middlemarch. All the ethical import of the "stealthy convergence of human lots" is nowhere to be found on the way to meeting the Vincys. Instead, this portion of "this particular web" of social life in Middlemarch brings together characters via the reliable operation of well-established social mechanisms, the picture of the predictable and non-stealthy convergence of human lots.

In case we were to miss the no-way-out nature of things here, the reflexive thinking of the provincial mind finds its way to the reader's ear as well: Lydgate can neither "be long" in Middlemarch, nor "belong" in Middlemarch, without knowing the Vincys. The iron logic and claustrophobic qualities of social organization within Middlemarch briefly inhabit the narrative voice, telling the reader twice what Lydgate never hears at all: no matter how aloof he believes himself, he will surely belong to Middlemarch, just as surely as he will meet the Vincys. Repeating at a syntactical level the inevitability of belonging within the plot, this line might seem rhetorically "noisy," introducing static by its double reading, an unintentional granular-level joke sneaking into Eliot's usually pellucid prose. Rather than noise making this message harder to hear, however, the static renders the joke—like knowing the Vincys—impossible to resist.

If this risks a bit of clunky over-reading, its cue comes from Eliot's prose in this passage, which seems to creak uncharacteristically here. Eliot's almost rote description, however, shows its laboring gears precisely at the moment it indicts the dullness and predictability of a social life that itself seems mass-produced—quite literally here an effect of the aggregate of those "of any consequence"—by the social mechanisms of Middlemarch society. Sympathetic understanding and reflective judgments about one's actions, the ethical centerpieces of Eliot's novel and her narration, in particular, are put under pressure by the apparently reflexive quality of social effects, their clockwork production by the structures of social life in Middlemarch.

The aesthetic and ethical problem that emerges in such a moment is increased by the novel's investment in maintaining a distinction between novelistic plot, in which action is undertaken purposively (at least ostensibly), and action that is simply the emanation of social structures. So, while Rosamond's perception is utterly attuned to the local social rules and networks of Middlemarch, that perception is itself figured as a mere effect of the social structures she inhabits, rather than as a thoughtful, reflective relation to those structures. Earlier in this chapter we saw one way the novel and sociology are at odds with one another, with the plotlessness and expansiveness of the sociological able to flicker into being only momentarily before being dialed down into the codifications of plot. Here plot, understood as entailing purposive action, risks being usurped by the densely interwoven social structures of Middlemarch itself, the "particular web" that exemplifies the novel's sociological achievement for many critics. In the Rosamond–Lydgate storyline, the meticulously fine social interrelations of Middlemarch seem to produce plot spontaneously, like a novel writing itself, and so superseding the kind of self-conscious and reflective relation to one's own actions the novel associates with sympathetic imagination. The distinction I am after here might be glossed by two different senses of reflexivity, one indicating self-consciousness and the second associated with reflex in the sense of a twitch, the merely automatic nature of the social effects that emerge from the network of social relations in Middlemarch. The social medium of *Middlemarch*, the system of interrelated social structures that are the usual backdrop for the central drama of (a great number of) individual lives in Eliot's novel, leaps here into the foreground, taking over the plot and briefly overwhelming any sense of intentionality in the actions undertaken by characters.

In effect, the fictional social structure of Middlemarch meticulously constructed by Eliot is too well, which is also to say too readily or instinctively, understood here by some who inhabit it. Coming only a few pages after the novel's meditation on the indifference of strangers and its prediction of surprising affiliations between unfamiliars, the story of Lydgate's acquaintance with the Vincy family is that moment's antitype, an instance and emblem of the kinds of social encounters that surprise no one at all. What we get in the Lydgate and Rosamond story is a scale model version of the novel's broad plot-sympathy paradigm. In that paradigm, personal transformation and a wider moral vision come about from surprising and ethically charged encounters with others, encounters that might allow us to recognize in others what the novel famously calls "an equivalent center of self." But in the Lydgate–Rosamond plot, we find ourselves reading what feels like a miniaturized pulp version of *Middlemarch* that has snuck inside *Middlemarch*, in which the pleasures of the reliable structural predictability of genre fiction, such as those we might find in the detective novel, temporarily supplant the more diffusive pleasures of deferral we have come to associate with *Middlemarch* itself in all its social and narrative complexity.

Whatever pleasures we might find in a plotline whose action unfolds like a reflex of Middlemarch's social body, in which the wider vision that might enable a grasp of the social whole takes the diminished form of a local aspiration to know the social scene, it is clear the novel wants us to find less of them. This antitype plot of social convergence, what we might think of as the purely structural or spoiled (in the sense of spoiling the surprise, but also in the sense of "gone bad," like spoiled milk) version of social convergence, banishes contingency from itself and from the minds of both readers and characters. The parameters on this scale model version of the social interconnection plot have already been well measured in advance. Measured both by the broad populace of Middlemarch, which is confident that everyone eventually will know the Vincys and that it knows a good social match when it sees one, and by Rosamond Vincy, who knows a good social match even before she sees one: "A stranger was absolutely necessary to Rosamond's social romance."

The difference here between the obscure, suspense-filled pathways of a "stealthy convergence" that surprises an "indifferent stare" and simply meeting the Vincys is all the difference in the world for Eliot. That difference is the one between social convergences too obvious and too mechanical, what might be called "too sociological," to be narrated by any but the gossipy, overly sociological Middlemarchers, and those more stealthy ones that occasion encounters and affects outside everyday social life. This latter type not only opens up spaces in Eliot's social and narrative fabric for great acts of sympathy between people, but it is also where novelistic narration asserts its superiority, and its claim upon our interest, over more overtly sociological forms of knowledge.

Eliot's most "sociological" character, Rosamond Vincy, with her sociologically eroticized incarnation of the "combination" of "correct sentiments, music, dancing drawing . . . and perfect blond loveliness which made the irresistible woman for the doomed man of that date" (268), her every perception acutely attuned to the social field of Middlemarch, is also arguably cast as the novel's most solipsistic. This suggests that to bear a sociological imagination at the level of character in Eliot might obliterate everything else about its bearer. To possess such knowledge or to adapt such a stance toward one's world is to carry a weight so heavy as to crush the capacity for all other forms of insight or being. *Middlemarch*'s imagination of a version of itself comprised by nothing but central characters, the novel maximalized with which this chapter began, finds its counterpart here in a character barely individuated enough to count as such in this description, distinctive only in her incarnation of the collective powers of the social itself. For all the sociological ethos of *Middlemarch*, its conviction that "there is no creature whose inward being . . .

is not greatly determined by what lies outside it" (838), the book carefully maintains its difference and its distance from that ethos through maneuvers stealthy enough to count as novelistic, to count as narrative and character, rather than mere sociological fact.

Flirting with Disaster

Tertius Lydgate comes to Middlemarch to escape the impinging, urban social world so as to pursue his vocation in solitude, but he finds there a woman who is never alone. Instead, "having always an audience in her consciousness" (167), Rosamond Vincy is surrounded by people, having always an audience in the consciousness of others as well. As we are told, "(every nerve and muscle in Rosamond was adjusted to the consciousness that she was being looked at)" (117). Eliot's narrative interruptions, I have argued, are responsive to the challenges of figuring social extensivity within the novel, momentary breaks from narrating the story of particular individuals in order to gesture toward a socius unbound, or to condense its own broad social field into a scale-model of itself, making it graspable with a glance. Here, however, this far less intrusive parenthetical comment—a narrative voice murmuring to itself rather than a question that abruptly halts narration—registers society's perceptual force, the mental parentheses, as it were, of an awareness of others that constitutes our sense of social being.

More vividly than anyone in the novel, Rosamond's hypersensitivity to the ways others see her incarnates society in this familiar form. But, her confidence in and awareness of her own social power in Middlemarch is at the heart of the grounds on which the novel makes Rosamond its primary exhibit in the case against an oversensitivity to social form. Rather than being the microscopic counterpart to the macroscopic roaming narrator detailing "the particular web," such local knowledge is a sure sign of ethical myopia in Eliot's world. Knowing how and when to be seen, a social knowledge converted into a local talent in Rosamond, is also the barrier to entry for an Eliotic sympathy predicated upon social unknowing. Seeking escape from the distractions of the overly peopled metropolis, Lydgate runs into the arms of a woman who carries a crowd of onlookers wherever she goes. As the narrator notes, "whatever Miss Vincy did must be remarked" (294).

Of course, whatever anyone does in the space surveyed by Eliot's own narrator must be remarked. And, the narrator has been training its reader in properly attending to others throughout, reminding us of the demands on narrative and ethical attention made by a densely populated novel. Too much interest in any one person, especially those who are beautiful, is one of the nets to be evaded by narrator and reader both. Those within the novel, however, find it hard to avert their eyes from Rosamond Vincy, and even for the reader such aversions are to be inferred from the narrator's quiet irony instead of being enjoined upon us. While "Why always Dorothea?" radiates out to illuminate the ethical and formal challenges of realist social multiplicity, the rhetorically understated irony used for the surplus of interest solicited by Rosamond—"(Every nerve and muscle in Rosamond . . .)"— remains fastened with surgical precision upon a local instance, cordoned off by its parentheses. And so, among the many blows dealt to Rosamond by the novel, an early one: unlike Dorothea, Rosamond occasions no reflection upon the demands of narrative attention, no bravura moment of the realist novel theorizing its own ideals and challenges. All of this passage's potential allegorical energies are drained away by the under-the-breath quality of a parenthetical aside.

Rosamond, however, does remind us that among the talents for handling the multitude of social claims produced by densely peopled social environments, few are as ready to hand as flirtation. While we might turn first to Jane Austen rather than George Eliot to learn how to flirt, the flirtation between Rosamond and Lydgate appears as a kind of test case of practical sociology in this novel, a means of contending with Middlemarch's surprising social density and multiplicity within its story space. Flirtation, a very public "play at being in love" (as Lydgate and Rosamond's relationship is first described), relies upon an artful self-conscious of the rules of the social sphere in which it transpires for its effectiveness. These qualities of self-consciousness suggest that flirtation itself, in the register of desire, constitutes a reflective relation to social structures more commonly associated with avowedly sociological thought. In its artfulness, flirtation also implies a relative if momentary freedom from a frictive social sphere, an erotic version of what Simmel calls sociability, the "play-form of association": "sociability distils . . . out of the realities of social life the pure essence of association . . . [and so is] spared the frictional relations of real life."[57] The appeal of sociability, Simmel makes clear, is in part its rendering something as complex and abstract as society into distilled, manageable form. Like sociability, flirtation is not simply an escape from society, but a way to experience society in leavened, game-like form. "While it is true that flirtation does no more than *play* with reality, yet it is still *reality* with which it plays."[58]

In drawing out a rhyme between forms of social understanding the realist novel produces and types of social sophistication such as flirtation, *Middlemarch*'s only true flirt, Rosamond Vincy, comes into view as an analogue at the level of character for the narrative's effort to properly attend amidst social numerousness. Rosamond's flirtatious navigation of a crowded social sphere (in which she is what everyone wants) in turn suggests narration itself in *Middlemarch* might be seen as a kind of flirting, a kind of erotic energy attaching itself to narration's need to lose interest. Parrying, without dismissing, the multitude of erotic possibilities within a crowded social world, flirtation resembles omniscient narration's own efforts to figure large numbers of characters without becoming absorbed by any single one of them. Thinking narration and character together, Rosamond and Lydgate's early flirtation, conducted ostentatiously in the public spaces of Middlemarch, thus also marks the persistence of the impersonal appeals of social extensivity in the novel, appeals that, under the regime of the novel genre's commitment to individuated character, narration itself can never quite embrace.

The story of Rosamond and Lydgate's flirtation also gives us one last impression of the ubiquity and the felt qualities of the social within *Middlemarch*. Their plot attests to a social fact as universal as any in this novel: any effort to remove oneself from the social scene in the myriad forms of being socially away—the civil inattentiveness of staring off into space, narration's own moment of "unfocused interaction," the playacting at romance by which Lydgate means to avoid broader social interaction, as we will see, cannot last for long in *Middlemarch*.

Lydgate imagines provincial life will be as close as he can get to being alone in a crowded modern world. Telling the Reverend Farebrother of his reasons for coming to Middlemarch, he surmises, "in the country, people . . . are less of companions . . . one makes less bad blood, and can follow one's own course more quietly" (174). Middlemarch for Lydgate is a space emptied of cumbersome sociality, a depopulated "medium for his work, a vehicle for his ideas" (180). In a word that illuminates both his desire to be free and the premodern, constraining character of social relations in his understanding, Lydgate insists he does not intend to be the banker Bulstrode's "vassal" and will not become indebted to him (179). Just about any social relation for Lydgate, however, feels like a claim akin to servitude upon him, and his story is largely of unsuccessful attempts to evade such claims. The issue of the Chaplaincy for the new hospital, for example, in which he is forced to cast the final lot in a vote for one of two candidates for a well-remunerated position, ensures that Lydgate's name will be associated with Bulstrode, an association that will ultimately help exile him from Middlemarch. Voting with the banker to spite those who assumed he would do so anyway out of self-interest, Lydgate feels for the first time the "hampering, threadlike pressure" and "frustrating complexity" (180) of the multiple social claims made upon him in Middlemarch. His recalcitrance toward the internal politics of Middlemarch in the case of the chaplaincy signals a broader social obduracy that pervades Lydgate's efforts to remain socially aloof so he might concentrate upon his work.

In an image of the complexity and reciprocity of social structure in Middlemarch, Lydgate later finds himself struggling amidst the myriad interconnections that link Middlemarchers: "I find myself that it's uncommonly difficult to make the right thing work: there are so many strings pulling at once" (494). Lydgate belatedly intuits here the condition of interdependence that nineteenth-century thinkers like Herbert Spencer and Auguste Comte identified as the hallmark of modern social structure, what Émile Durkheim later in the century would call social or "moral density." Contrary to Lydgate's expectations upon spurning London for the countryside, the relative small-ness, remoteness, and density of the Middlemarch community make for a great number, variety, and complexity of social interrelations.[59] Not only do the economic fortunes of the Vincys and the Bulstrodes "hang by the same nail," as Mr. Vincy puts it, but more complexly, this nail is connected by social threads to multiple other nails, which are, in turn, connected to each other.

While the Vincy family is not among his patients early on, Lydgate "had many patients among their connections and acquaintances" (95). Tracing out the multiple levels of social connection between the Vincys and each of the other major non-aristocratic characters of the novel brought about through intermarrying—the Bulstrodes, the Garths and Peter Featherstone—Eliot's narrator underscores the further interconnections brought on by gossip. The "socially uniting" Mrs. Cadwallader, the Rector's wife who is a well-employed carrier of gossip, demonstrates the social function of talking about one another to one another (53). There is "no report about [Lydgate] which was not retailed at the Vincys" (96), for example, by their medical attendant, Mr. Wrench. Wrench's professional jealousy brings him to gossip about the new doctor Lydgate to the Vincys, and these reports are the beginnings for Rosamond, who is "tired of the faces and figures she had always been used to" (96), of her wish that she might meet him. Lydgate is introduced to Rosamond primarily through the tremendous amount of talk about him that his arrival in Middlemarch elicits, rather than through a face-to-face meeting. We might say—and in doing so note the ominous implications for Lydgate's hermitic wishes—he and Rosamond first meet, or, at least Rosamond first makes Lydgate's acquaintance, through the "socially-uniting" medium of gossip.[60]

My point here is not simply that Lydgate's desire to socially withdraw is impossible, although this is certainly one of the lessons he learns. Rather, it is both through the mediations of communal gossip, as well as talk about the community in which they live, that Lydgate and Rosamond meet and begin to flirt. Sharing a distaste for the "commonness" of the Middlemarchers, Lydgate and Rosamond look at first to be the subjects of the usual story of courtship in the nineteenth-century novel: gradually drawing off into the more secluded exchanges of the couple, a romantically sanctioned negation of the larger social field. But Lydgate and Rosamond's erotic attraction concurs less with the negation of the social sphere around them, as one might expect of two confirmed snobs, than with its libidinalization. What is erotic for them proves ultimately to be produced not just in, but by, a broader social realm. In the scenes of sexual attraction between characters elsewhere in Eliot's work, Jeff Nunokawa has argued, just being alone together behind closed doors often can be enough to produce an erotic charge.[61] Lydgate and Rosamond's attraction, however, both transpires in, and is promoted by, being largely in public, even as they imagine themselves drawing away from the middle-class social scene in Middlemarch. It may take two to tango, but in *Middlemarch* three or more are needed to flirt.

By "general consent" Rosamond is the most beautiful young woman in Middlemarch (268). "General consent" is, of course, the mark of mediocrity in *Middlemarch*, but consensus itself is here less a description of Rosamond's popularity than the means by which it is constituted. "Having no unbecoming knowledge," with "that combination of correct sentiments," music, dancing, and more "which made the irresistible woman for the doomed man of that date," Rosamond's status as the "It girl" of Middlemarch is the target of the narrator's irony (268). A far cry from Dorothea who "never called everything by the same name that all the people about [her] did" (537), Rosamond appears here as a recognizable social type whose skills might include rarely being at a loss for names of the kind that Dorothea never uses. "Sentiments" that are "correct," socially approved, Rosamond incarnates social consensus, and in bodying it forth underscores how social consensus can produce libidinal attachments.

While the narrator's irony highlights Rosamond's mere type-ishness, those within Middlemarch find her all the more attractive for her performance and incarnation of a type. Like the felt force of "all ordinary life," the apprehension of Rosamond as a kind of sociological entity carries its own charge, one that makes the sociological affectively real within the novel. An aura of determinism hovers in this passage not just around Rosamond's description as a type, a "correct combination" that highlights her submission to the forces of fashion, but also its erotic effects. The correlation between her embodiment of a type and the social effect of this embodiment is as powerful and irresistible as a muscular reflex, one that "the doomed man of that date" has no hope of escaping. Like the reflex by which one "could not be long in Middlemarch" without knowing the Vincys, Rosamond embodies an irresistible erotic social fact.

Among Lydgate's charms to Rosamond is that he seems to her to not be anybody in particular: "a stranger was absolutely necessary to Rosamond's social romance" (118). If Rosamond's appeal to Middlemarch men is in part due to her impersonal qualities, she herself is no less attracted to the impersonality of a stranger. In this preference, Rosamond's erotic longings are conjoined with a paradoxical attachment to detachment. The stranger, Simmel writes, is "one [with whom one] has only certain *more general* qualities in common" and "as a group member ... is near and far *at the same time*."[62] Lydgate's own indifference and social aloofness are the very instrument of his attraction to Rosamond. The "flower of Middlemarch" appears to Lydgate less as inhabiting a social medium than as standing out in relief against it. His "general disbelief in Middlemarch charms, made a doubly effective background to this vision of Rosamond," and even her mother's lower station renders her all the more attractive. "The tinge of unpretentious, inoffensive vulgarity in Mrs. Vincy gave more effect to Rosamond's refinement" (116, 158). Sharing a disdainful consciousness of provincial life, Lydgate and Rosamond find much to talk about when they finally do speak face to face. At a dinner party in the Vincy home, the two "readily [get] into conversation" about the general "tuneless" state of Middlemarch music, save, it is implicitly understood, for Rosamond's own playing (159). Rosamond's comment that "'we are speaking very ill of our neighbours,'" halts only for the moment an extended flirtation conducted over the shortcomings of Middlemarch life. What brings them together is what they think sets them apart from the rest of the Middlemarch community.

What sets them apart, however, is also what fails to maintain a separation between the flirtatious pair and the rest of the Middlemarch community for long. The restiveness of flirtation defers desire by playing with desire. "Every conclusive decision brings flirtation to an end," Simmel writes.[63] It is precisely this sense of the deferral of both erotic and social obligations that most appeals to a man who views Middlemarch as thinly peopled, a "medium for his work, a vehicle for his ideas" (180). Deferred desire of the flirtatious sort in the nineteenth-century novel finds expression most frequently, of course, in verbal play, and Lydgate soon finds himself engaging in such games with Rosamond. His response to her assertion at a party that he will find little to like in Middlemarch: "'I have certainly found some charms in it which are much greater than I had expected.'" Rosamond's "simpl[e]" reply, "you mean the rides towards Tipton and Lowick; every one is pleased with those," elicits an oblique response from Lydgate, one whose open-endedness provides Rosamond with all the information she needs. "No, I mean something much nearer to me." In the substitution of a figure for a background, the substitution of the charms of Middlemarch, ones that "every one is pleased with," for those of Rosamond, we also get a glimpse of the error Lydgate is beginning to make. One cannot, Lydgate will learn, simply prefer the charms of the flower of Middlemarch and ignore the ground in which she is grown. That is, one cannot flirt in Middlemarch for long without someone taking notice.

The public social environments in which flirtation is conducted in this novel, the sites that help make flirtation what Richard Kaye has called "a private language enacted in public," are not restricted simply to physical drawing and dining rooms.[64] Rather, flirtation here is less about privacy in public than a recasting of the social itself as the site of the libidinal: the "public" of Lydgate and Rosamond's flirtation seeps into the speech and body language in which it is conducted, regardless of where. Having spent time alone together as a result of the doctor's attendance at the Vincy home during Rosamond's brother's illness, the two find themselves in "that intimacy of mutual embarrassment" (266) which arises from each thinking the other is feeling something. The embarrassment such self-conscious intimacy produces, however, is overcome not through a lessening, but an increase of self-consciousness: "Talk about the weather and other well-bred topics is apt to seem a hollow device, and behaviour can hardly become easy until unless it frankly recognizes a mutual fascination. . . . This was the way in which Rosamond and Lydgate slid gracefully into ease and made their intercourse lively again" (266).

Rosamond and Lydgate slip into new self-consciously theatrical, public roles, but do so in order to evade the implications of those roles. Lydgate "call[s] himself her captive—meaning, all the while, not to be her captive." "Flirtation, after all, was not necessarily a singeing process," and "this play at being a little in love was agreeable" (267). Flirtation for Lydgate is pretending to play in a play, a means of evading the social consequences of his relationship with Rosamond, which, after all, he reasons "did not interfere with graver pursuits" (267).

In treating flirtation as "play" in the sense of both game and theater, however, the public scene of flirtation becomes a part of their conversation and marks the self-conscious qualities of their exchanges. No longer uttered simply for themselves even when they are alone, such theatrically flirtatious speech combines John Stuart Mill's well-known definitions of eloquence and poetry. Eloquence is speech intended for others, while lyric poetry is defined by its asociality, an address "utter[ly] unconscious of a listener." "Eloquence is *heard*, poetry is *over*-heard," Mill writes.[65] Like a socialized version of lyric utterance, Lydgate and Rosamond hope to be both heard, and heard as overheard, by others. As the narrator remarks, "what they said had that superfluity of meaning for them, which is observable with some sense of flatness by a third person; still they had no interviews or asides from which a third person need have been excluded. In fact, they flirted" (268). More accurately, they had no interviews or asides that did not already incorporate an imagined third person as a condition of their speech.[66] How else to achieve the "superfluity of meaning" that constitutes the evasiveness and the pleasurable deferrals of signification in flirting if not always to have "an audience in [their] own mind[s]"? Nursing hopes to maintain his distance from the distractions of Middlemarch's social world, Lydgate takes up flirting as more sophisticated, and paradoxically less social, entertainment for himself. Demonstrating just how difficult securing such isolation can be in Middlemarch, however, the social sphere he hoped to escape returns as an eroticized imaginary third party to his flirtation, "an audience in [their] own mind[s]," becoming a condition of, and partner, to his pleasure.

Adroitly highlighting the conventions of their flirtation, "this play at being a little in love," Lydgate and Rosamond would appear thus to be beyond these conventions and the society that sponsors them—at least to the mind of Lydgate. The limitations of such practices, and the obduracy of a surprisingly complex social realm for Lydgate, are revealed in his mistaken belief that he can avoid society through an indifferent playing with its forms. Lydgate roots his certainty that they are only playing at being in love in a mutual sense of tact: he was "not [misunderstood], he believed, by Rosamond herself; she, he felt sure, took everything as lightly as he intended. She had an exquisite tact and insight in relation to all points of manners; but the people she lived among were blunderers and busybodies" (299). Lydgate understands tact as a kind of practical sociological knowledge, an "insight in relation to all points of manners." Conferring order upon an otherwise messy social sphere, tact bespeaks a social sensitivity responsive enough to smooth out any wrinkle. Tact is thus imagined by Lydgate as a form of social distinction that sepa-rates himself and Rosamond from the social blunderers of Middlemarch, but also as bringing the neutral, impersonal qualities of good social form to bear upon, and leaven, the intensity of their erotic relation.[67]

What the novel stages in this plotline, however, is precisely the failure of Lydgate's pretense to social knowledge and detachment from the local social claims of Middlemarch. The consequences that follow from Lydgate's confi-dence, simultaneously cast as both arrogance and ignorance, in turn affirms the novel's own firmer grip on such forms of social knowledge. Similar to the interplay between realist character and omniscient narration—in which narration is less a person or entity than an effect, created by its distinction from, and negation of, the limitations of anything-but-omniscient human characters—the demise of Lydgate and Rosamond's shared sense of being exempt from the social forms of Middlemarch render *Middlemarch*'s narrator all the more secure in its own claims to represent, and manage, the complex social environments that spell the frustration of these two characters.[68]

As Lydgate discovers, too late, "it was not more possible to find social isolation in that town than elsewhere" (294), and Middlemarchers begin to talk about his flirtation. The momentary suspension of social forces Lydgate achieved by distilling his social life into a flirtation with Rosamond ensures their return, endowed with even greater power in the form of a consensus whose powers of description are enough to bring into being what it purports to simply report on. "The certainty that Miss Vincy and Mr. Lydgate were engaged became general in Middlemarch without the aid of formal announce-ment" (346). Fittingly, for a character who learns the lesson of the intracta-bility and obduracy of Middlemarch's complex communal structures, it is the community, rather than Lydgate himself, who ratifies his engagement to be married. Erasing the distinction between the wider public of gossip and the act of publication, Lydgate and Rosamond's engagement appears as an effect of the consensus of Middlemarch's social networks, the same "gen-eral consent" that had found Rosamond to be "irresistible to the man of that date" (266). Lydgate and Rosamond merge at the moment of their engage-ment, not with each other, but with the web of communal relations whose reach they thought themselves beyond. From a marriage once envisioned as an antisocial paradise—a "being continually together, independent of others" (351)—they instead discover that to stand outside the community is merely another means of being part of the community. Affective identification and sympathy, the twin pillars of Eliot's fictional social worlds, are less important here than simply the fact of structural social interconnection that characterizes community formations.[69]

Lydgate the bachelor is last seen in *Middlemarch* hard at work for Middlemarch, spinning the "particular web" of communal relations he had come there to avoid, in the employ of the social forces he thought himself beyond. "Young love-making—that gossamer web! … And Lydgate fell to spinning that web from his inward self with wonderful rapidity.… As for Rosamond … she too was spinning industriously at this mutual web" (346). Having once nursed hopes to avoid social demands altogether within Middlemarch, and so to stand at some distance from the plot of *Middlemarch*, Lydgate's spinning at "this mutual web" puts him to work within a novel whose central image of itself and the social interrelations it depicts—"this particular web"—glimmers in its figurative interconnection with the gossamer strands he spins.

By its conclusion, the novel gives us to understand Lydgate's own aspirations to greatness in the sphere of medical research and reform as dashed, whereas Rosamond is accorded the lesser fate within the plot of getting what she wished for. Her desire to live apart from the middling Middlemarchers is granted after Lydgate's death in the form of a new husband who ministers to the gout of the wealthy residents of Bath.

In the different tones in which readers are encouraged to understand their fates, we also should recall how much closer Lydgate is to the affections and identifications of this novel and its author, so much so that Lydgate is at times accorded the aspirations of the novel itself. As a doctor, he "longs to demonstrate the more intimate relations of living structure," to gain knowledge that will allow him to "pierce the obscurity of those minute processes which prepare human misery and joy, those invisible thoroughfares which are the first lurking-places of anguish, mania, and crime" (148, 164). Readers of Eliot have noted that the talents of perspicacity ascribed to Lydgate's powers of imagination in this passage are shared by the narrator who grants them, suggesting that both seek, in different registers, to delineate the most intimate recesses of the human self. Promoting a continuity between the projects of the scientific researcher and the novelist, the powers of perception exercised by the narrator are momentarily extended to the scientist as well, though the scientist, unlike the narrator, fails to make good on such powers within *Middlemarch*.[70]

In other moments, however, Lydgate does not just share the realist novel's self-description, but himself uncannily seems to possess *Middlemarch*'s own vocabulary for itself and the social formation it depicts famously as a woven "particular web." The frustrations of social complexity experienced by Lydgate, as he attempts to steer his way through the political and social rivalries of Middlemarch, also lend him the idiom of webs and networks possessed by no other person within *Middlemarch*, possessed only by narration itself: "I find myself that it's uncommonly difficult to make the right thing work: there are so many strings pulling at once" (494). As if contemplating the nearly unimaginable act of writing *Middlemarch* himself, Lydgate describes his own social bafflement in a language borrowed from "this particular web" that keeps the narrator so busy. The clarifying, collating power for reader and narrator of "this particular web"—a distilled image of the novel's vast complex of interconnected social relations—when loaned to Lydgate in the vocabulary of "strings pulling at once," however, gives him no such insight, allows him no such clarity.

The barrier separating the space and vocabulary of omniscient narration and the space of character, here momentarily thinned out, would seem to be punishingly reasserted in Lydgate's cluelessness. A character is loaned a narrator's language, only to reinforce how far from that narrator's clear-eyed intelligence and perspicacity, as well as capacity to handle the complex social networks of the novel, that character is. However, at the moment when play-acting at love produces the same effect as love itself, we find that Lydgate is now less in possession of the vocabulary for this web, than put to work for that web's construction and expansion. Producing from his own unintended, not-so-stealthy convergence with Rosamond Vincy the very strings or threads of the social fabric he had hoped to avoid, the gossamer strands of "this particular web" enmesh him within the social world he thought he could distance himself from. And, even more strangely, as the web spins out from him, Lydgate would appear to be working not only for Middlemarch, but also for *Middlemarch*, giving readers the uncanny image of a novel and its social world—condensed by the narrator into the image of "this particular web"—unwittingly being produced by one of its characters. The strangeness of this image returns us to the idea of a *Middlemarch* as encompassing as all those who are not Dorothea, a novel diverting us away from its own always diverting characters, asking to be read for the ways in which it might make us, though not Lydgate, come alive to the expansiveness, the unbounded qualities, of the social.

In the convergence of the language of social interrelation and the language of novelistic form, sociality takes on a novelistic cast for Eliot; being socially intimate with another is modeled not just on reading, but also being in, or producing, a novel. Working not only against sociology but also character, as the privileged sites of knowing the social, Eliot posits the novel as able to produce a more affectively real and evanescent sense of the social at the moment that thinkers from Mill to Wilde are turning their attention thither. While Eliot's sense of the social is particularly novelistic, the novel itself is much transformed by this claim. Being with other people is not just modeled by the novel's depiction of psychic intimacy between two characters, intensively engaged with one another. Instead, we find ways of being with others in *Middlemarch* modeled not by the one-on-one close quarters of sympathy, but by the impersonal intimacies of free indirect discourse, by the extensive social landscapes of modernity, or by the charge of a felt responsiveness to "all ordinary life." The centrality of "noise" within *Middlemarch* asks us as well to reconsider accounts of Eliot and sympathy, noticing not only how people are drawn together in *Middlemarch* by conditions too complex to be reducible to the singular identifications of sympathy but also the felt appeals of turning from the one to the many, to all those who claim, however silently, the right to be imagined. That is, "Why always Dorothea?"

The modes of social life sponsored by forms far shorter than the novel, indeed by a literary form whose very brevity might well be a rebuke to the long-windedness and extensionality of the novel, will show us that being with other people is not represented and modeled only by the novel in the nineteenth century. The pleasures of getting away from others, or those of getting away from one person for the more impersonal social pleasures of the many, as we will see in the next chapter, finds its literary acme in the short-form epigrams of Oscar Wilde. The particular aesthetic, epistemological, and social problems posed by social density find their match in Wilde's own program for social brevity, a literary style and social ethos built out of none but the most ephemeral of social and aesthetic forms. We turn now from the maximalism and extensionality that I have stressed in *Middlemarch*, to the minimalist or miniature aesthetic and social ethos of the epigram.

Oscar Wilde's Ephemeral Form

The world of sociability . . . is an artificial world, made up of
beings who have renounced . . . the purely personal features of the
intensity and extensiveness of life in order to bring about among
themselves a pure interaction.

—GEORG SIMMEL, "SOCIABILITY"

Stranger, if you passing meet me and desire to speak to me, why should
you not speak to me? / And why should I not speak to you?

—WALT WHITMAN, "TO YOU"

A flattened Dublin, it has been said, could be rebuilt street-by-street, building-by-building, brick-by-brick, through a careful reading of Joyce's novel *Ulysses*. A book so detailed and thoroughly mapped onto its urban locale, *Ulysses* by these lights exemplifies a sense of even the formally innovative modernist novel as bearing a realist, quasi-sociological relationship to the European capitals in which it so often is set. So, given that his name is practically synonymous with the modes of style, urbanity, and sophistication reflexively associated with city life itself, we might do worse than turn to Oscar Wilde for a vision of London in the late nineteenth century, the geographic and imaginary epicenter of what I have been calling in this book the literature of social density. Who better, we might ask, to tell us about the spatial arrangements of the *fin-de-siècle* city and its society of strangers, or at least its more fashionable quarters, than Wilde?

In practice, however, a map of London as it is populated and traversed by characters from Wilde's plays, essays, and fiction would reveal that for all the vivacity of their social lives—Wilde's collected prose seemingly constituted around a series of dinner parties and dialogues in libraries and studios—his characters are practically agoraphobic shut-ins, rarely straying from the drawings rooms and libraries of homes on fashionable squares into the streets of the city. As if speaking for the entirety of Wilde's character population, one dandy declines an invitation even to sit in the garden and smoke cigarettes, protesting, "being out of doors makes one feel abstract and impersonal."[1] Even in his novel of lurid London, *The Picture of Dorian Gray*, the city is more location than locale: the passages describing the East End of London, for example, where Dorian goes to score opium, read as stock scenes with fog-shrouded streets that feel second-hand, as if cribbed from Charles Dickens's *The Mystery of Edwin Drood*. It is not just that Wilde cannot be bothered with producing his own realist detail. What is significant about Wilde's London versus, say, that of Dickens, is that it is above all small. An immense urban space has been recast as a social class; it is a compact, small-town version of a megalopolis where everyone knows your name.

The novel, of course, might be thought of as the city's made-to-measure literary form: both drawing for plot upon all the incident promised by the experience of urban accident and contingency—unexpected meetings of characters on city streets, networks of interrelated institutions and people—and reducing a city's chaos by transforming a potentially baffling urban scene into a plot, thinning the urban multitudes into a limited set of characters. But for Dorian Gray, so frequently recognized everywhere he goes in London that he flees for the "charm of a little village . . . where no one knew who he was," such distillations of urban complexity by plot feel akin to being crushed in a crowd on Regent Street, as if London were more rather than less densely populated for the fewer people such plots contain.[2]

The oddly shrunken social character of Wilde's little London, and the wish of Dorian to flee it, is the geographic expression of what I will show in this chapter to be an unexpected ambivalence about life with other people in Wilde. For all our association of both Wilde and his work with the vibrant sociality of a particular class and style of aristocratic Londoner and those who love them, people in Wilde are as much a problem as a pleasure. Unexpectedly, in a set of works constructed around a seemingly endless series of parties, drawing room dialogues, and flirtatious banter in the ballroom, we find a social ethos not just dedicated to the pleasures of the sociable moment but also besotted by that moment's termination. "All association must be quite voluntary," Wilde's edict goes in his essay "The Soul of Man under Socialism," and it is in Wilde's vision of voluntary attachments that we can mark the emergence of transient sociality as a full-fledged aesthetic project in the later nineteenth century, one that takes shape in Wilde, I will suggest, in response to the populousness of the social imaginary.[3]

While an antisocial ethos in Wilde is enunciated by Lord Goring in Wilde's play *An Ideal Husband*, who finds that "other people are quite dreadful," in this chapter I want to suggest that Wilde promotes less an antithesis than a continuity between Wilde's more familiar avidity for sociability, and that taste's seeming antitype, the antisocial Wilde. In the literature of social density, the particular form of sociability staked out by Wilde finds an endlessly renewed faith in those one does not know, most succinctly expressed by Algy's line in the original four-act version of the play: "I think people one hasn't met are charming." In tracing out the continuities between the sociable and the aloof, we will see the particular ways in which literary form in Wilde is responsive to, and shaped by, the felt force of the social that Wilde calls the "burden" of other people. Giving rise to innovative social and literary modes of both engaging and deferring the claims of others, such aesthetics of antisocial sociality will help illuminate one of Wilde's central projects: a wish to reconstitute society, to remake its forms, that is also at the center of the responses to the social forms of modernity we have been studying.

Plot itself is one of the means by which the novel manages social complexity, we have seen, by turning unwieldy populaces and complex spaces into a story, making London little by transforming strangers into familiars. I will turn in this chapter, however, to an extensive yet noticeably smaller program for dealing with populousness that takes shape across Wilde, most centrally at the level of a literary form that is arguably the realist novel's generic antonym. To do so means making the case for the importance of the apparently trivial in Wilde, the wide effects of a form of littleness so ubiquitous in Wilde's prose as to be easily overlooked: the small and slight but almost compulsively uttered literary form of the epigram. Well-known as playwright, novelist, poet, and essayist, it is at the level of the sharp, short, and witty line of the epigram where Wilde is the undisputed modern champion. We might try best to account for the ubiquity of Wilde's own signal compressed literary form not only as the acme of Wildean wit, in which we would note the pleasures afforded by a well-honed line, or as the mark of the thoroughly social orientation of his plays, novels, and essays, which constitute themselves around social scenes of gem-like witty conversation, or even by pointing out the epigram's proximity to the strategies of advertising slogans, as important as each of these accounts is to our understanding. Rather, the epigram, in all its minuteness, helps us to better understand something as diffuse as the contours of modern social life as it makes itself felt in Wilde. Finding in Wilde's epigram a means of managing social complexity as powerful as that of any realist novel, this chapter attends to the epigram's centrality in Wilde's work as an aesthetic correlative to the forms of social promiscuity—the flirtatious conversation, the witty banter, the brief encounter, the crush—around which Wilde constructs his plays, novel, and essays. In social transience, Wilde elaborates affiliative modes hard to tell from the wish to take one's leave of others, or to keep them at arm's length—familiars more than kin—modes thus suited to navigating the densely peopled social environments of the modern world.

In being attentive to Wilde's brief form, what we can better measure is the particular social effects and force of literary form in his work, in which a well-delivered *bon mot* can be as effective as a stiff arm in keeping others both close at hand and at arm's length. In Wilde's epigram, then, is the most marked formal instantiation of the overall valuation of the power of weak ties, wherein what is briefest or shortest is almost most lasting, that this book has been tracing out, to different effects, in a variety of generic and thematic contexts.[4]

By turning its attention to the epigram, this book thus finds an apt emblem as well of its own intertwined social and formal concerns. Literary form, we will see, becomes not just hard to tell easily apart from social effects in Wilde's epigrams, it also figures a utopic social wish to remake social relationality in its image. To be attentive to the felt attractions of social transience in Wilde is also, I hope, to return the force and distinctiveness of the social within his work amidst a critical tendency to assimilate all manner of social attachment in his work to the domain of the sexual. This is not to say that transient sociality does not have its sexual permutations, or its erotic dimensions. Nor is it to diminish the particularity of the felt force of the social, the threats of violence carried by the social, for a gay Irish writer in England at the end of the nineteenth century.[5] Instead, it is to make the case for the centrality of the social in Wilde so as to better understand Wilde as both a theorist not just of modern sexuality, but also of modern social life, as well as a theorist of the relational possibilities afforded by sociability itself. In the evanescent sociality of Wilde's characters, I want to locate not simply the means of articulating emergent sexual attachments, but the aptness of that form for navigating social multiplicity.

To give a sense of just how central the Wildean epigram is to the valuation of social brevity in his work, and that brevity's affordance of a respite from the claims of others, I will also situate epigrammatic breviloquence in Wilde within a range of broader, if perhaps less brilliantly voluble, ways in which Wilde's work is shaped by the effort to manage the social claims of a densely peopled social landscape. In brief, this chapter wants to suggest we should take seriously the brevity and apparent slightness of the epigram. I do so not by arguing that we have been mistaken in thinking it is slight or brief, pointing out the epigram's long and storied classical literary history, for example. Instead, in Wilde we find the import of slightness and brevity itself. What I trace out here are the implications and social effects of the claim in Wilde's long letter, *De Profundis* written while in the constraining space of Reading jail, a constriction that was, unlike the constrained form of the epigram, not of his own choosing: "I summed up all systems in phrase and all existence in an epigram."[6] It is in the confidence of that assertion, a certitude in speaking that is borne not just here but throughout Wilde by the epigram, that I will suggest we discover Wilde's convergence with some contemporary social theory's understanding of modernity as an era of chronic doubt, as well as the compensatory promises of a Wildean epigram that brooks no uncertainty.[7]

Short-Form Wilde

For all of the scenes of conviviality and sharp wit we associate with Wilde's work, life with other people is often articulated as a burden sooner shrugged off than avidly entered into. In "The Soul of Man under Socialism," the form of social coercion that Wilde calls the "sordid necessity of living for others," which "scarcely anyone at all escapes" (255), the "interference" of the "clamorous claims of others" (270) that "wound[ ] and maim[ ]" (262) reads as if Wilde were briefly channeling John Stuart Mill's vision of socialization and its discontents in "On Liberty." In Mill's account, like Wilde's, society too exercises its "interference," "restraint," and "compulsion" over the individual.[8] Unlike Mill's account of individual freedom and liberal government, however, the language of coercion used to describe the public in Wilde's essay, an English public that "tries to constrain and impede and warp the man who makes things that are beautiful" (277), is matched by a future utterly liberated from social relations entirely; an assertion of a glorious future in which society, under Wilde's version of socialism, will "leav[e] mankind alone" (266), making no "claims upon him at all" (284). Vividly evoked in this essay are the contradictions of determinism and freedom that resonate throughout Wilde's work, the antinomy of social life as both powerfully coercive, dominating of the individual, and possibly escapable. As Wilde phrases the central problem of modernity in *De Profundis*, "To be entirely free, and at the same time entirely dominated by law, is the eternal paradox of human life that we realize at every moment" (123). I will return to this essay as Wilde's most forthright articulation of the burdens of other people. But by glimpsing within it here the countertendency of a utopic evocation of the frictionless social life of a future society, we might ask about Wildean means of reshaping social life closer to hand so as to see what forms of sociality are imagined and licensed by Wilde's central rhetorical form.

The epigram's short and sharp form is at the heart of the passing exchanges central to Wilde, acting as image and instrument of both engaging the social and evading the more long-lasting aspects of social life. As anyone who has ever seen one of Wilde's plays knows, the enduring power of brevity also is what allows us to forget entire plotlines or the names of characters the moment we leave the theater while the one-liners remain firmly lodged in our heads. In the longer view of literary history, the brevity of Wilde's epigrams might also be thought of as a retort to the maximalism of the Victorian novel, an antidote not only to that form's own long-windedness but also to the novelistic forms of social extensionality we find in *Middlemarch* and *Bleak House* and the ethos of sympathetic, consequential attachment that has long been seen as its undergirding. Sleek, elegant, and cutting, at the level of form the epigram is everything the Victorian novel is not, which is to say that in being less, in some ways Wilde suggests, it is much more.

The epigram is Wilde's best known form, or the form that makes him best-known since so much of what lasts of Wilde are his one-liners: burbling up throughout his plays, essays, and in his novel in the mouths of characters, as well as the Preface to *The Picture of Dorian Gray*, which is comprised entirely by epigrams, and publications like the thirty-four epigrams that comprise

"Phrases and Philosophies for the Use of the Young," and the nineteen that make up "A Few Maxims for the Instruction of the Over-Educated." Wilde's epigrams bear the substantial wit and critical capacities they do because they operate as an intensified formalization of Wilde's satires of Victorian conventions and pieties. Simultaneously invoking and remaking conventional moral maxims, the epigram frequently reverses such maxims, leaving them both formally intact, and emptied of conventional moral messages (e.g., "ambition is the last refuge of the failure"; "if one tells the truth, one is sure, sooner or later, to be found out"). While brevity is the soul of wit, as well as Wilde's skewering of Victorian life, brevity also becomes a social mode in Wilde, one extending well beyond wit. So ubiquitous and generalized within Wilde's work as to nearly fade into the virtuosity of his overall prose style, the epigram is also more particularly at the heart of Wilde's exploration of the character of social relations under modernity.

As a condensed rhetorical form characterized by brevity, the epigram also becomes in Wilde a means of promoting such qualities as a social practice: a portable transient sociality of the city, as it were, everywhere one wants to be. In the words of one character, Lady Windermere, "I always like the last person who is introduced to me; but, as a rule, as soon as I know people I get tired of them."[9] Enamored with the social scene in general but tiring easily of the individuals she meets within it, Lady Windermere finds in the endless introductions to the many—strangers become familiars—relief from the boredom of the few. Or, the seemingly democratic ethos of *Dorian Gray*'s Lord Henry when it comes to friends is cast by Basil as a desire to be released from the enduring, individuating attachments of any particular relationship: "You like everyone; that is to say, you are indifferent to everyone" (*DG*, 8). But, as we know, it is not just what a character says in Wilde, it also how she says it. In phrasing her dedication to social transience in epigrammatic form, Lady Windermere allows us to see the epigram's social effects within Wilde, its aptness for relations that might last only long enough to deliver a good line. As the rhetorical crystallization of social ephemerality, a means of paradoxically sustaining social evanescence, the epigram also bears a particular relationship to the forms of familiarity and serial sociality associated with flirtation and parties. Like the epigram that sustains them in Wilde, such lighter-than-air social modes characteristically decline to consolidate into the intensities and obligations, the psychic intimacies of a durable relationship.

In their satirical brevity, Wilde's epigrams frequently bear a sort of lightning-strike sociological insight, able to startle readers into awareness of the artificial qualities of their own world and its social formations, denaturalizing institutions and social practices by diverting or reversing the usual meaning of a well-known maxim. As Amanda Anderson has noted in her study of Victorian efforts to develop positive forms of detachment and self-reflection, Wilde's epigram instances "an *ironic* detachment—it pulls back and comments upon a topic, a prior response, a set of conditions."[10] Irony is certainly one of the epigram's signal critical strategies, and in Anderson's terms the epigram is central to forms of ethical reflection and action in Wilde. But we might retexture her account of the epigram as ethical detachment by being equally attentive to the Wildean epigram's iterable or serial qualities, its particular affinity with a social transience that imagines detachment not as a one-time achievement, but an ongoing practice.

Alongside the epigram's general capacity for sociological insight, its more particular relationship to social momentariness brings it close to the sociology of short-form social encounters Erving Goffman developed in the mid-twentieth century. In what Goffman calls "interaction ritual"—a phrase that marks a continuity between Goffman's sociology of transient sociality and the writer who as much as any in the nineteenth century alerted readers to the weight born by the seemingly minor rituals of interaction—the social moment finds its twentieth-century chronicler:

> A sociology of occasions is here advocated. Social organization is the central theme, but what is organized is the co-mingling of persons and the temporary interactional enterprises that can arise therefrom. A normatively stabilized structure is at issue, a "social gathering," but this is a shifting entity, necessarily evanescent, created by arrivals and killed by departures. . . . A psychology is necessarily involved, but one stripped and cramped to suit the sociological study of conversation, track meets, banquets, jury trials, and street loitering. . . . Not then, men and their moments. Rather, moments and their men.[11]

What Goffman discovers in this study is the consequentiality of social brevity that is also at the heart of Wilde's understanding, the lasting effects of the smallest and most seemingly negligible of social moments. Society, Goffman argues here and across the work of his career, should not be seen as being constituted through the willed action of autonomous actors; instead, society crystallizes through the momentary, seemingly negligible social interactions of everyday life.

In taking up the ways in which the epigram registers and responds to the force of the social, this chapter carries out its own micro-sociology of literary form, deducing from the shape and function of the epigram a sense of what the social feels like in Wilde. The transient nature of the epigrammatic style, together with its inversions in Wilde of the "caprice" over the "lifelong passion," of the "faithless" over the "faithful," not only illuminates the epigram as a Wildean engine of transient sociality but also illuminates its recasting of the bonds of Victorian community into social evanescence.[12] The crystallized speech of the epigram exemplifies an effort—as hard as such effort can be to see amidst the social avidity and éclat of Wilde's speakers—to both cancel the constraints of the social and to reconstitute social life in the diminutive shape of the epigram, a social life whose affective intensities would be drawn from the brief encounters that find both their occasion and emblem within the epigram.

Although Wilde's work is thoroughly saturated with the consciousness of other people's presence, readers have been less attentive to Wilde's work as it responds to the difficulties of sustained relations and intersubjectivity in the social sphere that Mill describes as "interfering" with and "impinging" upon the individual in. Other people are as much a problem as they are a pleasure in Wilde, but they are crucially both: to choose one over the other—a fully sociable Wilde, with no party too small to pass up, or an anti-social Wilde, in which the social realm is evoked only to be negated through assertions of pure agency and freedom, as two recurrent critical views of Wilde in recent work have had it—is to miss the distinctive mode of serial sociality Wilde's rhetorical form promulgates, as well as that form's responsiveness to liberal understanding of society. To conclude from the wish to get away from others in Wilde that his was an aesthetic of social negation, or an instance of one strand of aestheticism's association with the inwardness of experience and the hermeticism of the aesthetic interior, or as manifesting an indifference to social forms of modernity, would be to miss the point of the passing social interests and attachments in Wilde.[13] While Mill envisions a social sphere with little middle ground between a social sphere that "interferes" with the individual and simply being left alone, Wilde's understanding of a self constituted out of our social encounters also produce a powerful sense of the oppressive tenuousness of that structure. But the structuring presence of weak social ties in Wilde also suggests that Mill's notion of an autonomous liberal subject is a fantasy that cannot be sustained.[14]

The epigram helps us better see how aestheticism's valuation of transient experience—most vividly in Walter Pater's understanding of art as giving "nothing but the highest quality to your moments as they pass, and only for those moments' sake"—finds its articulation in formal dimensions.[15] Critics of Wilde, with some notable exceptions such as Amanda Anderson, have tended to pass over his epigrams as an object of extended analysis, as if their wit, their status as mere wit, made them too transient, too slight to bear consequence. Their baldly propositional qualities—even as paradoxes, which, to be sure are as propositional in form as the maxims they invert—also make them resistant to styles of reading oriented toward the recessive or figurative aspects of writing in Wilde's aesthetic of connotation.[16] Anderson makes the epigram central to her understanding of Wilde's ethics, arguing that the epigram is the literary form of demystification, formally expressive of Wilde's project of critical detachment from, and critique of, the conventions of Victorian middle- and upper-class society. The epigram and its usual bearer, the dandy, instance the negative ironic critique that is both central, but ultimately in Anderson's argument, inadequate to a Wildean ethics that also seeks to limit the "free-floating detachment of the dandy" who utters them. In Anderson's account of the literary forms of liberal projects of distance, the epigram's portability, its capacity to be redeployed in multiple contexts, ends up reinscribing the limits of ironic critique, which cannot make normative propositions. That is, Wilde's ethical project struggles against its own forms of detachment. My understanding would suggest that this contextualization of the epigram into a normative ethical program underplays the critical potential of Wilde's promulgation of seriality and weak forms of relationality, by nature unavailable to propositional statements, but also that it underplays slightness itself, which is crucial to the powers of the Wildean epigram.

Consider the negligibility or what we could call the minorness of the diminutive epigram. Following Sianne Ngai's discussion of the minor aesthetics of cuteness in the twentieth-century avant-garde, we can see how minorness as a category conveys both the epigram's minuteness—the miniaturized dimensions of a bonsai rhetorical form that is, if not easily wrought, at least easy to pass along (on coffee mugs, T-shirts)—as well as the epigram's seeming inconsequentiality amidst the prolix rhetorical qualities of Victorian social criticism as embodied by, say, Carlyle's Hero as Man of Letters (and Carlyle's own prodigious literary production). In Ngai's account, however, the interest in avant-garde forms in the diminutive, the cute, such as Gertrude Stein's *Tender Buttons*, is the means of a meditation upon the "restricted agency" of art in a society defined by ends-means rationality. The epigram's smallness seems loosely to correlate to a kind of brash minorness, formal self-sufficiency as encapsulated critique. Not the lone and isolated voice of the Victorian sage enduring the wilderness, but a smart turn of phrase.[17] Critics may well have found little to say about epigram because everything has already been said by the self-contained, airtight, crystallized pithiness and certitude of the epigram itself. In a line that will be of central importance to this chapter's argument about the power of the confident speech borne by the epigram, as one dandy remarks, responding to a query of whether what he has just said is actually true: "It is perfectly phrased! and quite as true as any observation in civilized life should be."[18]

That Wilde thinks of his epigrams in *De Profundis* as the transistorization of the world, summing up "all existence in an epigram," and the miniaturization of "all systems" into the hard gem-like flame of the epigram's condensed rhetorical form, also places Wilde unexpectedly at the start of a longer line of short-form twentieth-century philosophical writing, such as Nietzsche's aphoristic works and Adorno's *Minima Moralia*, each of which find in the aphorism or the epigram a compelling formal mode for philosophical critique. With only a glance at the efflorescence of the aphoristic philosophical form among those who come after Wilde, we can ask what critical power breviloquence itself might bear in Wilde, and whether forms of reflection and critique less available in the novel (recall that while anthologies of "sayings" from George Eliot's novels were hugely popular, critics also complained that the appearance of aphorisms fragmented her works, interfering with one's ability to read the novel as a whole) might find their purchase in the seemingly trifling qualities of the epigram.[19] While the social effects borne by the epigram, its aptness as the coin of the realm of Wildean wit for fictional environments so thoroughly social as his, is the primary concern of this chapter, we can account along the way for the peculiar and possibly even pointedly limited critical force that might be carried by such a slight rhetorical form. The avowedly circumscribed form of its insights and the trivial or negligible regard the epigram solicits might be one place in which a Wilde intent on neither absolute constraint nor absolute freedom can come into view. Rather, in the epigram's combination of absolute rhetorical confidence and its pointedly trivial form, we can better find a Wilde concerned to mark art's power to signal its own limited powers in modernity.

The Soul of Man under Sociability

The desire to get some distance from other people is on display everywhere across Oscar Wilde's work. For those accustomed to reading Wilde as the pet dramatist of Victorian High Society, such a wish is phrased most familiarly as a form of snobbery. As we have been informed by Lord Goring in Wilde's play *An Ideal Husband*, "Other people are quite dreadful. The only possible society is oneself."[20] But as it is heard in this snobbish wish to reconstitute High Society as a party of one, the wit of the dandy, who could not do without the audience he disdains, provides cover for a broader program of managing social density in Wilde. The paradoxical inversions of a Lord Goring, who finds not three, but even two to be a crowd, are one arm of a more extensive program to evade the claims and obligations of communal bonds in Wilde's work. This program is broad enough to expand beyond its epigrammatic forms in Wilde, beyond the casual snubs of the dandy whose appeal only increases with his aloofness, to become what looks like a full-fledged project of social engineering. Not content to portray onstage the ever-widening circle of Victorian upper-class society as in need of the most Malthusian of plans—as Lady Markby remarks in the same play, "The fact is that our Society is terribly over-populated. Really, someone should arrange a proper scheme of assisted emigration"—Wilde undertakes just such a program of navigating the innumerable claims of the social throughout his work (*Husband*, 204).

Such a "scheme" for curtailing the demands of other people is hard at work not just in the self-regard of Lord Goring, for whom, famously, "to love oneself is the beginning of a lifelong romance" (*Husband*, 212). As Wilde's manifesto for renovating burdensome social bonds, "The Soul of Man under Socialism" suggests, not only is it "impossible for the artist to live with the people" (283), it may be impossible for all kinds of people to live with any people. "Assisted emigration" not being extensive enough to free one's self from the burdens posed by other people in general, Wilde elaborates a broad program for a world in which one might be released from the social sphere entirely. The constrictive powers of the social are registered by Wilde as the "blind forces" which govern action, as the "terror of society" (*DG*, 17) which "wounds," "maims," and "worries the individual" (SMS, 261), but also as the gentler forms of such power, forms unnoticeable enough to mask the fact that individuals are "thinking other people's thoughts" (SMS, 267).

The powers posed by society are countered by a broad enactment in a social register of what Wilde outlines in his critical essays as the principles of a specifically aesthetic freedom. "It is through Art, and through Art only . . . that we can shield ourselves from the sordid perils of actual existence."[21] In "The Decay of Lying," an essay devoted to the refuting realism's documentary mimeticism, Wilde institutes a zoning regulation for the appropriate subject matter of art so strict as to exclude from its concern any concern at all.

> The only beautiful things . . . are the things that do not concern us. As long as a thing is useful or necessary to us, or affects us in any way, either for pain or for pleasure, or appeals strongly to our sympathies, or is a vital part of the environment in which we live, it is outside the proper sphere of art. (*DL*, 299)

The forces of constraint identified with the social, and the modes of evading them, widespread enough in Wilde as to register even in the most minimal forms of interest in environments, things, or people, are the subject of his wider program for evading the claims of others. The doctrine of aesthetic-critical autonomy put forward in these essays on art and criticism evolves into a full-fledged scheme for escaping other people, finding its social ideal in the pleasures of a book that need not be read. People might, in a wish as strong as any in Wilde, be "shut . . . up, when they become wearisome, as easily as one can shut up a book of which one has grown wearied" (DL, 340). We might not at first glance recognize this book of Wilde's, one in which the wish that people might be "shut up" is realized. Or, rather, we might miss it amidst the wide range of methods for achieving such a wish that are employed in numerous works of Wilde including his most notorious one, a book in which even an attentive reader might be forgiven for failing to notice that a central character almost disappears before the story has even really begun.

No sooner are we introduced on the first page of *The Picture of Dorian Gray* to the man responsible for the "full-length portrait of a man of extraordinary beauty," "the artist himself, Basil Hallward," than do we find he is already transformed into a ghost of himself, a character imbued with the fatality of his future disappearance: "whose sudden disappearance some years ago caused, at the time, such public excitement, and gave rise to so many conjectures" (*DG*, 1). A "disappearance" no less "sudden" takes place here on the first page of the novel, but the casual tone of the prose with which it is accomplished forestalls any of the "excitement" or "conjecture" which followed this earlier disappearance, albeit fleetingly. In a book where world-weariness is worn as an emblem of the sensibility of the aesthete, it is as if *The Picture of Dorian Gray* is wearied enough of Basil Hallward to enlist him in a novelistic disappearing act the moment he appears on the page—and wearied enough to mention it as only the most passing piece of information that is quickly forgotten in the novel's forward momentum. In Basil's opening page disappearance, the book's beginning anticipates its end for this character, an end in which Basil, on the way to Paris, in his words "to shut myself up till I have finished a great picture," instead is murdered by Dorian Gray: "shut up" both within and like the book "of which one has grown wearied" (148). Basil's own anti-social impulse to "shut [himself] up" is preempted by another, more powerful one, that of *The Picture of Dorian Gray*.

The opening page of *The Picture of Dorian Gray* indicates in miniature a program in which the claims of others might be avoided "as easily as one can shut up a book." The wish that the incursive character of the social sphere might be as easily escaped as a boring book is tossed aside gives us an emblematic instance of how Wilde's aesthetic program also provides the model for a social practice. In Lord Goring's anti-social declaration that "the only possible society is oneself," we can detect the broader outlines of the determining social order he, and others in Wilde besides, wish to escape. The crowded character of this social order is registered even in a party at Lady Brandon's, one whose guest list undoubtedly is painstakingly culled and unquestionably elite, but which Basil refers to as "a crush" (*DG*, 6). The crowd violence lingering over a Society party phrased as a "crush" would seem out of place in the exclusive social *demi-monde* Wilde puts on stage and in his pages were it not so ubiquitous. Such violence, as Lady Markby in *An Ideal Husband* has already noted, is pretty much *de rigueur* for both High Society and Society in Wilde's work, societies that call into being the most extreme measures for escaping their crushing effects:

> The fact is, we all scramble and jostle so much nowadays that I wonder we
> have anything at all left on us at the end of an evening. I know myself that
> when I am coming back from the Drawing Room, I always feel as if I had-
> n't a shred on me, except a small shred of decent reputation, just enough
> to prevent the lower classes making painful observations through the win-
> dows of the carriage. The fact is that our Society is terribly over-populated.
> Really, someone should arrange a proper scheme of assisted emigration. It
> would do a great deal of good. (*Husband*, 204)

The "jostle" of an "over-populated" "Society" in which the push-and-shove of social life leaves one with barely a "shred" of clothing, or reputation, makes explicit the violence of the crowd implied in the "crush" at Lady Brandon's and elsewhere. Even in such presumably elite circles, the crowded social space Wilde understands as the condition of modernity is close enough to squeeze the breath out of the most experienced partygoer.[22]

That an emigration scheme of sorts is put into effect under the cover of art, among other modes, should not surprise us given Wilde's insistence on the freedom of the realm of the aesthetic from the kinds of determination and violence he associates with society. If some in Wilde simply "shut up" a book they weary of reading, and wish they could do the same with people, there also exist books in his estimate engaging enough to read through to the end. Such compelling books, like those of Balzac, can summon the magical talents to make people disappear, or thin them out into strangers, that in the analogy made between tiresome people and books one wearies of can otherwise only be wished for. "A steady course of Balzac reduces our living friends to shadows, and our acquaintances to the shadows of shades" (DL, 299). In moments like this, other people in Wilde take on the force of what Émile Durkheim calls a "social fact," something that is "capable of exercising on the individual an external constraint," and in the side effects of reading some novels, we also can see art's capacity to transform other people into something like antisocial facts.[23] Novels that turn "friends" and "acquaintances" into "shadows" and "shadows of shades" are no less a part of the general program of managing social density in Wilde for the softer tones under which it is put into effect. Rather, these softer tones take their place amidst a panoply of measures more and less direct for abating or deflecting the crushing powers and determining qualities of the social.

Wilde's work often is assimilated to the very social world he portrayed on stage and in his prose, making it easy to misread Wilde's representations of Society as a wish simply to belong to, rather than recast or remake, its forms. Such reformulations, however, are ubiquitous: in the voice of the dandy for whom "discord is to be forced to be in harmony with others" (DG, 68), and in manifestos for "socialism," which is to "relieve us from the sordid necessity of living for others which, in the present condition of things, presses so hardly upon almost everybody" (SMS, 255). Freedom from the "press" of others, others whose mere existence is a physical pressure akin to medieval torture on the rack, appears as a distant utopian goal in this essay, to be realized only in a projected future. Such a long-term plan for escaping the torture of the "press" of people is elsewhere realized in a moment, simply asserted with breathtaking elan by Lord Goring. If, as Wilde writes "scarcely anyone at all escapes" the "necessity of living for others," it is not for lack of effort.

At times this need to keep others at a distance can be hard to see as anything but a preference for the social scene in general over any of its particular inhabitants, as with the dandy who, in spite of finding "other people quite dreadful," also rarely refuses an invitation to a smart party. And such a need easily might also be seen as the particular quality of Wilde's work were it not of a piece with a historical condition so broad as to barely register as anything but everyday life. In Georg Simmel's social scientific understanding, Wilde voices a version of what we have come to recognize as the transformed social arrangements known as modernity. Simmel, glossing the effects of the loosened but more numerous social bonds in modernity, writes:

> While at an earlier stage man paid for the small number of his dependencies with the narrowness of personal relations . . . we are compensated for the great quantity of our dependencies by the indifference towards the respective persons and by our liberty to change them at will. And even though we are much more dependent on the whole of society . . . we are remarkably independent of every *specific* member of this society.[24]

In this light, we can see that Wilde's preference for the many over the few registers the transformation that theorists like Simmel identify as the social character of modernity. By this reading the "indifference towards the respective persons," the "remarkabl[e] independen[ce]" of the individual both wished for and on display in Wilde, is not simply stylized snobbery, or the triumph of Wilde's individualism. Rather, the desire to escape the obligations of the particular few by taking refuge in the many, or to evade the claims of the social altogether, marks a convergence between Wilde's aestheticism and sociological understandings of the crowded and transformed character of Victorian modernity.

If Lady Markby's scheme of assisted emigration suggests the historical method of transport to the colonies for thinning a crowded England, the promiscuous sociability of characters who never stop looking over one's shoulders for the next person to talk to indicates that those like Lady Markby have already arranged their own scheme for navigating the problems of overpopulation. The unending social circulation of characters in and out of scenes and drawing rooms in Wilde is mirrored by the epigram's own amenability to being lifted from one particular dramatic context and reused and repeated elsewhere, its own potential for unrestricted circulation found in its movement from mouth to mouth, from novel to play to essay.

The circulatory capacities of the epigram are suggested not least by Wilde's epigrams themselves, and not only in their self-conscious detachability and quotable character. In the hands of Lord Henry in *The Picture of Dorian Gray*, the transience of the epigram is also manifest in a preoccupation with promiscuity itself as its subject matter. "Those who are faithful know only the trivial side of love: it is the faithless who know love's tragedies" (12). "Faithfulness is in emotional life . . . simply a confession of failure" (49). "The only difference between a caprice and a lifelong passion is that a caprice lasts longer" (23).

And, in *The Importance of Being Earnest*, the hard truths of Wildean antisociality coincide with an avidity for a sociability that locates its most powerful
feelings within the momentariness of its bond: "It is always painful to part
from people whom one has known for a very brief space of time ... even
a moment's separation from anyone to whom one has just been introduced
is almost unbearable" (282). A form characterized by its fleetingness and its
brevity, the epigram also becomes a means of promoting such qualities as a
form of stranger sociality.

In the lines cited, the circulatory tendencies of the epigram at the level of
form merge with what I have suggested are one of its primary effects and concerns, the promulgation of transitory social relations. The transient qualities
of the epigrammatic style, together with its inversions here, of the "caprice"
over the "lifelong passion," of the "faithless" over the "faithful," illuminate
the epigram as an aesthetic form with a social correlative, a powerful means
of putting forward an ethic and art of none but the briefest engagements. The
rare instances when such an ethic of impermanence fails even a dedicated
flirt like Lord Henry is reason to mourn that which will not go away: "I once
wore nothing but violets all through one season, as a form of artistic mourn-
ing of a romance that would not die" (*DG*, 101).

The promiscuity both of, and promoted by, the epigram is the concentration of a more general condition of the social avidity and restlessness that
Wilde identifies as the paradigm for good talk: "Conversation should touch
everything, but concentrate itself on nothing" (AC, 372). At the heart of the
types of passing exchanges central to Wilde, exchanges that are pointedly
dedicated to the moment and no more, the epigram is the image and the
instrument of both engaging the social, and evading the more lasting consequences of social life. In the forms of address and leaving off that the epigram
both promotes and offers itself as alibi for, talk itself is a means of slipping
free, if only momentarily, from the constraints of the social.

Epigrammatic Address

In their combination of the keenness of interest with an indifference to the
durability of the attachment, Wilde's promiscuous talkers imagine ways of
experiencing the world that take their intensity not from the singularity of
any lasting relation to a particular person, but from the multiple qualities of
passing, serial affiliation. In its seeming preference for the social scene over
any one person in it, the serial sociality of the epigram thus defeats the logic
of having to make a single choice, locating its interests instead in what is "created by arrivals and killed by departures," as Goffman says. As the second epigraph to this chapter suggests, in Whitman's poetry we might find a related,
if also instructively distinct, valuing of the social and aesthetic possibilities

made available by social transience and relations tied to no person in particular. In Whitman's poem, "To You," the intimacy of poetic address is predicated on the momentariness and brevity that we have seen instantiated by the
epigram: "Stranger, if you passing meet me and desire to speak to me, why
should you not speak to me? / And why should I not speak to you?" The appeal
of speaker to stranger is predicated on the momentary qualities of a "passing" meeting, as well as in the social indistinction of the anonymous stranger
hailed. Encapsulating an attraction both singular ("*a* stranger") and generalized, since stranger-ness is a condition inhabited by an unbounded multiplicity of people unknown ("a *stranger*"), "To You" is exemplary of Whitman's
transformation of the "mutual non-knowledge" of strangers, as Michael
Warner argues—here, a poet and his reader, who finds himself arrested by
the hail of the poet, solicited through and across the printed page of the poem
he is reading—into a scene of intimacy.[25]

We might, along with Michael Warner, see that Whitman marks this scene
of strangers meeting and potentially speaking as an effort to make the structural anonymity of the writer-reader relation across the printed page into a
public, print-based medium of sexual solicitation. However, in the features of
a relationship that is more invoked than depicted with any specificity here—a
moment merely in passing, the social indistinction of the stranger hailed, a
landscape unmarked as either urban or rural, a proposal to speak rather than
the content and duration of conversation itself—it is also exemplary of a minimal form of sociality, an attachment whose neutrality and impermanence is
the most distinctive thing about it. Michael Moon has recently discussed such
transient desire within Whitman. Calling it Whitman's "butterfly passion,"
this passion takes its charge not from any enduring attachment to a single
person or thing, but in the "urge to flit," to move from one interest to the next,
an urge expressed in part by his poetry's "relative lack of interest in any single
or particular individual, himself included."[26]

Given their usual volubility, it is hard to imagine any character in Wilde,
much less Wilde himself, inhabiting such a suspended and contractual scene
of speech as in "To You," a moment in which talk is proposed rather than
simply carried out with elan. But, the implicitly serial qualities of the social
attachment of speaker to stranger—a scene of solicitation enacted each time
the poem is read by those to whom it is addressed ("To You")—underscore a
sense that in this poem, and in Whitman's many poems that are effectively
lists or catalogues of people and things, the world is experienced in ways resonant with Wilde's attachment to ephemerality. Whitman's catalogues of
people and things, his ambulatory poetics of the street and the urban scene,
encourages us to experience the world "as multiple, serial phenomena of richness and intensity so strong that one's response would perforce be an erotic
one."[27] Moon calls Whitman's an epistemology not of the closet, but of the
"street or ferry-boat or public assembly," in which the poet comes to know

the world through intimate contact with the throngs of men in public spaces in the city. I would suggest alongside this a more functional understanding of Whitman's stranger sociality, what is a difference of emphasis really, in which the serial interests, the catalogues of people encountered and then let go, are specifically understood as a means of contending with the proliferation of spaces of social density in the urban landscapes of modernity. To "flit" through such scenes is to form transient attachments, but it is also a way of making crowds less crowding, a poetic and social style of both encountering and managing social multiplicity through transient, minimal affiliations.

Although I have been suggesting that Wilde's characters are by and large homebodies by comparison with Whitman's peripatetic speakers of the streets, Whitman and Wilde each elaborate rhetorical modes that not only encompass, but crucially also manage, landscapes crowded by other people, inviting them in and leaving them behind in the same breath. To bring out the libidinalized qualities that each locates in serial sociality amidst densely peopled scenes, often specifically scenes of men in Whitman, is of course to recognize the emergent forms of attachment among men prior to the codification of some of those attachments as sexual in the sexology of later decades. But, it is also to see that libidinalizing social density through social promiscuity is also a way of navigating the social arrangements and landscapes of modernity, a means of managing the peopledness of their social imaginaries by flitting, by the transient engagements, that keep them both within range at a distance.

Whitman's poetic address is open-ended and solicitous of a stranger's own speech, both evoking a scene of mutely eloquent recognition, as Moon says, and envisioning an on-the-fly public sphere comprised by speech among strangers. By contrast, amidst the "crush" and volubility of those who comprise the Wildean social sphere, the epigram may well be the only form of speech that allows one to get a word in at all. In fictional worlds so thoroughly socially saturated, in which nearly every thought finds highly stylized expression in smart conversation, the epigram is the form of speech ideally suited to, even tailor-made for, navigating the densely populated social environments characteristic of Wilde's works.

Rare is the narration or description of anything like psychic interiority in Wilde, and even more remarkable is how infrequently any character is ever alone, not engaged in the conversation with other people out of which Wilde's works are almost entirely built, with Dorian Gray being the glaring exception that proves the rule.[28] That the crowded streets of Wilde's London are rarely strolled within a body of work where characters hardly ever leave the drawing rooms and libraries in which they talk and talk is a notable enough quality of his work for Wilde himself to remark upon it. Professing himself helpless to write anything but indoor forms—the drawing room fiction, drama, and dialogue-driven essays that are his dominant modes—he confesses in a letter: "I am afraid it is rather like my own life—all conversation and no action. I can't describe action; my people sit in chairs and banter."[29] Such a preference for the indoors to the outside is in part a reflection of a Wildean social aesthetic that finds not just in epigrammatic speech generally, but in conversation in particular, a means of contending with the crowdedness of a social sphere that extends its force to every corner within Wilde's works. In confessing his inability to write action, which he elsewhere describes as "a blind thing" "limited by accident" and "dependent on external influences" (CA, 358), Wilde also allies interior spaces, the drawing room beautiful, as it were, "where people sit in chairs and banter," with the real albeit limited power of talk to allay the powers of the social.

If Wilde's characters only infrequently hit the streets by comparison to Whitman's speakers, however, the force of London's population is still registered powerfully enough to penetrate even the most carefully arranged interiors of the aesthete's house beautiful. As we have heard already at the start of this chapter, "out of doors one becomes abstract and impersonal.... In a house we all feel of the proper proportions. Everything is subordinated to us, fashioned for our use and our pleasure" (DL, 291). A crowded social imaginary whose thrum and hubbub is heard in "the dim roar of London" that penetrates Basil Hallward's studio in the opening lines of Dorian Gray, cannot be fully shut out, not even by Wilde's self-professed limits as a writer of the indoors exclusively, or even by the most well-executed architecture of the house beautiful (DG, 1).

If the "dim roar" of the city's population cannot be silenced by a carefully arranged aesthetic interior, however, other resources are marshaled to counter the crowd that roars outside its door. Such a "dim roar" when it passes over the aestheticist house's threshold is drained of any sense of a threat—labor unrest, demonstrations for the franchise, a Wildean terror of inarticulacy suggested by a "roar"—that might be posed by the crowded society that produces that roar: "The dim roar of London was like the bourdon note of a distant organ." In an instant, the social's "dim roar" is transformed; no longer the sound of the crowd, but instead a "distant" musical "note" as it passes from the "out of doors" in which one "becomes abstract and impersonal" to the aesthetic interior in which "everything is subordinated to us." As if a magical threshold has been crossed, the coercive qualities elsewhere associated with the social sphere are suddenly made soft, "distant," and musical.

The transformative powers found in narrative description in the novel, changing the noise of the social's "roar" into a musical "note" as it passes into the house beautiful, however, are afforded as well to the stylish talkers who inhabit that house. The talk that takes place within such an aesthetic interior, where people "sit in chairs and banter," is at times itself equal to the task of subduing the forces of the social embodied by the densely peopled streets of London. In Wilde's dialogue "The Critic as Art," Gilbert and Ernest talk through the night in "the library of a house in Piccadilly, overlooking the Green Park." Through Gilbert and Ernest's discussion, the dialogue elaborates an account of criticism's superiority to realist art since criticism, unlike art, is freed from the demands of mimetic realism; criticism has no obligation to reproduce life, and so is "never trammeled by any shackles of verisimilitude" (CA, 365). And within the charmed circle of Ernest and Gilbert, the power of talk itself becomes a recurrent subject, but also an analogue to the autonomy of criticism from realist accounts of the world. Contrasted with action, speech, like criticism, is also independent from the obligation to take the world as its reference. "It is very much more difficult to talk about a thing than to do it" (359). Difficult it may be, but any appearance of labor disappears into the effortless style and "perfectly phrased" confidence with which Gilbert asserts "the world is made by the singer for the dreamer." Ernest's reply thus accords and confirms for speech its proper Wildean powers: "While you talk it seems to me to be so" (362). And, as if by an extension of the powers of autonomy from the social emblematized in a "roar" that becomes a "bourdon note," the normally crowded streets of Piccadilly are themselves emptied out by the dialogue's finish.

> Draw back the curtains and open the windows wide. How cool the morning air is! Piccadilly lies at our feet like a long riband of silver. A faint purple mist hangs over the park, and the shadows of the white houses are purple. It is too late to sleep. Let us go down to Covent Garden and look at the roses. Come! I am tired of thought. (*CA*, 407–8)

Gazing out upon an emptied socius, a "long riband of silver," the two talkers will go into the streets of London, streets containing no people, but only roses.

Similarly, in the dialogue "The Decay of Lying," the end of the conversation coincides with the end of the essay being unfolded within it, a termination that arrives not by the conclusion of a plot or even a closing argument, but is simply summoned by its declaration: "Come! We have talked long enough" (DL, 320); "Come! I am tired of thought" (CA, 408). A social engagement that can be terminated by fiat, Wilde's dialogues thus also imagine a world in which association similarly might be begun and ended by decree, might be "quite voluntary." In that voluntary quality, the powers of speech that brooks no objection to its decrees and can bend the world's will to its words is distinguished from those more lingering forms of attachment catalogued by Lord Henry in *Dorian Gray*: "The people who have adored me . . . have always insisted on living on, long after I had ceased to care for them, or they to care for me" (101).

Seeming to bear within itself the cadences and inflections of speech, the epigram feels spoken and so implicitly bears with it a scene of communication. But if Wildean epigrammatic speech seems to frequently command both a listener and a social scene, it as frequently is the escape route from quarters that have become too crowded for comfort. The stage-voice used for the epigram even in the closest of company in Wilde, announcing its reach far beyond those within earshot, underscores its broadcast effect: the epigram's tendency to address contexts and people well beyond the dramatic scene in which it is uttered. Addressing the many even as its scene of delivery is the relative few—the library, the drawing room—the epigram pulls away from its immediate environment without quite leaving it fully behind, both including and reaching beyond those closest at hand for an imagined broader sphere of circulation often leaving its immediate auditors speechless.

> "Those who are faithful know only the trivial side of love: it is the faithless who know love's tragedies." And Lord Henry struck a light on a dainty silver case, and began to smoke a cigarette with a self-conscious and satisfied air, as if he had summed up the world in a phrase. (14)

The dandy's talents for getting in the final word expand here to put an end to conversation altogether, leaving nothing to say at all about anything, it having already been said. Words that are "perfectly phrased," the silencing qualities of the epigram thus abet if not an escape, at least a neutralization, of a crowded social sphere by stunning it into silence with "a phrase" that in summing, also shuts, it up.

Putting an end to the conversation, by these lights, would appear as one of the most powerful versions of a Wildean sociable antisociality. However, the epigram also evokes, through its self-consciously quotable and endlessly redeployed qualities, the broader sphere of its circulation among a wider audience limned by publication itself. The inflection of even his essays with the patterns and structures of speech is one of the signatures of Wilde's style, and readers both in his day and our own have associated Wilde's writing style with its evocations of conversation, rooting Wilde's talent in a sort of pre-literate oral culture. For Robert Ross, Wilde's published work is merely the palest of fire cast by the light of actually talking with him face-to-face: Wilde's "personality and conversation were far more wonderful than anything he wrote, so that his written works give only a pale reflection of his power." Ross's assertion of the belated relation of Wilde's writing to his talking, Paul Saint-Amour suggests, is one of the constitutive features of print culture. However, "rather than naively imagine orality as a tonic to writing, as nature to writing's artifice, or as authenticity to the travesty of type, Wilde recognized that the longing for orality as origin, nature, or authentic prehistory may be the most characteristic thing about print culture."[30] Finding in Wilde's cultivated oral style a counterdiscourse to and dissent from the nineteenth-century culture of copyright and its privatization of literary property, Saint-Amour argues that Wilde self-consciously endows his writing with the properties of an imagined oral culture, and its notions of communally held property, freely plagiarizing from both his own work and that of others, as well as making his works appropriable by others.[31]

While its inflection as speech is, as I have been arguing, central to understanding the character and promiscuous effects of Wilde's epigrams, what seems most piquant about the spoken qualities of Wilde's signature short form is less its pre-print nostalgic orality, but rather its carrying with it an implicit aspiration toward the qualities of print. While the epigram does bear the cadences of spoken language, it is paradoxically a spoken language that aspires to a condition of print perfection in which words might become "perfectly phrased." That is, the epigram imagines a perfected speech scene, as if every word had been carefully planned, honed, drafted, edited, and redrafted in advance and then delivered as if it were spontaneous (Yeats, in fact, accused Wilde of doing just this in advance of dinner parties). By self-consciously exaggerating the precision and syntax available to written language, but within the pointedly casual, apparently spontaneous speech of a character, the epigram encapsulates a relationship to speech and print that is the inverse of the one proposed by Saint-Amour. In the epigram's merging of the attributes of print and spoken language, it preserves the sociable scene of talk alongside the technologies of drafting and rewriting that might enable a line, in Wilde's hands, to become "perfectly phrased." That the line "To love oneself is the beginning of a lifelong romance" is both spoken by Lord Goring in the play *An Ideal Husband* and can be found, verbatim, as a epigram in Wilde's quasi-essay, "Phrases and Philosophies for the Use of the Young," suggests not only the circulatable qualities of the epigram, its transposability, but also its dual character as both speech and print. From the perspective of the social effects sponsored by literary forms, the epigram offers another version of the impersonal intimacy that is associated with strangers: a speaker might simultaneously inhabit the qualities of anonymity and impersonality made available by print publication, circulating in the wider scene of publication's readership, while also retaining talk's sociable scene of face-to-face communication.

Whitman's "To You" draws upon its own distribution in print form among the impersonal, anonymous reading public of strangers to imagine reading as both the site of intimate social contact and the occasion for making intimacy a public event, turning print into a public scene of solicitation, Michael Warner argues. In imperfectly but still usefully related terms, Wilde's epigrams invoke a sociable scene of conversation whose talk draws its force from its implicitly written qualities, speech "perfectly phrased," invoking the conditions of publication—an address oriented not to the local social environment, but toward a mass public—as an escape route from the pressures of face-to-face social intimacy. If the Wildean epigram is insistently delivered in a voice ever-conscious of those not in the room, its signal place within Wildean conversation nonetheless locates it within the sociable world of talk. Welding together social propinquity and the neutralizing effects of print impersonality, the epigram's style and confidence drains it too of the hesitation and awkwardness of Whitman's speaker proposing to speak with a stranger, becoming instead "perfectly phrased."

The Wilde System

At times, the means of managing a crowded social sphere in Wilde is hard to tell from a more general economy found in his writing. In this economy, the excesses of pleasure and language that have been associated with Wilde and embodied by the character of the dandy, for whom the only way to overcome a desire is to succumb to it, stand in stark contrast with what turns out to be a fierce husbanding of textual resources, a conservation program that takes the form of frequent recycling of material from one work into another. The experience of reading, for example, a well-wrought line from *Lady Windermere's Fan* and encountering it again, in slightly different form, and in a different character's mouth, in *The Picture of Dorian Gray* is familiar to any who have read widely in Wilde's body of work.[32]

This practice of intertextual borrowing among Wilde's works is driven in part by what I have already suggested is the epigram's natural tendency toward generalized meaning. Its capacity to both comment on the dramatic situation at hand and be amenable to wider application—its generalizing and citable qualities—lends itself to the sorts of recontextualization and recycling Wilde made a habit of. The very extractability and ostentatiously quotable qualities of the epigram, its solicitation of its own repetition or repurposing in other contexts, has posed a problem for literary critical approaches that are oriented toward sustained engagements with individual works, or those that ground their thinking in genre. This is particularly the case for Wilde's works, which are so generically mixed—an essay in the form of a dialogue is hard to tell from a play, and a novel hard to tell from a sheaf of aphorisms.[33] To make matters worse, Wilde regularly recycles epigrams, transferring them from essays to novels to plays. A reader can find herself with the vague sense that she has heard this line somewhere before, a sense imparted by even the one-off epigram's bearing of a certain second-hand, made-for-quotation quality; or, with the uncanny feeling that Wilde's epigrams might be reproducing themselves, colonizing other works far-flung from their original context. What is more, Wilde's epigrams were as easily assimilated and put into circulation in the culture of Wilde's own day (reportedly, his most casually dropped witticisms even while at Oxford, found their way into the mouths of royalty like the Prince of Wales), as they have been into our contemporary culture, printed onto coffee mugs and collected into books of quotations by those who recognize the epigram's proximity to advertising copy and the apothegms of self-help.

The epigram's amenability to recirculation thus partakes of a broader habit in Wilde's work of reusing and redeploying names, words, and lines in different contexts, a tendency that when infrequently discussed has been pointed to by critics as illuminating Wilde's intuitions about the indeterminate or unfixed qualities of language and naming.[34] What looks like the ceaseless circulation and the promiscuous tendencies of language from one angle, however, from another resembles nothing so much as a well-run conservation program, an ecologically minded "green" sort of modular authorship—iterable phrases with multiple textual lives—in which the efficient reuse of resources, the fullest use of every bit of writing produced, is maximized. It is not just that Wilde's language often underscores the tendency of words and their meanings to travel beyond their usual contexts and ambits. Even the capacity to recognize such qualities in language has a strange way of drifting from one textual setting and into another. Lord Henry's plan for "rechristening everything" in *Dorian Gray* (193), for example, is realized at least in part in Wilde's play *The Importance of Being Earnest*, where Jack and Algernon hastily arrange to have themselves christened "Ernest" in order to be acceptable spouses to two women who declare they will marry only someone of that name. The seeming arbitrariness of a character's declaration that in order for her to marry, "the only really safe name is Ernest" (263), is matched by the seeming arbitrariness with which the name, free-floating as an unexplained ideal until this point, descends upon the man formerly known as Jack, who is finally disclosed at the play's end, via the discovery of his true parentage, as being "naturally . . . Ernest" (306).

Such rechristenings and redeployments are familiar to us now from one camp of deconstructive reading which early on claimed Wilde, like the railroad cloak-room in Victoria Station in which Jack was left as a baby in *The Importance of Being Earnest*, as that moment of criticism's terminus and origin both. Less remarked in readings that have taken up the multivalency of the name Ernest and the double life of secrecy and meaning licensed by the name Bunbury, however, has been the fact that names in Wilde are also oddly hard to come by. It is not only that both Jack and Algernon must, if only momentarily, huddle together under the single shared name of Ernest if they wish to make it to the altar with Gwendolen and Cecily. Even an incomplete survey reveals that characters everywhere in Wilde's work must make do with sharing names, which on evidence of the texts are remarkably scarce. There is Markby, Markby, and Markby, solicitors, in *The Importance of Being Earnest*, for example. But Lady Windermere is both the name of the idealistic title character of *Lady Windermere's Fan* and the epigrammatic female dandy of Wilde's short story "Lord Arthur Savile's Crime." Ernest is not only the name that sets the passing mark of a litmus test of eligibility for marriage in *Earnest*, as well as being the "natural" name of Jack all along. The name Ernest is also assigned to the character who plays straight man to the paradoxes and aesthetic doctrines elaborated by Gilbert in "The Critic as Artist." In the "Decay of Lying" Wilde uses his own children's names for the dialogists, Cyril and Vivian, with a slightly different spelling of Vyvyan, his son's name. In addition, another Cyril, Cyril Graham, appears as the beautiful boy-actor who is responsible for the forgery of a painting purporting to reveal the true addressee and beloved of Shakespeare's sonnets in "The Portrait of Mr. W.H." While Mr. Erskine of Treadley lunches with Lord Henry and Dorian Gray at Aunt Agatha's in *Dorian Gray*, a character named Erskine is the possessor of the forged portrait in "The Portrait of Mr. W.H." And Mrs. Erlynne, besides being the name of the fallen mother to Lady Windermere in *Lady Windermere's Fan*, is also given a brief, non-speaking role at Lady Narborough's dinner party in *Dorian Gray*.[35]

In one sense, the various names that float across different works of Wilde might suggest his corpus constitutes something akin to a self-referring network of textual circulation, one whose strategies of borrowing are as familiar to us as those of television networks, in which popular characters from one situation comedy make occasional guest appearances on another to boost sliding ratings. Aaron Kunin has recently argued, in a revival of renaissance understandings of character, that all character works in this way, since character is a type rather than a singularity, one that exists beyond the particularity of any single literary work.[36] Such wily cross-marketing, however, seems less to the point here than a plan to shrink the named populace of Wilde's works, as if in a counter-movement to the nineteenth-century realist novel's own taste for multitudes of characters. In fact, the recurring names in Wilde attach themselves to different characters across these works, showing up not as guest-stars in another play or story, but as different people altogether. A dandified woman in one work becomes a less jaded one by the same name in another, so the Lady Windermere of "Lord Arthur Savile's Crime" is quite another thing from the Lady Windermere who takes the title role of Wilde's play. Rather than underscoring the free-floating nature of language in Wilde, we would better understand the miserly allotment of names among characters as helping to counter a problem of overcrowdedness in Wilde's fictional social world. And, those names that are not with the program of managing populousness, are against it, paying for it with the fate of unremitting sociality that accompanies the wrong name: "And I pity any woman who is married to a man called John. She would probably never be allowed to know the entrancing pleasure of a single moment's solitude" (*Earnest*, 263). Less strident than other more Draconian schemes of population management, such as assisted emigration, which appear elsewhere in his work, Wilde nevertheless manages at least to keep up the appearance of keeping down the numbers by allocating fewer names than there are characters in his work, hiding the surplus of people behind names that do double-duty, as if he were fudging the numbers in a census of his fictional populace.

In letting some of his characters hide themselves behind or beneath the names of other characters, what even constitutes a single character—how we might tell where one person ends and another begins—begins to fade from importance in Wilde's works. Understood in this way, Wilde thus nudges us away from the kinds of coherence we are inclined to ascribe to literary characters in general as a result of our being trained up by the association of the realist novel with psychologically textured representations of interiority. That Wilde's characters often share names seems something that would jump out to any reader. Who could miss such a thing, for example, in novels by James or Eliot, or even Dickens for that matter, in whose works names frequently index the traits (*Our Mutual Friend*'s the Veneerings, to just take one)—so unchangeable, so utterly defining—of both individual characters and the constraining qualities of character itself? However, even those characters in Wilde who are afforded the differentiating powers of a unique name can seem so interchangeable and indistinct from one another as a result of Wilde's thin modes of characterization. With characters appearing to be almost duplicate types of one another, it can be hard to see the trees (individual characters), as it were, for the forest (the totality of Wilde's system of characters).

The characters who inhabit his dialogues, "The Decay of Lying" and "The Critic as Artist," for example, are only intensified versions of the numerous characters in Wilde who exist largely as rhetorical effects, emanations of a style of speech engaged in repartee and argument, rather than being defined by the texture of psychic singularity. And it is just these characters' wit and dedication to the dilatory pleasures of speech itself that make them so alike as to be hard to tell apart. With the structuring effects of characterological coherence diminished, it is the sociable setting of the dialogues itself, rather than any single character, that becomes the central structure in these works. The shared elaboration of a sociable scene of critical discussion, in which to "talk about a thing is much harder than to do it," deflects the specification of either of the speakers into fully fledged individuals. To recognize the de-specified or flat qualities of characters in Wilde's work more generally brings us to the familiar critical grounds on which we recognize the truth of style over personhood in Wilde ("the first rule in life is to assume a pose"), the insistently shallow forms of interiority we find in characters who are nothing but talk. As I have been arguing about the epigram's aspirations to reshape the demands of sociality, the rhetorical existence of Wilde's characters exemplifies the limited but nonetheless substantial powers of talk and of accomplished conversation to mitigate those demands. But, it also cancels the realist imperatives of character psychology. The practice of sharing names across characters diverts us away from readerly identification with, or often even of, individual characters.

While the anti-realist approaches to character in aestheticism have been well-documented, more generally and more unexpectedly, I want to notice that names shared across distinct works of Wilde, alongside the always-recycle ethos of reusing lines across multiple texts, also nudge us away from the experience of any particular individual play, story, dialogue, or novel as a discrete work, as freestanding and unitary in even the provisional ways something like the realist novel asks to be experienced. This is not to say, of course, that Wilde's works have by and large been read or his plays attended in anything but single-text-sized servings by the vastly greater part of his readers and audience. However, we should notice that a critical inclination to approach his work through the overarching category of "Wilde" in general, such as Alan Sinfield's *The Wilde Century*, as distinct from discrete treatments of a single work intuits and turns into a critical method something like just this experience of finding iterations of the same names, if arguably not the same characters, in multiple textual locales. That is, Wilde particularly invites critical approaches that take as their object not simply an individual text, but a more miscellaneous tracing out of histories of identity, tropes, styles, and more across multiple works, an attention to what we might call an overall ecology or "the Wilde system." Or, at least we would give it that name if consistency and systematicity, like faithfulness, were considered anything but a failure of imagination by Wilde's own estimate.[37]

In the case of characters, as a result both of their distributed or shared names and slender psychological characterization, the effect of this deflection away from the singular persona is not simply the familiar Wildean valorization of surface over depth or style over essence. Rather, or in addition, I want to pull out the implication of my earlier observations about character and suggest that this deflection cultivates readerly attachments that instead find their model within Wilde's own serial social aesthetic. Thwarting our identification with any one character, instead a reader is encouraged to cathect what arises between characters: the sociable scenes themselves that are brought into being through Wildean conversation. In this regard, Wilde's thin characters share properties less with the flatness of the minor characters in the realist novel, whose minorness helps by way of contrast to produce the depth and centrality of the protagonists, than with eighteenth-century precursors in which the truth of character was not yet fully associated with deep interiority. This calls to mind the dynamic that Deidre Lynch, in her study of the creation of character in the eighteenth century calls that century's "hesitancy about creating individuals" via character, which she suggests should be seen in relation its other vast discursive project, the trans-individual one of creating society. The stylized thinness of Wilde's characters deflects our attention from interiority, like the flat or impersonal modes of character Lynch identifies, and thus enables Wilde to emphasize the social moments that arise between characters, a discursive project of bringing into view the powers of sociability and the nature of the social bond more generally.[38] Not "men and their moments" in Erving Goffman's words, but selves constituted out of their fleeting encounters, "moments and their men."

To think of Wilde in these terms—as cultivating in his readers and characters both an attachment to no single person but instead to the scene and qualities of sociability itself—is to take up sociability in the more specialized sense of Georg Simmel's understanding, which we have encountered in other moments in this book. For Simmel, sociability expresses an impulse to association itself, a taste for a form of contentless relationality whose distinctiveness is in bearing no wider purpose, mission, or intention, and so no appeal other than the "feeling for . . . a satisfaction in, the very fact that one is associated with others."[39] In sociability, whose exemplary instance is the party, Simmel identifies a structural impulse toward being with others in and of itself, outlining what is effectively an aestheticist account of association, a structure whose very unmotivated quality allies it with art and play. "The world of sociability . . . is an *artificial* world, made up of beings who have renounced . . . the purely personal features of the intensity and extensiveness of life in order to bring about among themselves a pure interaction," "the most adequate fulfillment of a relation, which is, so to speak, nothing but relationship."[40] In sociability all the messiness of intersubjectivity, as well as the passions and interests of the "purely personal," are thinned out in a dedication to "the success of the sociable moment" and its necessarily evanescent existence.[41] Most strikingly, sociability's neutralization of the personal and its dedication to a relationality drained of purpose or intensity bears its own attractions, Simmel suggests, what Wilde might have called sociability for sociability's sake.

Sociability's emphasis on the impersonal, as well as tact and social form, allies it with Roland Barthes's notion of the Neutral, a "familiarity singularly tinged with aloofness," as I discussed in this book's introduction. These qualities also draw Simmel's sociology into close range with the intertwining of social and aesthetic form in Wilde, the consonance between sociability and the Wildean epigram. But we should also see how the impersonal attractions of sociability are not only depicted in Wilde's work, they are also transferred to the reader, who, in finding little purchase for attachments to the distinctive qualities of characters, hard-pressed at times even to differentiate one character from another, instead takes the sociable scene's "artificial world" as the site of readerly cathexis. The appeal of structure and neutrality, instanced here as the appeal of the "Wilde system" over an individual character or individual text, is related to what Leo Bersani has in mind in a recent essay, "Sociability and Cruising," which also draws upon Simmel's notion of sociability to elaborate upon what I have been calling thin social ties. Bersani rephrases the impersonality and neutrality of sociability in Simmel as "a form of relationality uncontaminated by desire." Extending Simmel's account of the impersonality of sociability to cruising as a form of "sexual sociability," Bersani finds in cruising's promiscuity, its evasion of more permanent relations, an orientation toward new forms of relationality untainted by desire, and in turn the violence and futurity allied with heterosexual desire and its oedipal conflicts.[42] In Bersani's work on the realist novel, such forms of relationality are precisely what realism's requirement that every action bear meaning within the structure of narrative, what he calls "significant form," as well as its demand for "coherently structured character," is inhospitable to. In realism's negation of "the sensual intensities and fragmented variety of human desires," and its demand for durable, meaningful (i.e., plot-furthering) social relationships, Bersani writes, "the novel makes aesthetic sense out of social anarchy."[43] Although the essay on Simmel is not overtly interested in literary form, another way of phrasing what Bersani uncovers in sociability is that it is a site of an appealingly "a-significant form." A sense-conferring structure or architecture that nevertheless de-realizes any content or purpose, sociability might be said to produce an anti-plot, and thus anti-realist, dedication to the sociable moment and the social bond, and no more.

In Wilde, I have been arguing, the force of the epigram and the sociability that is its occasion enables such an anti-plot, or anti-novelistic, structure to become the central achievement of his work. In the extension, or contraction, of the impersonal appeals of sociability to sexuality, Bersani underscores possible continuities between the social and the sexual that have been less attended to in the recent history of queer criticism, as well as suggests how classical sociology might be a theoretical resource and underpinning of some versions of queer theory, including those most dedicated to challenging "the value of the social itself."[44] However, moving from the social to the sexual is also the route by which the sociological imagination of Wilde's work has largely been eclipsed in recent Wilde criticism, which has mostly tended to exclude the social on its way to specifying the sexual.[45] This imagination finds it most vivid expression precisely in Wilde's Simmelean interest in sociability for its own sake, and an aesthetic of social evanescence. Richard Sennett's critique of Erving Goffman as depicting a social imaginary comprised by actors without passion thus also feels apt to Wilde. But aptness here would mean recasting Sennett's understanding of Goffman's insufficiency as a formal achievement in Wilde: "Here [in Goffman] is a picture of society in which there are scenes but no plot."[46] Scenes but no plot: it is in the evanescence of both the epigram and sociability, forms of scene that become independent of plot, that Wilde's anti-novelistic aesthetic of "weak ties" most endures.[47]

The "impulse to sociability" may find its expression not only in the party, as it does in both Simmel and Wilde, but in the felt attractions of a reader for sociability's figuration within Wilde's pages. And in this relation's impermanence or only passing qualities, the codifying energies of, say, the marriage plot, are also forestalled, thwarting its coalescence into any more enduring attachment. Uncodified, the momentariness of such attachments also assures that they never find their conclusion or satisfaction in one single person, never reach the target of the church altar toward which the trajectory of the marriage plot inevitably bends. In this, what sociability underscores is recognizably of a piece with the Wilde that queer criticism has so illuminated over the past two decades, in which the inevitability of marrying a man named Ernest is shadowed by the satire of the marriage plot whose iron law demands it. Such impulses and appeals are registered too, however, we should notice, in the familiar after-effects of reading Wilde. Even as entire plotlines and characters may fade from memory, it is not only the epigram but also the felt appeal of the sociable scene brought into existence by the "perfectly phrased" epigram that remains, a Cheshire cat smile of the sociable moment that lingers well past the time when the play is over or the book is "shut up."

Certain Speech

Wilde's taxonomies of the poles of freedom and constraint under modern social life are at times as familiar and as close to home as the distinction between the country and the city. In *Earnest*, we are told, "When one is in town one amuses oneself. When one is in the country one amuses other people" (254). Going by a variety of designations—Ferdinand Tönnies's notions of *Gemeinschaft* and *Gesellschaft*, Émile Durkheim's mechanical and organic forms of solidarity—the transformation from traditional, kin-based forms of obligatory social relations to the more elective forms of belonging within modernity, what is sociology's Great Divide, is recast by Wilde as the difference between a night to one's self in the city and a day spent being a gracious guest in the country. Sociology's epochal transformation, however, has in Wilde none of its epoch-making qualities. Instead, this gap is in Wilde's play a distance whose traversal is as easily accomplished as a round-trip train fare from London and a change of names, famously from "Ernest in town to Jack in the country" (257). The obligations imposed by traditional forms of community such as are found in the country, obligations phrased in Wilde as the duty to "amuse[ ] other people," are easily shrugged off in this play by a return to the city on a train that makes frequent trips. According to this travel schedule, modernity and tradition are mapped onto familiar contiguous geographic fields rather than successive ages, traversable neighboring landscapes.

By the lights of "The Soul of Man under Socialism," however, no trip back to the city will relieve us from the "sordid necessity of living for others which, in the present condition of things, presses so hardly upon almost everybody" (255). Instead, nothing less than a "scheme for the reconstruction of society" (288), one that will purify the social sphere of any form of obligation or constraint, will do. The obligatory social bonds that Wilde keeps safely contained in the country in *The Importance of Being Earnest*, are everywhere in the present day in this essay. "All association must be quite voluntary" (260) and "socialism" will only have achieved its ends when we can live "without exercising constraint on others, or suffering it ever" (288). Even, or even especially, the gentler modes of societal compulsion must be abolished:

> People . . . are less conscious of the horrible pressure that is being put on them, and so go through their lives in a sort of coarse comfort . . . without realising that they are probably thinking other people's thoughts, living by other people's standards, wearing practically what one may call other people's second-hand clothes. (267)

The utopian wish for a society in which one might be utterly released from "the clamorous claims of others" (255) projects a form of community that is drained of any of its qualities of social obligation. In one of this essay's many logical and tonal swerves, however, Wilde's plan for "the reconstruction of society" is seen to be not one of negation or escape from society entirely, but rather, an un-social sociability: "The ideals we owe to Christ are the ideals of the man who abandons society entirely, or of the man who resists society absolutely." But, the passage continues, "man is naturally social" (287–8). Wilde's model citizen both "resists society absolutely" and is called back to the sphere of others by natural inclination, being "naturally social." In this future society, the "horrible pressure" and "press" of other people will become as light as air, a "sordid necessity" of "living for others" changed into a "voluntary" "association." In this utopic projection of a society freed from the burdens of intersubjective entanglements, but not negated by such freedom, Wilde imagines a social world emptied of its coercive and obligatory qualities (256).

In *The Importance of Being Earnest*, however, no such program of social renovation is called for. Instead, geography and social attachments are as famously malleable as desire itself in this play, wherein one might fall in love with a name before a person, and simply saying something with style and confidence can make it so. As Gwendolyn says of the name Ernest: "my ideal has always been to love someone by the name of Ernest . . . It is a divine name. It has a music of its own. It produces vibrations" (275). Geography similarly bends to the perfectly confident style of Lady Bracknell's way of speaking as she interviews Jack as a suitor for her daughter. Expressing doubts about his house's location on the unfashionable side of Belgrave square, undeterred she declares "that could easily be altered." Queried whether she means the fashion, or the side, Lady Bracknell overcomes fashion and geography in a single irrefutable line: "Both, if necessary." So too, with a perfectly phrased response, the urban landscape of London can be declared to permeate even in the most rustic of locales. Gwendolyn on a day trip to the country from London where she resides declines an invitation to climb a hill offering an overlook of five counties, demurring: "Five counties! I don't think I should like that. I hate crowds" (283). As easily reterritorialized as the crowded streets of London are by a vision and voice intent on finding an urban scene in the country, social life is also characterized by a paradoxical confidence in both its predictability and its endless malleability. The fact that Gwendolyn will marry someone named Ernest brooks no doubt. That she is in love with someone named Jack is no barrier to this, and, as the play discovers in the end, he really is named Ernest, rechristened with a name he already had. Certain of her marital future, Gwendolyn makes that future bend to her certitude.

It is in this combination, even amidst a play as self-consciously trivial as this one, that Wilde's particular view, if not quite a theory, of modernity comes into view. The social and epistemological understandings of characters who inhabit stances of absolute confidence, as well as possess a sense that the world will bend to that confidence, index the condition of living under what recent sociological theory calls "reflexive modernity." Modernity, Anthony Giddens suggests, is characterized by its "wholesale reflexivity," the chronic reexamination and revision of social practices in the light of new knowledge about them, which in turn alters the character of those social practices. Or, as Lady Bracknell, turning to the Victorian science of social statistics for marital guidance, puts it:

> I do not know if there is anything peculiarly exciting in the air of this par-
> ticular part of Hertfordshire, but the number of engagements that go on
> seems to me considerably above the proper average that statistics have laid
> down for our guidance. (*Earnest*, 292)

Honoring this statistical law even in the breach, in her turn to statistical accounts of marriage to justify the proper number of engagements in "this particular part of Hertfordshire," Lady Bracknell exemplifies the reflexive character of Wilde's social landscape. This landscape is constituted not just by the felt force of social density; it is constituted by reflection upon itself, incorporating, for example, its own statistical image within that reflection. While reason was the basis for the Enlightenment promise of rationality and scientific knowledge as the replacement for tradition, Giddens argues that the reflexivity of knowledge in modernity means "we can never be sure that any given element of that knowledge will not be revised." Modernity thus "effectively involves the institutionalization of doubt."[48]

The condition of persistent doubt Giddens identifies with reflexive modernity may seem a far cry from the certitude displayed by speakers everywhere in Wilde. Amidst the chronically revisable nature of social practices in modernity, in which both the side of Belgrave square and its fashionableness might be changed, however, the generalized uncertainty of reflexive modernity finds its compensatory formation in Wilde: a rhetorical style of absolute confidence. Modernity's condition of chronic doubt is most forcefully articulated in that doubt's refutation, the assertion of inerrancy in declarations judged not by whether they are true, but by being "perfectly phrased." The paradoxical coexistence of certitude about the predictable (it can be known in advance) and revisable (it can change, and be changed) nature of social organization exemplified throughout Wilde, what is most modern about this most modern of authors, finds its most perfect condensation in the perfect condensation of the epigram. By the very certainty of its formulations, that truth is simply a matter of being "perfectly phrased," Wilde's epigrams both bypass claims to truth or logic and overcome, at least for the moment, the conditions of chronic doubt that characterize reflexive modernity. Through the epigram's endless recirculations and repetitions, the efflorescence every-where in Wilde of an avidity for sociable scenes, and in the persistence of the certain speech of the epigram and its serial, repetitive qualities, we can detect within Wilde the chronic doubt of modernity. It is this doubt over and against which the epigram offers its speakers the chance to possess, however briefly, the certitude of perfect speech.

Reaching back to the observations about social transience and Wilde's sig-nal short rhetorical form with which this chapter began, we can now also see better the broader context for my claims about the modernity of the epigram within the literature of social density. The assuredness of the epigram is one manifestation of reflexive modernity, but it is also the form of speech built for a world increasingly felt as populated by those unknown, by strangers. The epigram's own confidence instances a form of confidence in social relations that depends not on the transparency of selves, of knowable others, or psy-chic intimacy. Instead, this confidence rests on the impersonal perfections of social form itself, the thinned-out selves through which the "closed charm" of Simmel's sociability comes into being, in which no greater knowledge of another person is requisite than the impulse to sociability itself, and the com-plexities of social life are distilled into the formal essence of sociability. The absolute certitude of "perfectly phrased" talk, then, combined with the end-lessly revisable qualities of conversation in Simmel's sociability—talk that "spins itself out, deepens, loosens, cuts itself off purely according to impulse and opportunity—that is a miniature picture of the social ideal that one might call the freedom of bondage"—this is Wilde's emblem of and response to reflexive modernity.[49]

Simultaneously absolutely certain in what they say and endlessly revisable, endlessly reworded and recontextualized from character to character, novel to essay to play, Wilde's epigrams turn the "dim roar" of the city that thrums outside the house beautiful into a nearly static-less social form. That the price of such certainty is its compression into the slight, ephemeral, "minor" form of the epigram, is the most forceful mark of Wilde's engagement with the anything but minor conditions of modernity.

Henry James and the Art of Distance

Midway through his well-known essay on the realist novel, "The Knowable Community," Raymond Williams seems almost embarrassed. Williams is discussing what might be called the demographics of characters in novels, remarking on a shift between those written by Jane Austen at the start of the nineteenth century and George Eliot toward its latter decades. Sharing Austen's own education and class background, her novels' characters would have no trouble reading the books in which they appear, Williams notes. Eliot's comparatively broader novelistic canvas, by contrast, draws characters from a wider range of economic and educational backgrounds, including those with little ability to read; so, for many of those characters, reading an Eliot novel would be something close to an impossibility. In Eliot, whom Williams admires deeply, we see the "failure of continuity between the necessary language of the novelist and the recorded language of many of the characters." While Austen's omniscient narrator can seamlessly lend characters its own qualities of perception and language, qualities recognizably those of Austen herself, when Eliot's narrators voice the thoughts of rustic characters, "the strain of impersonation" becomes palpable to the reader. She turns them into mere types; or, when individuated, she turns them into "surrogate[s]" "of her own consciousness," mouthpieces for her thinking rather than bearers of distinctive, singular minds of their own.[1]

In describing Eliot's tendency to squeeze her capacious, agile, and learned narrator's consciousness into the minds of characters whose limitations make them unlikely vessels, Williams underscores the structural challenges of Eliot's inclusive aesthetics, her novelistic enfranchisement of characters who find little room on the pages of Austen. Eliot is "not *with* anyone" of her characters, he writes. The democratizing expansion of the novel to include broader classes of characters also produces torque on the narrator's capacity to enter their minds. In those passages of free indirect style in which a character's thoughts are made known to us by the narrator's voice, to speak "*with*" them in their own modes of perception has become more difficult after Austen due to the novel's expansiveness. Williams is making a historical point about the novel here, but in doing so, he also sounds something like a note of frustration with Eliot herself.

It is at this moment that Williams suddenly stops, as if embarrassed. He reassures us that he is not just trading on history here, calling Eliot out for a Victorian intellectual's condescension. Rather, he feels close to the problems Eliot faced in democratizing the novel's character populace, close enough, he writes, that "I could make these points in her presence; that I am, in a sense, making them in her presence, since her particular intelligence, in a particular structure of feeling, persists and connects."[2] It is an odd moment and a slightly dizzying one. Williams breaks critical frame, as it were, asserting not only that he would say such things to Eliot, but that he effectively is saying them to her: "I am, in a sense, making them in her presence." Williams develops what he calls a "structure of feeling" elsewhere in his work in order to get at "social experiences in solution," the felt qualities associated with particular historical periods before they have been defined or classified. This particular "structure of feeling," however, feels personal for Williams. It is as if Eliot's acts of authorial "impersonation," where she cannot resist taking up cognitive residence within characters she identifies with, have become contagious; Williams conjures Eliot within his own scene of writing, a critical essay inadvertently turned séance. Or, more precisely and more vertiginously, the essay becomes a séance turned on its head (if séances have heads), with the critic cum medium Raymond Williams less conjuring than being conjured up by Eliot's spirit.

In a relatively straightforward sense, Williams is recognizing the legacies of Eliot for the novel and for twentieth-century British and American culture, suggesting we also inhabit outlooks and ways of experiencing the world that Eliot and the realist novel have bequeathed to us. But Williams's shift to the first person pronoun here nudges his essay away from general critical claims about the novels and the world we inhabit, and toward his individual experience, as he casts himself as kin to a character in a novel written by Eliot, an inhabitant of her "structure of feeling," which seems here both a quality within her novels and a part of her cultural legacy. Or, to say it another way, the essay seems briefly taken over by a George Eliot novel, with Raymond Williams rather than, say, Hetty Sorel of *Adam Bede*, being inhabited by Eliot's consciousness.

In claiming an intimacy with Eliot herself in this passage, Williams writes himself into something like a structural rhyme with his discussion of Eliot's problem of authorial surrogacy. What Williams has been discussing as the ill fit between a perceptually acute narrative consciousness and the thoughts of rustic characters, however, are replaced in this rhyme by something a little more bespoke, a nearly made-to-measure fit between Williams himself and Eliot. A critic's identification with an author in an essay might not be much of a surprise, of course, but the wish fulfillment that takes place across the semicolon in Williams's passage is. The move from the conditional "I *would* make these remarks in her presence" to the "I *am*, in a sense, making these remarks in her presence" vivifies Eliot's "intelligence" and "structure of feeling" into a "presence" that could actually hear Williams's "remarks." Briefly imagining the essay not as print but as speech, words spoken to Eliot herself, Williams turns the essay into a scene of social intimacy, an encounter between critic and novelist that takes place within or across the medium of the essay itself. Williams's near-embarrassment, detectable only in his protestation that he would not be embarrassed at all to say such things to Eliot's face, is alleviated by his essay's conversion into something like a meeting with George Eliot, a sociable séance conducted under the auspices of literary criticism.

I start here with Raymond Williams because his experience with George Eliot turns out not to be unique. In fact, it reads as a repetition of an earlier eminent critic and writer's experience of finding himself slightly, or perhaps even more than slightly, embarrassed in Eliot's presence, actual or otherwise. Meeting George Eliot for the first time, a young, ambitious writer of fiction named Henry James finds himself beguiled—sort of: the "deliciously hideous" Eliot has a "beauty . . . that steals forth and charms the mind." "Behold me in love with this great horse-faced blue-stocking," he writes in a letter to his father.[3] James's account here in his letter of a beauty immaterial enough to overcome not only Eliot's body but his own as well—to charm his "mind" without exciting the carnal senses—indirectly suggests that James's relations with Eliot were a bit smoother on paper, easier for being routed through the mediation of writing, than they were in person. A similar sense of writing's mediating power and reparative social charms emerges from reading James's mostly laudatory reviews of Eliot's work alongside his recollections of two painfully awkward visits he made to the home of the author he saw as the greatest living English novelist, a writer James considered to have nearly finished off the "old-fashioned" realist novel by perfecting it with *Middlemarch*. In each case, the essay form serves to mediate the relations between an author and critic, opening up a space somewhere between being with another person face to face and disinterestedly reading or writing about their work.

This chapter takes up Henry James's particular and peculiar forms of engagements with George Eliot in his reviews and in life in order to demonstrate their effects on James's own theory and practice of the novel, and in turn on the Anglo-American novel criticism that develops after James. From the apparently trivial encounters between James and Eliot within his reviews of her work and in the visits to her home that James recounts in his memoir *The Middle Years*, I want to build an understanding of James's renovations of the realist novel and the early development of professional novel criticism as it is saturated by the language of sociality. The Prefaces James wrote for the New York Edition of his revised novels are the occasion for a reflection upon his earlier work, but they also constitute an important part of James's legacy for theories of the novel that would develop over the twentieth century. In returning to these novels, James famously understands his project as a social encounter with his earlier authorial self, a coming to critical self-consciousness through this meeting of his two distinct selves. In emphasizing the difference, the alterity between his earlier authorial self and his present self, James begins in the Prefaces to ground a theory of the genre of the novel in a social encounter, one characterized by a curious combination of intimacy and distance—a younger James, who is both familiar and distant to his present self. Drawing out the interrelation of social intimacy and literary form at the turn of the century, I turn to the particularly powerful relation between James and Eliot, showing how reading or writing about George Eliot not only figures, but comes to stand in for, the pleasures of intimacy at a distance that this book has been tracing out. It is through James's intimacy with Eliot—an intimacy paradoxically most powerful when he is at a distance from her, when it is mediated through his essays on her that also imagine themselves as a moment of social intimacy or ghostly co-authorship—that the critical practice of close reading begins to be specified, one whose practices continue to shape contemporary critical approaches to literary study.

James's own fiction is often read as a transitional node in the history of the novel, a switch point between nineteenth-century realism's dramas of social convergence and the modernist novel's dramas of consciousness and phenomenology, one that marks the ostensible waning of the novel's realist social imagination in favor of dramas of perception. Against this common critical narrative, here I will offer an account that is more transformational than transitional, showing that James's essays on Eliot are significant moments in the emergence both of twentieth-century novel criticism and of the Jamesian novel. The Jamesian novel's dramas of perception and consciousness emerge from the social grounds of literary form: James develops his thinking about the formal dimensions of the novel through a series of awkward encounters, both with Eliot's books in his essays on her work and with Eliot herself.

"The way to become an acquaintance was first to become an intimate," a character remarks at the start of James's *The Aspern Papers*, a story deeply interested in the mediation of social life through writing.[4] That this novella glosses an intimacy that would give rise to acquaintanceship—rather than the more familiar trajectory of an initial acquaintance growing into deeper intimacy—marks its own investments in the powers of intimacy at a remove. This line from *The Aspern Papers* also obliquely glosses James's two visits to Eliot's home, visits after which James suggests the "sublimity" of his relation to Eliot increases the more it is conducted not face-to-face, but through the medium of her books. In looking at James's encounters with George Eliot, we can see how fiction and writing about fiction are not only valued by James for the forms of social life and social distance they might sponsor. We can also see that social intimacy itself takes its shape and draws its charge from its mediation in writing. In this account, Jamesian social propinquity, in brief, can only be sustained when it is remade into a form of mediated or distanciated intimacy. Where the preceding chapters of this book have examined the interrelation of aesthetic and social effects within a text, here I suggest that such effects also can bleed into social relations in the world outside the novel, "mediating" social life by routing it both through and alongside literary works.

My claim for a social reading of Jamesian novel criticism builds upon a critical school that has found James to be, as Leo Bersani puts it in his discussion of the importance of talk in James, "one of our most sociable novelists." In different terms, Ross Posnock's reading of James within the pragmatist tradition also emphasizes the sociable "Jamesian self," which "is perpetually negotiating an identity out of its interaction with various others." Likewise, it is in the vein of Jamesian sociability that my introduction discusses James's preference for a London emptied of those he does know so as to better sense the infinitely greater number of people he does not. Another of James's most powerful critics, Sharon Cameron, also locates a Jamesian preoccupation with sociability in his "mediation of consciousness or . . . its externalization," a tendency to project thought outward, with consciousness thus located not in a psychologized interiority, but both in and between people.[5]

The story I want to tell here of James and his legacy for novel criticism thus shares Bersani's and Cameron's understanding of the sociability of James's writing as de-psychologizing, in spite of having been understood, and presented himself, as the great novelist of psychological interiority. For James's novels' "desire is always designed," and their "avoidance of undeflected, unmodulated desire . . . is thus eminently social," Bersani writes.[6] The phenomenological confusion around consciousness that Cameron identifies finds a material referent in James's later move to dictating his novels, his mediation of his writing through another person. But the sense of a medium—a space between that connects as well as distances—is crucial, I suggest, to understanding James's own essays as a mediation of his relation to Eliot, and to the consequences of that relationship for Jamesian criticism of the novel that relies upon a notion of mediation. Mediation itself, I suggest, might also become the object or site of a designed desire.

While communication across distance (which can be physical, but also notional or psychological) is the condition for the possibility of media, mediation can become a pleasure in and of itself, like the pleasure of sending a text or talking on the phone, as John Guillory has argued in his account of the genesis of the concept of media.[7] It is the specific appeal of mediation that Mark Goble identifies in a recent account of the technology of the telegraph in Henry James. Amidst the new technology of the telegraph, he argues that James's fiction is particularly responsive to the pleasures of communication.

Goble locates that pleasure in the medium of communication itself rather than in the more familiar sites of Jamesian stylistics of obliquity, linguistic displacement, and circuitousness that might emerge from the compressed writing of telegraphic messages. James's "telegraphic fictions," Goble argues, confirm that the pleasure in relations at a distance is not a substitute for something else in these works, a displacement of an erotic desire, for instance. Instead, James's fictions show that "there are pleasures in the world of media that are particular and native to that world ... that persist and thrive on being mediated."[8] If we think of mediation as not standing in for something else, not a second-best to a face-to-face meeting between James and Eliot, between critic and author, we can begin to see mediation's own appeals and challenges, the pleasures as much as the powers of distance.

One aim of this chapter is to show how James's encounters with Eliot, on the page and in person, are formative for later practices of what we might call critical intimacy. In James, we find an early centering of novel criticism around moments of close, tactful engagement with a literary text—a critic's job is "to lend himself, to project himself, and to steep himself" in a text, as James says—that resemble some aspects of the practice of close reading.[9] By turning to the realist novel's signature narrative technique, free indirect style, and that style's unexpected efflorescence far from the novel's fictional world in the pages of a critical essay, we can see how James remakes free indirect style from novelistic technique into a critical mode that is rooted in a particular form of textual or mediate intimacy. The contagion of free indirect style in Raymond Williams, in which the awkward fit between a narrative voice and a character becomes a moment of closeness to Eliot herself, indicates how the novel might afford ways of being close to, without actually being near, other people. As a means of bringing close what can never touch—in a realist novel, the omniscient narrator and a character—the "impersonal intimacy" of free indirect style offers James a means of negotiating his fraught relations with the novelist whose work he saw as rival to his own.

In thinking through the Jamesian grounds of textual intimacy, and the social grounds of Jamesian novel criticism, we can also mark James's understanding of novelist, character, and reader as themselves in a social relationship. This understanding is part of the legacy left by James to a broad range of novel theory across the twentieth century, Dorothy Hale argues, what she calls the "social formalism" of this theory. "Social formalism," Hale writes, is the "belief that the novel can formally both encapsulate and fix a social world."[10] Hale argues that James's central contribution to novel theory is the elaboration of "point of view." Not simply a narrative technique, as most have understood it, Hale argues that "point of view" is understood by James as itself intimately bound up with the constitution of human identity, and through it he constructs an ethics of alterity. "Social formalists," James first among them, thus understand the social (which Hale sees as narrowed to the interpersonal) not simply as the privileged representational interest and content of the novel. Instead, the social is instantiated within novelistic form itself, and so "relationality" needs to be understood "as a formal property of the novel."[11] James also regards the act of fiction writing itself as a social one, as with this remark, which not coincidentally appears in his essay on Eliot: "In every novel the work is divided between the writer and the reader; but the writer makes the reader very much as he makes his characters."[12] In the move from one type of making (character) to another type of making (reader), James asserts a social relation across the ontological gap dividing fictional characters and real world readers in the act of reading. In James's adaptation of the novelistic narrative technique of free indirect style into a critical mode, we will see how central it is to the style of close, personal engagement between critic and novel that Jamesian criticism evolves.[13]

My thinking here thus brings Hale's account of social formalism together with the emphasis on medium and mediation found in Guillory and Goble. In doing so, this chapter's account of James's mediation of Eliot underscores early Jamesian novel theory's orientation to the medium of the novel, an orientation that emerges from both the novel's newness as theoretical object, as well as James's social conception of the relation of artist, character, and reader. By medium, I refer to something that includes but is broader than the technical medium of print. I also mean the sense of the novel as itself a mediation—a space of communication—among author and reader, author and character, the social world and the fictive social world of the novel. Through James's theory of the novel, his understanding of that theory as itself a mediation of the novel, the medium of the novel, and its theory, begins to thicken. That is, it draws our attention to its mediated nature, its possession of a substance of its own, as it were, rather than being something just to be read through for content.[14] In this, contemporary practices of close reading, to the extent that such reading might self-consciously imagine a form of social intimacy with a text and so mark it as a medium, are not simply ontologically naïve and fantasized social encounters. They also might be the occasion for returning a consideration of mediation to current critical thinking about the novel, which tends to focus on representational content.

This chapter thus catches James mid-stride as he begins to codify a distinct set of practices that would help institutionalize the novel as an object of literary study. In recent histories of the rise of criticism about the novel, James's critical writings, in essays like "The Art of Fiction" and "The Science of Criticism," as well as his Prefaces, constitute one starting point for Anglo-American novel criticism's attempt to establish itself as a set of practices relatively distinct from writing about culture more generally, as well as the more established practices of writing about poetry, drama, and the fine arts. James labors to remake the novel itself from a genre generally considered as a mass media form in the nineteenth century into the "art novel," whose formal complexity and difficulty would ally it with the fine arts of poetry, drama, and painting. Such an "art novel" would in turn necessitate a critical practice that would legitimate the novel's elevation into high art status, providing it with the theoretical underpinnings James believed it had up to that point been lacking.[15]

By turning to James's essays on Eliot as a formative moment in James's practice and theory of the novel, we will see his criticism developing the language of social form and manners, "tact" in James's phrase, to talk about the novel. The project of elevating the novel from a mass form into an art form is undertaken in part by a criticism that invokes the tenets of tact and good social form. As a way of thinking about something as diffuse as novelistic form, "tact" thus roots criticism's practice in the vagaries of individual taste and good social form. But it does so even as James sets novel criticism on its way to codification and eventual institutionalization in the university. James's own attentiveness to good form in his fiction is a critical commonplace, expressed in his renovations of the novel of manners for a modern world and in his own wish to write a novel like *Middlemarch*, as he says in a letter, but with "less brain" and "more form." In seeing how free indirect style is adapted into both a social and critical mode by James, we can see how the "impersonal intimacy" it grants offers a means of negotiating a relation to Eliot and her texts that is at once intimate and tactful. It is through the turn to tact that James negotiates the questions of aesthetic and social distance, the proper relation between critic and text, between social and aesthetic form, and between intimacy and impersonality that become so central to writing about the novel. And in that turn to tact, we will see how difficult it becomes in the James–Eliot nexus to tell social form and literary effects apart.

Elsewhere, James links Eliot's aloofness from the social world, her wish to live the life of the mind rather than be the life of the party, with the faults he finds with her works: "If her relations with the world had been easier, in a word, her books would have been less difficult."[16] It is as if Eliot's reluctance to mix socially (famously, she preferred to be visited rather than to visit) made her novels more difficult to read, the intimidating intellect, erudition, and social critique of her fiction an emanation of her preference for a quiet evening in.[17] If the insufficiency of Eliot's sociality inhibits the novelistic here by James's lights, I want to follow out this continuity between the social and the novel to ends different from those of James, to mark sociality's deep imbrication with the novelistic as it is conceived by James via Eliot. With the particularly novelized qualities of sociality and the felt presence of others that we discovered in *Middlemarch* in mind, in this chapter we will see that James's essays—on, about, possibly even to, George Eliot—are the means by which James imagines a social intimacy predicated on its deflection into writing, on that social relation's mediated qualities.

Swarm

"A treasurehouse of details, but an indifferent whole," Henry James famously declared *Middlemarch* in his 1873 review of the novel.[18] For James, Eliot's novel's attention to the smallest details of ordinary individuals' regular lives and the nearly microscopically evoked ambient texture of a provincial town magnifies small subjects into high drama, rendering her realist novel a veritable Empire of the Little. But *Middlemarch*'s promise in its early chapters that this empire would take formal integrated shape through the skillful apportioning of its multitude of plots and characters is never quite fulfilled in James's view. For James, of course, the overextended realist novels he called formless "baggy monsters" are what he sets out to transform over the course of his writing life with his own vision of formally svelte novelistic representation. A "treasurehouse of details" is a great deal different from a "baggy monster," as James's admiration of the novel under review makes clear. But Eliot's book does not achieve the fine Jamesian balance by which a multitude of detail and people is winnowed to its essence. As he puts it in his preface to *Roderick Hudson*, the most formally accomplished novels turn on the proper management of fictional multitudinousness, making a potentially vast and unruly fictional populace into a well-heeled, discrete set of characters: "the mere procession of items and profiles is not only . . . superseded, but is, for essential quality, almost 'compromised.' . . . It is only by doing such things that art becomes exquisite."[19]

James expresses his disappointment in *Middlemarch*'s close-but-not-quite attempt to turn the crowdedness of this novel, "a mere procession of items and profiles," and "details" into exquisite art. However, in registering this disappointment, a rhyme emerges between what *Middlemarch* called "watching keenly the stealthy convergence of human lots" and James's description of the experience of reading Eliot's novel as a high drama, but not, notably, of characters whose lives dramatically intersect through "stealthy convergence[s]."

> We can all remember how keenly we wondered, while its early chapters unfolded themselves, what turn in the way of form the story would take—that of an organized, moulded, balanced composition, gratifying the reader with a sense of design and construction, or a mere chain of episodes, broken into accidental lengths and unconscious of the influence of a plan (M, 74–75).

The central dramatic experience of the book, as he describes it, is not the story of Dorothea's two marriages, Lydgate's entanglement with Bulstrode, or Featherstone's will. Instead, for James, the gradual formal development and promise of coherence ("an organized, moulded, balanced composition") over the course of its serial publication makes *Middlemarch* less about the suspense of the "stealthy convergence" of a multitude of characters' lives, than a gripping drama of formal coalescence.

More surprisingly, James's language and syntax here seem to mime that of *Middlemarch* itself, echoing Eliot's own passage as he turns *Middlemarch*'s plot and social drama into a corollary drama of novelistic form. In the barely noticeable conscription of Eliot's passage into his own prose, Eliot's "keenly watching" is transformed into "keenly wonder[ing]" in James's review, and the social drama of "the stealthy convergence of human lots" within *Middlemarch* pointedly becomes a formal drama about reading *Middlemarch*, a drama structured around a tension between "design" and "construction," on the one side, and an "unconscious" "mere chain of episodes," on the other.

James draws upon and echoes *Middlemarch*'s language, syntax, and tone throughout this review, though he never marks it as such. So, "ardent" and "yearning," key words used to describe Dorothea in Eliot's novel, recur multiple times in James's description of Dorothea, without the designation of quotation marks, as does a phrase from *Middlemarch*'s "Prelude," "meanness of opportunity," with which latter day Theresas, *Middlemarch* tells us, will find their spiritual aspirations ill-matched. James's simultaneous disinclination to quote directly from *Middlemarch* and silent assimilation of Eliot's novel's language to his own essay function as both a form of homage and a critique. Having "marked innumerable passages [in *Middlemarch*] for quotation and comment," James writes, "we lack space and the work is so ample that half a dozen extracts would be an ineffective illustration." In fact, the review does not properly quote a single phrase from the novel. James shows his appreciation of Eliot not by compiling a common-place book of quotations within the review, as had become a popular practice among Eliot's reviewers, who recognized and furthered Eliot's particular quotability.[20] Instead, by silently channeling the novel's language and syntax through his own prose, James grants his readers a taste of the vocabulary, sentence structure, and style of *Middlemarch* not through a common-place book of quotations, but by reading it *through* and *as* James's essay.

In some respects, James's essay reflects an intensified form of the inter-genre competition we might find in any review of a novel. Within the protocols of the genre of the essay, the review does its best to represent, praise, or critique the generically quite different aims and achievements of the novel. While generic boundaries are leaky at best, and the miscellaneous, omnivorous qualities of the novel mean that it can house essays, poems, plays easily within its pages and still be recognized as a novel, it is worth noting that what James finds fault with in *Middlemarch* is what we might well call this novel's essayistic qualities. James admires *Middlemarch*'s "*brain*," he says, its wide range of reference and its "constant presence of thought," but he also finds fault with Eliot's "wish to say too many things, and to say them too well," which makes the "discursive portions" of the novel "too clever by half" (M,

81). Put another way, while the novel is so different in scope and kind from the essay—as narrative fiction rather than critical prose, and, as James has remarked in his review, in the novel being too big to quote to any useful effect in a review—*Middlemarch* fails as a novel in no small part because it is also too much like an essay in James's view.

James discreetly calls Eliot out on her novel being, by his lights, too essay-istic and written for the likes of scientists such as T. H. Huxley and Herbert Spencer rather than general readers. However, the review also enacts this cri-tique at the level of style. James embeds a more powerful version of his claims about the essay and the novel within the style of his own writing precisely by not citing his use of Eliot's language, by smoothly integrating without remark her novel's language and syntax, even the granular-level structural rhyme of "keenly watching" and "keenly wondering," into his essay. If *Middlemarch*'s novelistic language and syntax can be assimilated invisibly, silently to the review essay form—marked neither by quotation marks, nor by any awk-wardness or dissonance with the essay's prose style or structure—then Eliot's book is insufficiently novelistic. James here both pays *Middlemarch* hom-age in slyly purloining Eliot's novel for his own essay, and takes critical aim at what he regards as the sententious and overly essayistic tendencies of its author, what we might also see as an effort to purify the realist novel of its narrator's pedagogic tendencies. And this being James, he has done so almost entirely with style.[21]

In asserting a sharp distinction between the novel and the essay in his critique of Eliot, we can see the beginning of the Jamesian novel, on the one hand, and Jamesian novel criticism, on the other, a division predicated in part on an idea of generic specialization, the growing division of literary labor over the next decades into a professional distinction between novelist and critic. But in asserting that division of labor by way of its abrogation, pur-loining Eliot's novel within his essay even as he argues that her novel is too essayistic, James's essay remains marked by the problem of criticism's critical distance from what it analyzes, the question of where his own language and thinking begins and that of Eliot ends.

James finds much to like in Eliot's novel too, admiring the scope as well as the social density I have suggested is so central to *Middlemarch*. The novel is "crowded with antique figures," its "large group of [characters] begotten of the super-abundance of the author's creative instinct," its pages "vast, swarming . . . crowded with episode" (M, 75). Amidst what seems like admi-ration, however, for James there may be too much of a good thing here, or at least too many of a good thing. In describing the vastness of people and episodes in *Middlemarch* as a "swarm," the novel would seem to suggestively float between morphologically opposed poles: blobby shapelessness, on the one hand, and, on the other, the spontaneously self-organizing collectivity of innumerable small things, bees or locusts in a swarm. A novel "swarming" is

thus James's version of the oscillation or toggling between the unboundedness of social extensionality and the locatable networks of "this particular
web" that I argued in chapter 2 is central to *Middlemarch*'s account of the
social. James's language here evokes an anxiety about populousness within
Eliot's novel, a sensitivity to the democratizing pressures of social density and
multiplicity on novelistic technique and form, echoes of which later can be
heard in his essay about the consequences of the novel form's vastly expanding audience, an audience he refers to in "The Future of the Novel" as the
"multitude" and "total swarm."[22]

Social vastness is precisely the problem that form promises, but fails, to
address in Eliot's book. As James notes elsewhere, the extensional, unbounded
qualities of the social is one of the great challenges for any realist novelist: "Really, universally, relations stop nowhere, and the exquisite problem of
the artist is eternally but to draw, by a geometry of his own, the circle within
which they shall *appear* to do so."[23] Impressed by *Middlemarch*'s aspirations
toward formal integrity and its panoramic qualities, James makes clear his
wish that Eliot's novel had given better shape and structure to the "crowd" of
incident and people it contains, a form that would have made it "the first of
English novels" in his estimate.

It seems then to be nearly with a sense of relief that James turns his
attention in the review to the vividness of Dorothea Brooke, a character whose emergence in contrast to this swarming over-abundance of
fictional life and liveliness in *Middlemarch* is both occasion for James's
obvious relief, and an instance of relief in the pictorial sense, as visual
contrast. Standing apart from the crowded social and aesthetic scene of
the novel that earns James's admiration and frustration, Dorothea Brooke
also would seem to have stepped outside its pages: "We believe in her as a
woman we might providentially meet some fine day when we should find
ourselves doubting the immortality of the soul" (M, 76). Following closely
upon the review's half-praise and half-blame of the novel as "swarming"
and "crowded," Dorothea's singular quality within this passage of the
essay develops against the backdrop of crowdedness. It is as if to the great
relief of all involved (James, his readers, the essay itself) we had suddenly
come upon Dorothea gazing upon us in the streets of London amidst the
five o'clock rush hour.[24] Breaking off from his description of Dorothea
as "the perfect flower of [Eliot's] conception," James briefly narrates just
such a little scene of chance meeting, allowing his essay to indulge a little
genre-envy, to become, however momentarily, like a novel.[25] Ditching its
genre by submitting the most minimal of novelistic scenes as evidence of
Dorothea's vividness as fictional character—"a woman we might providentially meet some fine day"—James's relief in meeting Dorothea again
echoes, more faintly this time but also more novelistically than an essay
otherwise might, Eliot's line about the stealthy convergence of human lots.

The review's own dip into the novelistic might be read as compensatory to what James takes to be *Middlemarch*'s formal loose threads and imbalances, imbalances signified above all by the book's failure to give its heroine adequate plot, since Dorothea's life is not made central enough by James's estimate, having to share space with the likes of Fred Vincy and other lesser creations. By relocating Dorothea outside the pages of the novel, James in effect also gives her an extra scene. In fact, James often couches the acting of writing fiction in the idiom of interpersonal relations, as if his characters were real people. "I get down into the arena and do my best to live and breathe and rub shoulders and converse with the persons engaged in the struggle that provides for the others in the circling tiers the entertainment of the great game."[26] Rather than descending into the "arena" of the novel under composition, an author living and rubbing shoulders with his own characters, in this instance James transports the character Dorothea out of the novel and into the world so as to encounter her under altered conditions. There James and his readers can meet Dorothea through her real-world avatars, not through the chance encounters of what *Middlemarch* calls "sarcastic" "destiny," but in the more divinely perfect form of a "providential" "meeting" apart from the thickly populated pages of the novel. A salvational one-on-one encounter with Dorothea outside the book, as James imagines, both lends this character more plot than the comparatively meager allotment she receives in Eliot's novel and acts as a crowd-thinning corrective to the swarm of people and episodes that seem to make *Middlemarch*'s overstuffed form bulge unpleasantly to James's assiduous critical eye.

In this respect, James's essay on *Middlemarch* coheres with the reading I pursued in my chapter on Eliot, one in which the novel seems to imagine its characters as not only inhabitants of a fictional world that the narrator is in the business of describing and substantiating but also as being able to inhabit the very space of narrative discourse itself. Narration affords an alternate site of a sociality, one situated just beyond the represented novelistic world these characters otherwise inhabit, where characters might meet one another in ways unimagined by the novel's own plot. In these moments, we can glimpse the novel's imagination of sociality, both within and outside its pages, as overcoming even its own plot devices that might otherwise keep characters apart.

We can see how James's critique on formal, aesthetic grounds of *Middlemarch* is enacted through an imagined social convergence of another sort, one involving James and Eliot herself in the faint outline of collective authorship his essay gives us. In an essay that is imagined as affording an impossible social contact between novelist and critic, James begins to recast the realist novel into its eventual Jamesian version by first rewriting one that is not his own. James in this essay begins to reshape *Middlemarch* a bit, mitigating his sense of the novel's formal shortcomings by channeling its language and syntax, recontextualizing a phrase here and there, suggesting another scene for its heroine, as if he were collaborating with Eliot on a book she's already written. In this oblique revision of Eliot, a rewriting of her novel without really changing it, we also get a preview of how James understood his revisions for the New York edition as not really changing his novels, but simply unearthing "the buried, latent life of past composition."[27]

In this, James's review returns us to the various ways in which Eliot's readers would catalogue her characters in writing about the novel, rearticulating them into relations undreamed of by the novel's plot. But it also takes us to what Andrew Miller calls the "optative" mode of reflection so central to the realist novel, the sense of the singularity of an individual life that comes about by its comparison with and reflection upon "lives unled."[28] Anticipating his own later fiction's frequent phrasing of thought in grammatical terms of the subjunctive—the "would have" qualities of experience that we find in *The Awkward Age* and other works—James here imagines a *Middlemarch* that might have been otherwise. He here makes the review into the occasion of this novel's rewriting. But, he also makes the review essay into the medium of a social encounter with its author, one in which the medium of communication itself provides its own attractions.

As we have seen, James thought of his creation of novelistic characters within the idiom of sociality, imagining writing as a passionately intense relation between author and characters that can tend even to the vampiric: "A beautiful infatuation this, always, I think, the intensity of the creative effort to get into the skin of the creature; the act of personal possession of one being by another at its completest—and with the highest enhancement, ever, that it is, by the same stroke, the effort of the artist to preserve for this subject that unity."[29] "Personal possession of one being by another": one can know a character only by inhabiting or being inhabited by her, as is the case with what has been called James's "inordinate receptivity," and experience is known by placing it within oneself, replacing "theory with practice . . . information with immersion."[30] This vampiric aspect of James, I want to suggest, is not limited to his relation to his characters. Here in James's review *Middlemarch* is ingested, diffused into the style and structure of his writing, an essay that paradoxically takes within its comparatively small contours a novel far too large to fit, shrinking and shaping a crowded, swarming *Middlemarch* into a more Jamesian, less populous and more formally manageable, iteration of itself.

In James's distillation of *Middlemarch*'s prose into his own, a social relation in print, we can recognize the marks upon contemporary practices of close novel reading left by James. If silently translating *Middlemarch* into one's own critical prose seems a far remove from contemporary critical practice, D. A. Miller suggests in his discussion of style and Jane Austen that just such an identificatory wish is what lies behind close reading itself, "an almost infantile desire to be . . . as close as one can get without literal plagiarism":

The practice of close reading has always been radically cloven: here, on one side, my ambition to master a text, to write *over* its language and refashion it to the cut of my argument . . . there, on the other, my longing to write *in* this language, to identify and combine with it. The adept in close reading must assert an autonomy of which he must continually betray the weak and easily overwhelmed defenses.[31]

To think of close reading in these terms (and to be sure, not every critic thinks, or writes, as Miller does) is to bring criticism into close quarters with the practices of narrative intimacy already touched upon earlier in this book, that of free indirect style, a "fantasmatics of *close writing*," Miller says.[32] What Miller articulates then are the novelistic qualities of close reading, and in particular the centrality for close reading of an especially powerful—that is to say, appealing and intense—closeness granted to novelistic character and narrative voice in moments of free indirect style, a technique that I argued in chapter 2 figures an impossible social relation between these entities. Rather than thinking of free indirect style as the moment of merging between a narrator's voice and a character's thoughts, Miller writes, free indirect style "attenuates the stark opposition between character and narration" only to "perform this opposition at *ostentatiously close quarters.*" This opposition amidst propinquity, "narration's persistence in detachment from character, no matter how intimate one becomes with the other," enables "an impersonal intimacy" that "grants us at one and the same time the experience of a character's inner life as she herself lives it, and an experience of that same inner life as she never could."[33] Finding its metaphor in narrative technique, these "fantasmatics" of close reading, which in spite of turns to historical or distant reading continue to shape criticism on the realist novel today, could be thought of as what Andrew Miller has called critical free indirect discourse.[34]

While both Millers describe free indirect style as granting us access to the inner life of a character but from a perspective not her own, as she herself has not experienced it, it is also the case that free indirect style, in its report of thoughts and experiences in a voice other than that of the subject experiencing them, puts into question precisely to whom the narrated experience belongs. Anne-Lise Francois argues that in "making available to the reader an inner life that it also leaves, in some sense, unlived by the protagonist, free indirect style might be called 'de-realizing' rather than simply expressive or concretizing" of a character's experience.[35] In thinking about critical free indirect style, what I want to bring out here in James are the de-realized and para- or quasi-social, as it were, qualities of this form of critical relationship, as well as the appeals of mediation—through print, through critical free indirect discourse—that it names, and names precisely as an escape from a "swarm[ing]" and "crowded" fictional world. The fictional subject of free indirect style is often left quiet, Francois suggests, set apart from others even, in moments of having her thoughts narrated by a voice not her own, and so is granted a certain freedom. What we might recognize here, then, is the particular form of "unsocial sociability" lodged as an ideal within free indirect style, a way of being with others without the burdens of strong in-person attachment.[36] While we should notice in this instance the uncertainty of the relationship between critic and text produced within close reading—the critic at once "within and beyond the writing he is studying"[37] as Andrew Miller puts it—what is most interesting in James's writing about *Middlemarch* here is the appeal of an impersonal intimacy that would seem afforded to James by the review itself, a means of both being alone with and not being with *Middlemarch* and its author at the same time.

James's yearning here toward co-authorship and toward the fantasmatics of free indirect style, in his *Middlemarch* essay, however, is notably drained of any of the intensities of the vampiric charge associated with his sociable authorship, his understanding of novel writing as a merging with a fictional character while in the act of composing that character.[38] By James's own account, his reading of *Middlemarch* in the wake of the experience of having met Eliot gives his reading experience a uniquely social cast. His "relation" to Eliot, he would write later in *The Middle Years*, is "intimately concerned in my perusal of *Middlemarch*."[39] James's "perusal" suggests a state of reading somewhat less than absorbed, of course, a slightly defensive construction by a fellow novelist that would seem belied by the Eliotic language of his own review. But the skimmingly light or dispersive way of reading implied by "perusal" accords with the involved detachment, the impersonally intimate qualities, of the relation James's essay bears to *Middlemarch*. Where René Wellek understands Jamesian criticism as founded on "sympathy, identification with the work of art," the Eliot pieces help us see a more complex form of sociality at stake in this understanding of criticism, one predicated upon the play of a distanced intimacy rather than identification.[40]

Unlike James's intensely vampiric experience of composing fictional characters, the essay form here bears its own neutralizing effects, the power to manage and make mild relational intensities in writing imagined as social intimacy—the "beautiful infatuation" of producing a character, or, in his review, of meeting George Eliot.[41] In his review, James remakes the "swarm" of Eliot's multitudinous fictional population into a transformational meeting with Dorothea, and, in turn with Dorothea's creator. This social neutralization calls to mind Erving Goffman's notion of the everyday strategies of "civil inattention," such as averting one's eyes on the bus, without which the millions of micro-social claims made upon us in the stranger-filled public settings of modern city life would be "unbearably sticky."[42] James also finds in his essay a way of lightening, without simply negating, both Eliot's swarm and the felt presence of Eliot herself by deflecting their relation into the civil attention of his critical essay.

In the section that follows, we will see how the intertwined relation of social and aesthetic form within James's review of *Middlemarch* becomes a question of good manners more generally in his attempts to develop a specialized critical language for the novel, a language that depends upon notions like tact. Casting his review of Eliot's *Daniel Deronda* in the form of a dialogue, James hedges his bets by dramatizing contradictory responses to a novel that felt to him, and to many of Eliot's first readers as well, particularly formally fragmented and inconsistent. The review puts in more pointed terms a question that bubbles up in James's review of *Middlemarch*, and more generally in Jamesian notions of critical refinement: Does good social form blunt or sharpen critical acuity? James's *Middlemarch* review phrases its harshest points about Eliot's novel in submerged and diffuse ways, part homage and part critique. And, we might think James is simply being polite in his criticisms of an author he regarded with some awe, as spiritual kin. In the review of *Deronda*, however, James has it both ways, turning that novel's bad form into polite conversation.

Good Critical Form

While James's essay review of *Middlemarch* exemplifies a mediated form of sociability, in what follows we will see how good social form can also be a means of holding a novel, or one's criticism of it, at a polite arm's length. James's famously formalist conception of the novel and his development of a critical idiom for writing about the novel emerges intertwined with the language of manners and good social form across his writing on Eliot. Tactful social form lends James a language adept in the kinds of vagueness, capaciousness, and ineffability that pester any attempt to actually define, or even write about, something as slippery as novelistic form. In merging a novel into an essay, and imbuing a work of criticism with social impulses, James's *Middlemarch* essay anticipates the dialogue form of his infamous review of *Daniel Deronda*, which comprises a social gathering of readers of that novel.

"I say it under my breath—I began to feel an occasional temptation to skip." So says Constantius, the book reviewer and novelist in James's review of *Deronda*. Constantius, James's stand-in for himself, is here trying his *sotto voce* best to speak about poor novelistic form while maintaining good social form. Registering the force of Eliot's public and critical popularity by lowering his voice, Constantius's whispered declaration suggests that to speak ill of George Eliot would be bad manners indeed. Confessing to those within earshot, politeness also seems to require Constantius to muffle his voice so as to avoid offending ears a bit farther off. His confession, as with Mill's famous description of the speaker of lyric poetry as "not heard but *overheard*," is to be heard as overheard. In muffling but still voicing his confession, Constantius suggests too that one could be too polite about Eliot, that a criticism that did not at least make room for the *sotto voce* vulgar, would not be worth its salt.

Eliot famously complained of those who praised *Daniel Deronda* by taking over its authorship, suggesting improvements even as they lauded it, praising even as they "cut the book up into scraps and talk of nothing in it but Gwendolyn."[43] Eliot's response to those who would have her excise the Mordecai plot, or make the love match in the novel between Gwendolyn and Deronda rather than Deronda and Mirah, underscores her view of the novel as seamlessly integrated: "I meant everything in the book to be related to everything else there."[44] However, "*Daniel Deronda*: A Conversation" is what James's review was titled when it appeared in 1876 in the *Atlantic Monthly*, suggesting that readers and reviewers alike were of more than one mind about a book that would be described notoriously as having "two halves." "Conversation" on this account invokes both the ample talk stirred up by the book, in no small part due to its treatment of Jewish characters and its interest in the relation of Jewish identity and English national culture, and the related sense of the book's lack of formal integration, the so-called "Jewish" and "non-Jewish" portions of the novel, which are so split for James as apparently to resist reconciliation even in their treatment within a form as capacious as the review essay. But "*Daniel Deronda*: A Conversation" as a title also seems to transform the novel itself into talk, draining it of all but its dialogue.

In dramatizing interchange about the novel in a dialogue that draws upon the language of "manner" and "tact" as a way of thinking about the novel's formal features, James also transforms a fictional form into the occasion for the practice of, but also reflection upon, social form. In James's one-act play of sociable criticism, what is described in the review as the novel's "importuning" qualities, its "want of tact," can be underscored in critiques by individual characters. But in being underscored within the more and less tactful tones of Jamesian conversation staged among a set of friends, rather than the usual genre of the review essay, Eliot's fragmented, "tactless" novel is one site at which James elaborates the terms and language of novel criticism through the idiom of manners.

James's remaking of the novel from a democratized mass media form into an ostensibly more complex, and less mass (more boutique, as it were), aesthetic form finds its counterpart in James's wish to make novel criticism more sophisticated. Until recently, James writes in "The Art of Fiction," the novel in England and America has been "*naïf*," with "no air of having a theory . . . a consciousness of itself behind it."[45] With such an un-theorized aesthetic artifact as its object, criticism of the novel in England, he contends, has been likewise haphazard and unserious: "We blunder in and out of the affair as if it were a railway station—the easiest and most public of arts."[46] James's description of the relative youth of the genre of the realist novel in the language of naiveté and unselfconsciousness, and his image of criticism's boorish amateurishness, casts the eventual maturation of the novel and its criticism as an issue of becoming both more sophisticated and more specialized, in a word, becoming professional practices under the divisions and specialization of labor characteristic of modernity.

What is notable about James's case for specialization and professionalism for the novel and novel criticism, however, is that it is made in a vocabulary more readily associated with etiquette manuals than with anything like the rationalizations of labor practices in, say, Taylorization, or even the codifications of prosody and meter one might find in critical handbooks on poetry.[47] If James's project of turning the mass media genre of the novel into a fine art form is recognizably of a piece with broader transformations of the rationalization and specialization of labor, intellectual and otherwise, the language of social form in which he couches that project would seem both to enlist and be not particularly amenable to codification and rationalization. Criticism in its amateur form is uncouth, "blundered" in and out of like so many unthinking people in a train station, requiring neither commitments nor qualifications. And the novel, while not totally boorish, has been until now untutored and "naïve," unaware and unconscious of its own form. James's program for renovating the novel and its critical apparatus would be, in these terms, a lesson in manners, a program in acquiring the kinds of graceful self-awareness outlined by the etiquette books and conduct manuals that flourished amidst the increasing social mobility and shifting grounds of social authority in nineteenth-century Britain, and that make for good social form.

The realist novel's own long-standing interest in the details and pleasures of bourgeois sociability is itself reflected in the special attentiveness and weight it gives to social form, to the seemingly small matters of good manners. James's particular interest in manners, Nancy Bentley suggests, rests on an understanding of fiction's capacity at the turn of the century, one driven in part by a competition for cultural status with the new science of ethnography, to make "manners . . . intelligible as the stuff of a larger totality . . . endow[ing] the minutiae of social manners with their meaning."[48] In setting up a newly more sophisticated novel criticism as a kind of finishing school for a charmingly naïve realist novel in need of some further refinement and elegance, James is drawing upon the realist novel's keen eye for the self-consciousness about life with other people that manners reflect.

If James grounds novel criticism in the language of etiquette, however, such ground had become particularly soft and shifting over the course of the nineteenth century, with etiquette increasingly associated not with an autonomous code of ethics or conduct, but with the ever-changing fluidity of fashion over the course of the nineteenth century. The rise of the etiquette book in the 1830s alongside the nineteenth-century novel of manners, Kent Puckett has recently argued, marks just how interrelated novelistic form and social form become under realism and also indicates the novel's anxious relationship to its own formal features. Within the familiar tendency of realist characters to make social mistakes—to say the wrong thing, to wear the wrong hat—Puckett discovers a species of "bad form." By his account, "bad form" is what indicates the character effect of depth (to err is human, he points out) as well as the fraught relation between human, mistake-prone characters, and the unembodied entity known as the mistake-less omniscient narrator, who is lent coherence by its difference from, and negation of the all-too-human limits of such bumbling characters. Finding the novel structured by the narrative effects of such mistakes, Puckett joins a range of thinkers who see the novel as constituted by the interrelation of aesthetic and social form, and the occasion at which literary form might itself become a "source of identification, anxiety, and aggression." Literary form, by these critical lights, is not just the reflection of particular psychic or social conditions but also should be understood "as a point at which social, psychic, and literary effects cannot be told cleanly apart. To understand literary form is, in other words, to understand how it is both generally and at particular moments coincident with or identical to social form."[49]

But would it mean to say that a novel itself is, at least to Henry James, tactless? James's language of social form is of a piece with cultural distinction as Pierre Bourdieu understands it, the means by which class distinction emerges from and depends upon differential amounts of cultural capital—a function of taste, as well as manners—and thus also of a piece with the broader project of rendering the art novel's readership more specialized, more distinguished by forms of intellectual capacities that would become associated with reading aesthetically complex works.[50] In his development of a set of terms for talking about the novel, the habits of self-consciousness associated with manners and tact enable James to assert the at least plausibly codifiable criteria by which one might think about novelistic form, thus linking it to the qualities of objectivity and reproducibility associated with a professionalizing field of critical writing, rather than amateurishness or non-specialization. At the same time, the ineffability of good social form as ideal that is always provisional and socially interdependent, the vagueness and globalizing character of terms like "tact," for James offers a sort of refuge from the forms of rationalization and systematization under market society that are corrosive to the artist.[51]

Tact, then, while offering a refuge from rationalization and systematization, also becomes visible as their reflection; the need for a generically specified novel criticism taking its place amidst the division of labor and professionalization at the turn of the century. Even while seeking to endow novel criticism with a more specialized and iterative theory and practice, James thus places less tangible or reproducible qualities like tact at the center of critical consciousness and analysis. Like James's gloss of Walter Besant's rule that young novelists should take many notes, in which James points out that what notes to take, "[one] can never learn in any manual," social and novelistic form might be codifiable in theory, but not in practice.

Those who have written about the relation between James and Eliot in recent years have been attentive to the ways in which Jamesian notions of literary "mastery" are transacted through forms of identification and dis-identification with Eliot and her implicitly "feminized" form of authorship, as well as through the modes by which James effaces his appropriations of, and dependence upon, the plots of women's fiction.[52] James's sense of himself as the elder Eliot's rival, as writing alongside and against the example of Eliot and the ways in which her form of realism had reshaped the novel, is one of the lines of discussion followed by nearly all those who write on them; and, for good reason, given James's own avowals that the books he would write might resemble *Middlemarch*, albeit with "less brain" and "more form."[53] A rivalrous relationship, of course, can involve feelings more mixed dwelling alongside the anxious forms of identification and dis-identification many critics tend to focus on when thinking of James's relationship to Eliot. Manners, rather than mastery, might allow us better to see James on the way to codifying the novel into doctrine for literary criticism but also to see how the social desire that takes shape in James's critical writings on Eliot also informs that criticism.

In no small part, James's review is self-satire, with the male character—like James at that point in his life a book reviewer with a single novel under his belt—a model of critical equanimity while he agrees with nearly every conflicting assessment rendered by the two female characters. Critical neutrality makes for model politeness, if not necessarily model literary critique: "I see what you mean," Constantius says again and again in response to divergent and conflicting declarations made by Theodora and Pulcheria, who have just finished reading Eliot's latest novel aloud. Deronda, having married his co-religionist Mirah rather than the beautiful heroine of the novel, has left for the vague territory of "the East" in the novel's final pages with the intention of giving Jews "a national centre." Asked what she thinks Deronda "accomplished in the east" after the novel ends, Pulcheria underscores an association of social form not with good manners, but with boring conventionality: "Oh, they had tea-parties in Jerusalem, exclusively of ladies, and he sat in their midst and stirred his tea and made high-toned remarks. And then Mirah would sing a little, but just a little."[54] For those less than taken with Eliot's novel, Deronda's nearly passionless good manners and moral rectitude are of as little import as the dullest and most conventional of social scenes possible.

In including the sarcastic jibes of Pulcheria, as well as a slight echo of cattiness that resonates occasionally in Constantius's critical equanimity, within the sociable scene of polite conversation, James asks whether good manners might annul or at least mitigate the capacity for critical insight, whether critical acuity is only possible on precondition of shedding one's social commitments. The dialogue's scene of sociable criticism allows James to place the strongest judgments about Eliot's novel's formal failures in the mouth of a character less than constrained by politeness. Pulcheria, the reader in this dialogue most likely to mock social form, is also most liable to speak her dissatisfactions with *Daniel Deronda*'s poor form: "An artist could never have put a story together so monstrously ill. She has no sense of form." As Pulcheria mocks Deronda's desexualizing good manners and chastises Eliot for her formal shortcomings, social form becomes both the occasion and idiom for assessing novelistic form. James ironically suggests the possibility through his least-well-mannered character that social form might, in fact, provide the terms for critical appraisal of novelistic form. In doing so, what may make the blundering forms of novel criticism James hopes to renovate into something less naïve, something more sophisticated, may be not an unthinking adherence to the rules of decorum. Instead, the best form might be that which can admit the vulgar within it, being sophisticated enough to possess more than mere social, or formal, correctness. As Joseph Litvak argues, in his critique of Bourdieu's account of taste as a form of distinction that distances itself from the bodily appetites, to think of sophistication in its fullest sense is to recover "sophistication's inherent vulgarity."[55] Social knowingness, as it is instanced within the critical idiom of tact that James is evolving, means also knowing when refinement itself might become a form of bad taste.

In its irreducibility to a single quality or criteria, the language of manners and tact accords with the global ambit of inchoate novel criticism, which takes on a literary genre as diffuse, miscellaneous, as "loose, baggy" and "monst[rous]" as the novel. Constantius's polite critical circumspection informs his globalizing vocabulary in discussing the novel's shortcomings: "In the manner of the book, throughout, there is something that one may call a want of tact. The epigraphs in verse are a want of tact; they are sometimes, I think, a trifle more pretentious than really pregnant; the importunity of moral reflections is a want of tact; the very diffuseness is a want of tact."[56] Constantius's assessment of *Daniel Deronda* as showing a "want of tact" draws its language and force from manners. But it shares as well the self-canceling practices of good etiquette, since even to draw attention to one's manner is bad manners. In effect, *Deronda*'s bad novelistic form is indistinguishable from bad manners in James's review: the epigraphs are "pretentious," a word that suggests they have overstepped the rules of good decorum by appearing to be not just what they are not, but in trying to seem better than they are, by being fussy. Constantius's complaint about the forwardness of the book's moral reflections underscores the fact that indirection and obliquity for James are the soul of good form, both aesthetic and social. But the repetitions of Constantius in his judgment of Eliot's novel as perhaps over serious, his wish to say in so many words, and his failure to just come right out and say that Eliot's novel might be too polite, implicates him in his own critique. That is, Constantius himself comes off as over-fussy himself, an adherent to good form to a fault.

Whether Eliot's novel's "want [of] tact" constitutes a momentary and regrettable but tolerable lapse, or is grounds for dismissal of the book altogether as a formal failure, balances on the same paranoia-inducing razor's edge as good breeding. By the lights of good social form, any lapse in etiquette however minor or momentary might stigmatize one as having bad form in general. But, doggedly fulfilling even every single one of the mandates in Emily Post's book will not add up to good breeding in its most ideal mode, in which the effortlessness of good social form by those to the manner born means that social form's overall effect will always exceeds the sum of its parts. Particular mistakes might betray either a minor and passing lapse in good manners, or one's total lack of the same, as with sententious epigraphs and moral reflections that insist a bit too loudly on their own importance. (The difficulty of distinguishing between a failure that signals mere momentary lapse and one that indicates utter lack is one of the strategies by which manners keeps those who care on their toes, seeking to avoid even the slightest of *faux pas.*) But these particular wrong moves or mistakes, such as those of a pretentious epigraph or an importuning morality, or when manner shades over into mannered, are bracketed on either side in Constantius's discussion by far less specific, diffuse indictments of "diffuseness" and "manner," indictments of problems that are too vague, too global to be rehabilitated by any correctional program or guide to good novelistic form that instructs its users in particulars.[57]

"Manner" and "tact": the globalizing terms here underscore how much what both James and Constantius refer to as formal failures eludes specification—etiquette manuals and James's theory of the novel notwithstanding—as well as how closely James's critical vocabulary of aesthetic form draws its power from and depends upon its social correlative. The meaning of "tact" as "touch" underscores its exemplarity of the kind of unconscious and artful sensibility or "feel for the game," what Pierre Bourdieu calls "practical sense," that cannot be codified into principles, a feel or sensibility that is as frequently known through its breach as in its successful practice.[58] James phrases his formal critique of Eliot's novel in the vocabulary of tact, but he also enacts it, renders it dramatic, through the dialogue form's valuation of interpersonal good graces, its implicit contract, in this case anyway, to disagree without being disagreeable. In Constantius, however, James makes clear the perils of too much tact. Agreeing with everyone in the dialogue, replying to every judgment in favor and against the novel with "I understand," Constantius marks the fussiness of a good form that cannot take a side, that cannot be sophisticated enough to arrive at a judgment that might offend.

James's review does a generic end-run around the essay into the dramatic dialogue, and from one angle looks like an effort both to soft-pedal his harshest judgments (and strongest praise) of Eliot's book by parceling them out among characters. However, we can also recognize that the critical dialogue is less end-run around the essay than its formal extension in Adorno's sense that the essay "thinks in fragments, just as reality is fragmentary, and finds its unity in and through breaks and not by glossing them over." The dialogue intensifies the essay's anti-systemic qualities and amenability to divergent or contradictory claims, by creating characters to voice those conflicting claims.[59] Although he wrote many of them, a Jamesian taste for form might find itself foreclosed or at least put off by the generic parameters of the essay, a genre whose stylistic tendency toward fragmentary, non-systemic thinking makes it temperamentally disinclined to ideals of morphological wholeness. However, we can also see that the dramatic dialogue allows James to imbue the fragmentary, blobby essay genre with an aspiration toward coherence, but it is the social coherence granted by a scene of sociable criticism, a review pitched in the form of social interchange. James's recasting of the critical essay's mode, from that of being the record of an encounter between solitary reader and text to the more social registers I have been tracing here, encourages an attention to the turns to the language of social form in James's review. James's review thus takes the occasion to apply the social as salve to the aesthetic, to transform Eliot's fragmented novel into a scene of eloquent speech.

As a scene of sociable discussion, the review anticipates the centrality of talk in James's later fiction, in which talk in and of itself comes to hold its own interest, the surface of wit not covering up some deeper meanings glossed over, but offering pleasures of its own. In Leo Bersani's understanding of James as one of our "most sociable novelists" because of his talent for talk, we find another way of phrasing the valuation of the social form that Georg Simmel calls sociability or the "social work of art" in which association itself, freed of any particular purpose, is its own end: that is "the fulfillment of a relation which is . . . nothing but relationship."[60] This utopic description of a conversational ideal, of sociability as its own pleasure, is visible in Bersani's account of talk in James as a "dream of detaching instruments of sublimation (speech and thought) from the activity of repression. . . . Language would no longer reveal character or refer to desires 'behind' words; it would be the unfolding of an improvised and never completed psychological design."[61]

Simmel's description of sociability underscores the coolly erotic dimension of social form, of the conditions under which conversation itself, rather than its content, becomes the object of desire; thus, in Simmel's light, even the conversation of three people disagreeing about a novel might, through a collective desire for social form, become the basis for the "art form of society." In his account of the latent, semi-utopic aspiration of conversation to a pure relation uninflected by any particular social conditions or purpose, society is rendered more manageable, transformed from a messy, chaotic social sphere into an art form as close to home as a dinner party. Simmel's abstraction of social life from particular contents into its formal qualities thus registers in a sociological sense the social and formal wish of James's essays on Eliot.

Before I turn to James's social calls on Eliot herself in the final section of this chapter, I want to note one more reverberation within James of the impersonally intimate qualities of Simmel's sociability, here in James's account in his preface of his creation of Isabel Archer, the central character of *The Portrait of a Lady*. Coming to him not out of the usual "germ" of a story overheard, or a situation experienced, Isabel has the distinction of being first conceived not as an actor within a plot, or one among a wider social constellation, but through his "grasp of a single character" "in perfect isolation": "Thus I had my vivid individual—vivid, so strangely, in spite of being still at large, not confined by the conditions, not engaged in the tangle, to which we look for much of the impress that constitutes an identity."[62] The singularity of his grasp is intense enough for James to first imagine Isabel as apart not only from the novel and from all other people, but even from the grounds of distinct identity, the "impress that constitutes identity."

James's uncharacteristically antisocial creation, Isabel Archer in "perfect isolation," may seem far from the sociable desire of Simmel's account; in fact, she would appear to be its antitype, in isolation. Yet, James's description of his creation Isabel Archer as pre-existing social life itself, not yet written and not yet dwelling in the "house" of fiction that he will construct around her in writing *Portrait of a Lady*, as "vivid, so strangely, in spite of being still at large," we can sense the kindred spirit of Simmel's sociable scene. In Simmel, as in James, the abstraction (or freedom) from the "impress" of identity and the "entanglement" of particular social conditions or purposes, is presented as precisely the means by which social or fictional entities—"society" for Simmel via sociability, a novelistic character "at large" for James—can best be made known. Although the novel itself goes on to show how wrong is Isabel Archer's own belief that she can live as if she were, or anyone could be, exempt from social circumstances, as Sharon Cameron has pointed out, the preface to the novel invokes precisely this freedom, nostalgically, as a way of valuing her character. Isabel Archer is vivid because she is bracketed, apart from social conditions on James's first conception of her.[63]

What such bracketing leaves out, however, is the other half of the twin genesis story James gives of *Portrait of a Lady*. Isabel Archer's movement from the "perfect isolation" of her initial conception to being placed amidst a social world of other characters is already conditioned, James also notes, by her precedents in Eliot's own fiction. In Rosamond Vincy from *Middlemarch* and Gwendolyn Harleth from *Daniel Deronda*, each of whom, in spite of their seeming "slim insubstantiality," "insist on mattering," James tells us he finds his challenge, a spur to make of such a "slim insubstantiality" the center of a novel. She is both plucked from Eliot's densely populated pages and conceived in "perfect isolation" by James in his account: my point here is less that

Isabel Archer represents a confusion in James about where one character ends and another begins, as Cameron remarks of James's experiments with consciousness and character, or a confusion as to where Eliot's novels stop and James's start. Instead, we should see that his account of Isabel Archer suggests she houses a social ideal in which detachment from the "impress" of social identity is not the negation of the social, but rather the enabling condition of knowledge, and a desire for sociability purely for its own sake.

Also bracketed in James's first account of the creation of Isabel Archer in vivid "isolation," of course, is plot, a story that will place the character within the "entanglements" of particular social relations. But even once James begins to answer his own question of what Archer will do in this novel, by his own account he emphasizes not the particulars of the social world into which she will be placed, but that world's formal qualities. The rest of the characters in the book, those who will people the world of Isabel Archer once she is removed from her initial conceptual isolation, will be "like the group of attendants and entertainers who come down by train when people in the country are giving a party; they represent the contract for carrying the party on."[64] James's functional description of the novel's secondary characters emphasizes vividly his sense of the novelist's first duty, which is to bring pleasure to readers, "to carry the party on as it were." The figure underscores the social dimensions of that pleasure, as well as reiterating the usefulness of the idiom of social form for James's thinking about novelistic form. If the recurrent Jamesian subject is freedom, as Bersani suggests, it is arguably freedom of the liberal kind framed by John Stuart Mill, whose *On Liberty* outlined what we could call socialization and its discontents; it is freedom from other people as James frames it. The contractual language that James draws on here likewise suggests *Portrait of a Lady* itself is a novel utterly bound up with promises, with obligations entailed in one's promise, and with nostalgic fantasies of negative liberty.[65]

James's description invokes however not just negative freedom and not just the pleasurable obligations of a party. He also casts writing a novel as a social obligation of sorts, "the contract for carrying the party on," and casts those obligations in terms of social pleasure. Less a pure fantasy of the negative freedom associated with Mill, then, this account of the social and the novelistic as voluntarily and contractually undertaken envisions freedom on the model of sociability, a relation that wants only to be a relation. As a phrase to describe his own "socialization" of Isabel Archer by surrounding her with more characters, the "contract for carrying the party on," in which James moves her from the "isolation" of his initial conception into a novel populated by others, is as good a description as any of sociability. "The art form of society" in which the air of voluntary obligation that attaches to a word like "contract" becomes hard to tell from the desire for the pleasure to be found in the voluntary form of association known as the party, whose dedication is itself a vision of a species of freedom, however displaced or attenuated, a dedication purely to "the success of the sociable moment."[66]

Henry James's Sublime Attachment

James's autobiography *The Middle Years* recounts the two memorable, and memorably awkward, visits by James to pay his respects to George Eliot. He dwells at some length on the social anxieties provoked by meeting an author of such intellectual stature, as well as the intimate relation for James between reading, and meeting, Eliot. During his first visit to Eliot at her home with George Henry Lewes in Regents Park, the young James's own nervousness over meeting the great Eliot is both assuaged and compounded by the presence of a gravely ill and greatly suffering son of Lewes's. James helplessly tries to comfort Lewes's son, who is suffering from tuberculosis of the spine, a moment during which James, as he labors to make natural conversation, recalls wondering "what conversation *was* natural" (*MY*, 69). Amidst the difficult scene, James is glad to make himself valuable, taking on the job of leaving the scene to help fetch the doctor. This task, James writes, allows him both to end "the strain of the scene and yet prolong[ ] the sublime connection" with Eliot.

James's reflection on this moment of physical suffering and social awkwardness allows him to articulate the social ideal that is lodged within his reviews of Eliot. It is in connections sublime rather than awkward, sublime because removed from the embodied, face-to-face social encounters, that this social ideal might be realized. Reading his essays on Eliot alongside these autobiographical accounts, it becomes clear James regards the sublimity of his relation to Eliot as increasing, rather than fading, the more mediated it is by her novels and his reviews. And the printed words of Eliot themselves become the more sublime for James having encountered the flesh and blood author. So, James goes on to say, his experience of meeting Eliot in person inflects all he reads of Eliot after; his meeting Eliot, he writes, is "intimately concerned in [his] perusal of *Middlemarch*," published soon after the visit, and his "relation" to Eliot "helped [him] to squeeze further values from the intrinsic substance" of the novels Eliot writes in the years after their meeting (*MY*, 72).

A social relation to George Eliot, James suggests, is best experienced while not in her physical presence, best experienced either writing about or reading her novels. There, it seems, the awkward social form of his encounters with her, the failures of etiquette large and small, might be better mediated or repaired. Eliot's and Lewes's famous intellects, and James's sense of their home as the site of too much heavy thinking even to bother with tea (James notes the absence of anything but the instruments of writing and reading on his second visit to the Lewes–Eliot home, in spite of the hour being appropriate for tea time), plays no small part in James's modest presentation of himself as a less intellectual and less accomplished writer in awe of Eliot and her achievements on the occasions of his visits. And *The Middle Years* explicitly plays up the contrast between the intellectual ferocity and moral seriousness of Eliot's home and the pleasant fatuity of the Greville home nearby, where James is staying when he goes on his second visit to the Lewes's. From what James calls "sharp truths" the Greville home is rendered immune by not only good furnishings and a dedication to leisure but also by a dedication to social forms whose highest aims are pleasantness. "I confess without scruple to have found again and again ... an attaching charm in the general exhibition of enjoyed immunity [at the Greville home], paid for as it was almost always by personal amenity, the practice of all sorts of pleasantness" (*MY*, 76). This less-than-sacred but utterly charming social order, lingered over by James for a number of pages as he defers recounting the details of his ill-fated visit to the Lewes–Eliot home, lends contrast both comic and dramatic to his description of that austere home.

Arriving for a second visit on a rainy day some years later he finds a "bland, benign, commiserating" Eliot in the "chill desert of a room" amidst the tea-less atmosphere of "Olympus," as James wryly calls their home, but otherwise known as Witley Villa, where Eliot and Lewes were staying at the time. On this visit, James is unrelieved by any urgent errand, and it is obvious to him that his timing is once again off. In spite of Eliot's and Lewes's adherence to social form in greeting them kindly upon their arrival, James remarks, "their liking us to have come, with our terribly trivial contribution, [was] mainly from a prevision of how they should more devoutly like it when we departed." By contrast with the frivolous witticisms in which the Greville social life traded, James recalls only silence among the visitors and the visited at Witley Villa, "no single echo of a remark on the part of any of us" comes back to him in his recollection of the event, until their parting moment when Lewes, "*then* above all conversingly," escorts them out. Just about to get into his carriage, James is asked by Lewes to wait a moment as he fetches some books, returning soon and begging James to return fetched volumes to their lender, Mrs. Greville: "Ah, those books—take them away, please, away, away!" Lewes exclaims to James (*MY*, 83). Only after the carriage has departed does James discover that what Lewes thrust into his hands with such disdain was James's own novel, *The Europeans*. In this anecdote of awkwardness the (possibly unwitting) bad social form of Lewes in returning the books with urgent distaste might be understood by James as an act of humiliating forgetfulness, in which Lewes is hardly aware of who his visitor is. Or worse, Lewes might know precisely who James is, delivering the most short-hand form of bad book review possible, and one done in the flesh, face-to-face rather than by the usual distancing mediation of print publication.[67]

In making a social act into a book review, as James understand Lewes's act, this episode becomes an insult not added to, but more accurately an extension of, the social injury already incurred by James in being a less than welcome guest in the Lewes–Eliot home. For James, Lewes's breach of social form and his own subsequent embarrassment is the review. That James's reviews of Eliot's *Daniel Deronda* and *Middlemarch* are structured by a social desire, in forms that suggest the review itself might be the space in which James might better meet Eliot, and under social and textual conditions of his own making, makes Lewes's slight all the more painful. Where in James's reviews of Eliot the print medium becomes a social pleasure itself, this textual sociality finds its obverse in the episode with Lewes, in which the social sleight becomes both the medium and locale of a literary insult.

James is humiliated at the time by Lewes's sociable volubility only finding its voice once the social moment's end has come within sight. But with the perspective of years, James is able to recuperate the lapses of social form his visit occasioned by converting this episode into an anecdote, by making it something to be repeated on social occasions for amusement, as James confesses to "having in my own person enjoyed adorning such a tale" (*MY*, 85). And in turning social shame into an anecdote, James not only transforms and contains his humiliation by the very fact of it becoming something to be told at parties, giving it dramatic shape (the comic and dramatic contrast of the Grevilles and Lewes–Eliot), and an "ideal logic" in the sequence of events, he also confirms its aesthetic "rightness." "This particular wrong—inflicted all unawares, which exactly made it sublime—was the only rightness of our visit" (*MY*, 84).

In his "failure to penetrate there" James transmutes shame by finding—like the account of the novel in "The Art of Fiction," in which the novel's only duty is to be "interesting"—instead the "*interest*" of Eliot and Lewes's "inaccessibility."[68] That is to say, its novelistic qualities. In its open-endedness, the "interest" James finds within the episode expresses the hard-to-pin-down qualities of his relationship with Eliot, somewhere between professional envy and yearning, between being face-to-face and at a far remove. The seeming disregard by Eliot and Lewes for social etiquette—no tea, no conversation that he can recall—in this episode turns out to be a species of professional good form. It is "right" precisely because, James writes, while Eliot is "engaged in my own pursuit" of realist fiction, she is "yet detached by a pitch of intellectual life, from all that made it actual to myself" (*MY*, 85–86). From the vantage point of his own success later in life, James is able to turn awkwardness to account, to make of the poor manners and antisocial reception by Eliot and Lewes, and of his own humiliation, a testimony to Eliot's greatness, and in so doing nearly conscripts himself into one of her own novels: "I was to become, I was to remain—I take pleasure in repeating—even a very Derondist of Derondists, for my own wanton joy" (*MY*, 86).

A "pleasure in repeating" not only this proclamation of his membership among Eliot's readers but also in her cast of characters, James has become one of Eliot's own, a Derondist of Derondists. And in taking "pleasure in repeating" to others this anecdote of his humiliation, James renovates the spoiled social scene of his visit to Eliot into the coin of the realm in Simmel's "ideal sociological world" of sociability, the "only case in which talk is a legitimate end in itself": the "telling of tales, witticisms, anecdotes" in which all personal interest is suspended in the interest of a "relation, which is . . . nothing but relationship [which is] its own self-sufficient context."[69] In the end, James's Eliot bears not the "interest" of the lengthy and diffusive Jamesian novel, but the well-crafted sociable form of the anecdote, what we might call the rhetorical form of social interest itself. Simmel's lines articulate the impersonal appeal of the emptied out qualities of the comfort of strangers, a relationship of attractive neutrality that is less expressive of an antisocial ethos or indifference to others than an attraction to an ideal of momentary sociability that this book has been tracing out in a variety of texts and in a diversity of genres.

The social yearning that appears across James's essays on Eliot is incited by non-knowledge—of Eliot herself, with whose "horse-faced" beauty James declares himself in love; of the "swarm" of *Middlemarch*'s multitudinous social extravagance. Granting this yearning something like the structure of the erotic, it is a structure drained of an erotic object, turning the medium of the essay itself into the site of social pleasure. In this neutral space of the essay, what this book has been calling the power of weak ties finds one of its most highly articulated instances in the transformations of the Victorian novel into its modernist heir: in the relation between Eliot and James, between the champion of the "old-fashioned English novel" and its renovator. James inaugurates criticism of the novel as its own special practice and its own kind of social form, by way of his encounters and negotiations with—face-to-face and on the page, in situations more and less tactful, in good and bad form—George Eliot. From such seemingly trivial encounters—"necessarily evanescent, created by arrivals and killed by departures" as Goffman describes the social transience out of which modern society crystallizes—we find the Anglo-American novel and its criticism reshaped.

"The way to become an acquaintance was first to become an intimate," we are told at the start of James's *The Aspern Papers*. The story concerns an unnamed critic trying to gain possession of the papers of his hero, the dead poet Aspern, from Aspern's aged former lover and addressee of his lyrics, Juliana. Its plot is structured around the critic's efforts to find his way into the home, and the papers, of Juliana. Her earlier life as the beloved of Aspern's lyrics seems now to have left her a recluse, as if her own former status as lyric addressee—at a remove from the poetic speaker who addresses her—has now left her alone, shut up in a house in Venice with her niece. Pretending to be a lodger in need of room so as to gain access to the house—becoming an acquaintance with Juliana by way of being an intimate—the critic is fascinated with the poet and his mediums, which take the form both of his letters and of Juliana herself. The letters appear to him not just as valuable artifacts, but as a social medium that connects him to Aspern: "they made my life continuous, in a fashion, with the illustrious life they had touched at the other end" (*Aspern*, 28). And, in meeting the former lover and subject of lyric address herself, the unnamed critic who narrates the story finds in her an even more powerful medium for Aspern:

> I was really face to face with the Juliana of some of Aspern's most exquisite and most renowned lyrics. I grew used to her afterwards, though never completely; but as she sat there before me my heart began to beat as fast as if the miracle of resurrection had taken place for my benefit. Her presence seemed somehow to contain and express his own, and I felt nearer to him at that first moment of seeing her than I ever had been before or ever been since. (*Aspern*, 14)

The narrator here dwells on the miraculous surrogacy by which one person's presence expresses that of another—"her presence seemed somehow to contain and express his own"—a séance of sorts with Juliana as medium. In the next moment, however, the narrator finds the medium interfering with the message, as it were. Alone with the aged Juliana, their company unalloyed by the presence of Juliana's niece, with whom the narrator has largely been interacting in his effort to secure a room at their home so as to better find his way to the letters he is after, he finds "[Juliana] was too strange, too literally resurgent" (*Aspern*, 15).

In the unnerving resurrection of Aspern from the dead within Juliana's own person, the narrator has suddenly come "too literally" face-to-face with the poet he worships, through the body of a surrogate: a medium that fails to mediate. The multiple relations of distance that undergird lyric poetry—the distance separating lyric speaker and lyric addressee that is the condition of lyric utterance; the distance between author and reader in which lyric address as speech uttered in isolation (not "heard, but *overheard*" as Mill's account goes) is doubled by the distanced, print-mediated relation of a poet and his readers—have collapsed.[70] In the dissolution of any difference between medium and message, between distance and propinquity—"too literally resurgent"—James marks the outside limits of the appeals of the medium of communication in and of itself, collapsing in on itself and on alterity. To see here the overwhelming, unbearable nature of social intimacy in face-to-face contact, and to have seen how such intimacy can be neutralized by its deflection into writing, however, is to trace out to its modernist moment the trajectory of thinned-out or weak sociality, the comfort of strangers that is not the negation of a sociable desire, but one of its strongest expressions.

Afterword

ALL ORDINARY LIFE

This book has been an effort to make visible and account for the power of the weak social ties of nineteenth-century "stranger society" and their consequences for literary form. Never able to be brought fully into representational focus, whether novelistic or poetic, the stranger is at once the emblem of a nineteenth-century modernity the novel in particular took as its own field of interest, and notably reluctant or fugitive to literary figuration. The moment a stranger catches novelistic narration's eye, for instance, the anonymity and contentless sociality that defines strangers begins to dissolve, transforming into the particularized traits of characterhood, social specificity, and interiority in which realist literary forms traffic. The society of strangers that is a feature of nineteenth-century British life is at once novel and utterly quotidian, a remarkable feature of modernity and so ordinary as to barely merit notice on one's way to the omnibus for work. And yet, it finds itself largely barred from figuration in the very realist literary practices that sought to register the complexity, fears, and pleasures of that modern society: this is the central paradox I have tried to bring out in *The Comfort of Strangers*.

Strangers, the dark matter of the social universe as I suggested at the start of this book, nonetheless produce a range of torquing effects upon literary form as it registers the vast invisible presence of those unknown, a countercurrent to the specifying engines of plot and individuated character. Henry James's attunement to the presence of everyone he does not know in the great wen of London once his friends leave town, for example, finds its way into his imagination of a novel as socially infinite as "unvisited" London itself, a wish also gestured toward by *Middlemarch*'s narrator's urge to tell the story of everyone who is not Dorothea, to bring forth the experience of "all ordinary life." The nineteenth-century realist novel, rather than being the constitutive literary form that makes and ratifies individual psychological inwardness and privacy, appears in this study as bearer of an aesthetic of social extensiveness, marking out an avidity for sublime social expansiveness that dwells quietly alongside the novel's careful and textured narration of the lives of a necessarily limited group of characters. In slightly different terms, the lyric lovers in Matthew Arnold's poetry appear within a space that is constituted less by retreat from the world's crowded streets, as lyric withdrawal would typically have it, than by the socialization of lyric intimacy. His poetry marks out a form and space of engaged disengagement that is also central to his account of a place for the public effects of otherwise inward, *bildung*-oriented culture in his essay *Culture and Anarchy*. For Oscar Wilde, social promiscuity is the great engine of his signal literary mode of the aphorism. Wilde's one-liners function as the rhetorical crystallization of social evanescence across his works, as if every verbal exchange were dedicated to the establishment and dissolution of social encounters all the more powerful for being brief. Finally, the essay form itself becomes the site of impersonal social intimacy in Henry James's writings on George Eliot, a medium through which the literary critic might both remain physically distanced from and yet "prolong[ ] the sublime connection" with Eliot, as James puts it.[1] In James's essays on Eliot's novels, we also saw the beginnings of the essay form as site of a textually mediated social intimacy whose afterlife can be discovered in the practice of close reading within literary studies. Across these works, the weakness of the social ties of the stranger, the crowd, of intimacy at a distance, turn out to be surprisingly powerful and durable, becoming a recurrent preoccupation that is nonetheless difficult to own amidst a realist form and era governed by an ethos of sympathetic connection.

In discovering the effects of the power of weak ties upon literary form, this book has made frequent recourse to a set of sociological writers—primarily Erving Goffman and Georg Simmel—who are themselves deeply attuned to the complexities of modern social life, and the ways that face-to-face interaction is shaped by and responsive to those complexities. While from its earliest stages of writing this book turned to sociological thought that considered the importance and strength of weak social ties as complement to the literature of social density, over time what also emerged was a productive friction between literature and sociology as two competing ways of thinking about the social. Nineteenth-century proto-sociological thought and its emergent claims to social explanation—alongside and even against those of literature—impelled Arnold's and Eliot's claims for the socially ameliorative effects of literature and culture, I argued. But, sociology's own neutral, descriptive modes in its observations about social life also enabled ways for me to think about socially multitudinous environments, and the social more generally, that were less committed to the amelioration of modern anomie or the revitalization of sympathetic ties than literature as understood by Eliot and Arnold. Such neutral states of attentiveness—like Erving Goffman's notions of "unfocused interaction" and "civil inattention," the means by which the multitudinous social environments of the city are prevented from becoming an "unbear-ably sticky" set of social claims for someone walking the street—thus shows up in these literary works as a mode of dealing with social complexity, for characters, novelistic narration, essayists, and more. The particular status of attention amidst social complexity, as well as its accompanying states of distraction and absorption, along with the difficulty for narrators of *losing interest* in novelistic characters, is thus central to the story of modernity and literary form this book tells. Both intimate and impersonal, the modes of civil inattention and unfocused interaction described by Goffman are not simply not paying attention; rather, they describe a delicate calibration of attention within public social spaces, the way we remain sensitized to others even, or even especially, while staying detached.

"Unfocused interaction," however, might also serve as a half-serious description of the methodological approach of this book as it tried to attend to social neutrality in these literary works by sometimes turning away from some of the usual sites of the social and its figuration, such as novelistic plot, or to show resistances to plot's transformation of strangers into familiars. At the same time, this book's obvious investment in the careful attention to the nearly micrological features of prose and poetry known as close reading, as well as its partner, the close writing of free indirect critical style, would seem far removed from civil inattentiveness. The attentiveness involved in close reading, however, like other forms of attention, can at times be hard to tell apart from the reverie and distraction that are attention's presumptive opposite—the moment when a particular reading feels like it has gone off into some other register, far from the text under consideration. Such oscilla-tions, however, along with being a feature of many of the works considered in this book, are also what enables the registration of structures or systems—of social interconnection, of sublime social expansiveness—that otherwise elude realist representation. In maintaining a sense that the slide between absorp-tion and distraction is a characteristic feature of both the inhabitants of nineteenth-century urban environments and beyond, as well as the prose and poetic techniques of the literature of social density, however, I hope also to have made the case for these modes as a method of reading apt to such liter-ary environments and forms. In this, the subject and method of this book appear together at the site of states where absorption and attention start to merge. This merging might be thought of as a version of the condition of social sensitivity Michael Fried ascribes to Zinedine Zidane in a recent essay on a film about the French soccer player. Fried, in an extension of his work on absorption and theatricality in the eighteenth century and minimalist art to photography, focuses on Zidane's utter absorption in the game he is play-ing, even as Zidane describes himself as impossibly, selectively hyperaware of the crowd around him, down to the ticking of a single wristwatch—"you are never alone" Zidane remarks. Fried describes this mode of absorption as "a state of mindedness almost unremittingly intense and at the same time . . . somehow bare and minimal."[2] It would be disingenuous, of course, to suggest that this book's method of attending to literary texts has been precisely or consistently bare or minimal. But in the oscillation between a critical minimality and intensity, or minimality and expansiveness, I have tried to register these texts' own toggling between the singularity of face-to-face interaction and an awareness of or sensitivity to the expansiveness or sublimity of the modern social field that characterizes a society of strangers.

Some recent work at the intersection of literature and sociology has sought to rethink close reading along such lines, proposing to model it on forms of close attentiveness associated with sociological observation. Turning to Goffman's descriptive sociology offers a way out of the usual humanistic interpretive and depth hermeneutics of close reading, for example, in Heather Love's recent argument for a style of close reading that is descriptive rather than interpretive. Similar to Fried's account of absorption above (though not Fried's methods), such reading methods would be both intensely engaged with the text and minimally attentive to human motivation or interiority, interested instead in describing procedures and interactions, what Love calls reading that is "close but not deep."[3]

Love's, however, is among a range of recent work in literary study that has, like this book, turned to sociology as a possible resource for rethinking a variety of methodological and theoretical investments in the discipline of English. This work is varied—ranging from sociologies of the institutions of literature, to turns to the descriptivist methods of sociologists like Goffman in order to move away from the depth-oriented hermeneutics of close reading, or approaches that bring out productively defamiliarizing visions of methods of literary analysis by the juxtaposition of literature with sociology. But one recent strand of such work, as I noted briefly in my discussion of *Middlemarch*, moves away from the examination of single literary texts in favor of data-driven, macroscopic approaches that bring into view vast histories and geographies of literature, an approach associated most closely with the work done by Franco Moretti.[4] Putting the literature of social density, with its frequent turns toward sublime social expansiveness, alongside distant reading underscores a rhyme between this book's subject and the vast fields of literary data—systems, morphological branches, new sub-genres—produced by the quantitative turn in literary study. What is especially interesting about this pairing is that it allows us to see that each offers accounts of literary texts—for Moretti, a data set; for this book, the social sublime of a novel about everyone—that are not available to our own phenomenological experience, or what might be thought of as its literary critical equivalent, close reading. That is, knowledge about the text is pried away from the experience of reading a text, the experience of submitting oneself to the duration of reading a long novel like *Middlemarch*, for example, which has been the long-standing basis

for the teaching of literature and writing about it. These are works—both
critical studies based on data sets and literary texts—that have no equivalent
object in lived experience. In *Middlemarch* the "keen vision and feeling for all
ordinary life," or a novel as large as everyone who is not Dorothea, point to
intense experiences that are most powerful for not actually being experienced
by anybody in particular, as I put it in my discussion of that novel in chapter 2.
My own approach to social expansiveness, even as it has turned to modes of
sociological attention, has retained the protocols of close reading that Moretti
eschews in part because close reading enables us to attend to the vast oscillations in scale, between the minimal and the massive, the "squirrel's heart
beat" and "all ordinary life" that for *Middlemarch*, and not just *Middlemarch*,
indexes the great representational aspiration of realist literary form.

In its final stages, this book was written at a desk underneath a set of photographs of people who are reading books as they ride the New York City
subway, all printed out from among the hundreds found on a website called
Underground New York Public Library. Lost in a book amidst fellow subway
riders, each photographed person instances reading in public as a paradigmatic instance of both absorption and Goffmanian awayness: the book as
involvement shield amidst strangers, as well as observational lure to fellow
passengers (and the photographer) who want to know what they are reading (figure A.1). Strangers in various acts of civil inattention, traveling about
a metropolis in the 21st century: each photograph is recognizably a scene of
everyday modernity. But, that is also to say that this modernity's roots are in
the nineteenth century and its society of strangers, the rise of mass transpo-
ration and inexpensive editions of novels. While resonant with the forms
of stranger sociality that this book is interested in, it is also the case that
these pictures show photography's capacity to do what I have shown realism, and in particular the novel, to find so hard: letting strangers remain as
such—anonymous, unscripted into narratives of social convergence, trajectories by which those unknown become kin. Arrested in the moment of being
photographed, even as we know the station at which they will get off the train
and leave the frame of the photograph cannot be far away, their enduring
transience is visual correlative to the power of weak ties.[5]

In closing, one last instance of the aspiration toward social expansiveness
that might be thought of as the afterlife of the nineteenth-century representational urge I have been tracing out. Much of the work of the Japanese conceptual artist On Kawara is interested in time, and among his more well-known
works is a series of postcards and telegrams, sent each day, with either the
time he woke up that day, e.g., "I got up at 7:50 am," or a note, "I am still alive."
Conveying a simple message, the most minimal of gestures, these works share
an interest of 1970s conceptual art in information and its networks of circulation. But Kawara's postcards and telegrams are a form of minimal and expansive (the cards and telegrams were sent over a period of years) textual sociality

FIGURE A.1 *Underground New York Public Library.*

that resonates with Wilde's brief aphorisms, as well as James's essays that enable a social apartness as well as connection. As a review of Kawara's 2014 show *On Silence* at the Guggenheim Museum put it, these works are akin to a wave from a person on board a boat to those on shore as they pass by, a minor form of passing social courtesy the review phrases as "a sensitive consideration for strangers."[6] But the particular work of Kawara's that feels most compellingly interested in social expansives is *One Million Years (Past)*, which is comprised by ten plain black books of 200 pages each, with each page containing 500 years written out, beginning with 998,031 B.C. and ending with 1969 A.D. (figure A.1). A kind of bureaucratic sublime opens up here when one considers how long it took to compile these books (two years).[7] But, there is also something nonetheless novelistic here about an aspiration, obviously unrealized, in Kawara's work to produce an immense and completed history of everybody, a work—not a novel, but perhaps novelistic—that would be about everyone. Kawara dedicated this work to "All those who have lived and died."

While Kawara's conceptualism and Eliot's realism may seem not just ages, or countries, but worlds apart, I want us to hear an echo in *One Million Years (Past)*, however minimal or soft, of a wish as strong as any in *Middlemarch*, a wish to have a "keen vision and feeling for *all* ordinary life." This is one last site of the afterlife of the comfort of strangers. Drained of plot, of narrative, of character, leaving only social vastness itself behind, like the grin of the Cheshire Cat in *Alice in Wonderland*, in Kawara's *One Million Years (Past)* and its dedication, we find an afterimage of an aesthetic of social expansiveness that finds its early expression in the literature of social density.

{ NOTES }

Introduction

1. Henry James, "London," in *Essays in London and Elsewhere* (New York: Harper & Brothers Publishers, 1893), 30.

2. Georg Simmel, "Sociology of the Senses: Visual Interaction," in *Introduction to the Science of Sociology*, ed. Robert E. Park and Ernest W. Burgess (Chicago: University of Chicago Press, 1921), 360–61, quoted in Chris Otter, *The Victorian Eye: A Political History of Light and Vision in Britain, 1800–1910* (Chicago: University of Chicago Press, 2008), 23–24.

3. Erving Goffman, *Behavior in Public Places: Notes on the Social Organization of Gatherings* (New York: Free Press, 1963), 41. Involvement shields are tasks or activities that allow one to withdraw from unwanted interaction in public, while still maintaining what Goffman calls "the impression of proper involvement" (ibid.).

4. Herman Melville, "Bartleby," in *Billy Budd and Other Stories* (New York: Penguin, 1986), 12.

5. Henry James, *The Critical Muse: Selected Literary Criticism*, ed. Roger Gard (New York: Penguin, 1987), 485. This sense of opportunity for the novel occasioned by a vast social scale governs James's own well-known theory of novelistic narration in his preface to *Portrait of a Lady*. There, the novel's proper subject is a social sphere that, like an "infinite" London, is marked by its expansiveness, as I remarked, "the spreading field, the human scene" (ibid.). While James's theory of narrative perspective is subjectivizing—each unique narrative eye recording "an impression distinct from every other"—the subjective perspectives in "the house of fiction" are themselves multiplied, amplified into a social scale as vast as London's own one million inhabitants: "The house of fiction has in short not one window, but a million" (ibid.). In assigning London's one million each their own narrative viewpoint, James outlines here his "scenic method," the technique by which individual characters focalize narration in the novel, orienting narrative perspective through their own subjective experience. The Jamesian renovation of nineteenth-century realism, by this light, might mostly look like a means of dialing down the Victorian novel's social populousness, a way of individuating and shrinking a social field into a smaller size than we find in, say, the thickly peopled multi-plot novels of Charles Dickens or George Eliot. This might be one shorthand way of differentiating the Jamesian novel from its nineteenth-century British precursors: James's novels have fewer people in them. In granting the nearly "infinite" unvisited London of one million each a place at "the house of fiction," however, James's theory of the novel, while recognizably a means of giving form to an otherwise thrillingly amorphous population of those unknown—which as a novel can only tell the story of a limited number of characters, so would necessarily radically reduce that population's size—nonetheless retains an impulse toward the socially "infinite," or at least the vast. In a well-known passage from his preface to *Roderick Hudson*, James defines the novel by its necessary conferral

of sense-making form upon social fields otherwise so extensive as to escape figuration. "Really, universally, relations stop nowhere, and the exquisite problem of the artist is eternally but to draw, by a geometry of his own, the circle within which they shall happily *appear* to do so." *The Critical Muse*, 452. We will return to this consideration of the realist novel's binding-straining impulse to figure the entirety of the social world in the chapter on George Eliot's *Middlemarch*.

6. James Vernon, *Distant Strangers: How Britain Became Modern* (Berkeley: University of California Press, 2014), 9. Vernon points out that London was, in 1880, the world's largest city, larger than Paris, New York, Tokyo, Beijing, and Mexico City put together.

7. Zygmunt Bauman, *Liquid Love: On the Frailty of Human Bonds* (Cambridge: Polity, 2003), 105.

8. "The Metropolis and Mental Life," in *The Sociology of Georg Simmel*, trans. and ed. Kurt H. Wolff (New York: Free Press, 1950), 169. See also Walter Benjamin, "Baudelaire," in *Illuminations*, ed. Hannah Arendt, trans. Harry Zohn (New York: Schocken, 1969), and Mark Seltzer, *Serial Killers: Death and Life in America's Wound Culture* (New York: Routledge, 1998).

9. I am indebted to an anonymous reader at Oxford University Press for the formulation of strangers in this study as the "dark matter" of the social universe.

10. The scholarship on the public/private divide is vast and I draw here upon two particularly influential accounts of the emergence of that divide as central to modernity. Richard Sennett, *The Fall of Public Man* (New York: W. W. Norton, 1992), and Jürgen Habermas, *The Structural Transformation of the Public Sphere: An Inquiry into a Category of Bourgeois Society*, trans. Thomas Burger with Frederick Lawrence (Cambridge, MA: MIT Press, 1991).

11. On the decline of the public sphere and the rise of the novel, as well as the novel's association with inwardness, among the most prominent critical works are Ian Watt, *The Rise of the Novel: Studies in Defoe, Richardson and Fielding* (Berkeley: University of California Press, 1971); John Kucich, *Repression in Victorian Fiction: Charlotte Brontë, George Eliot, and Charles Dickens* (Berkeley: University of California Press, 1987); Nancy Armstrong, *Desire and Domestic Fiction: A Political History of the Novel* (Oxford: Oxford University Press, 1987); D. A. Miller, *The Novel and the Police* (Berkeley: University of California Press, 1989). On the novel and transformation of the everyday into the sphere of meaning, see Franco Moretti, *The Way of the World: The Bildungsroman in European Culture* (London: Verso, 2000), and "Serious Century," in *The Novel*, Volume 1: *History, Geography, and Culture*, ed. Franco Moretti (Princeton, NJ: Princeton University Press, 2006), 364–400. Other recent accounts, whose aims my own project has learned from and is largely in sympathy with, have begun to retexture this long-standing association of the novel and nineteenth-century realist form more generally with privacy. Sharon Marcus's account of urban fiction in nineteenth-century Paris and London emphasizes communicability, rather than separation, between private and public spaces. Marcus also critiques critical investment in accounts of the decline of the public sphere and its separation from the private, as well as a critical consensus that apportions those spheres distinct genders. Sharon Marcus, *Apartment Stories: City and Home in Nineteenth-Century Paris and London* (Berkeley: University of California Press, 1999). John Plotz's *The Crowd: British Literature and Public Politics* (Berkeley: University of California Press, 2000) has been particularly important for my thinking about literary form's relation to the collective life of the crowd,

as well as the ambiguous or incomplete ways in which the public sphere is dissolved into private subjecthood in the novel. The later thinking in this project has especially benefited from conversations with David Kurnick and his work on the "novel of inwardness," and the novelistic afterlife of a wish for the necessarily public collective social scene of theater. David Kurnick, *Empty Houses: Theatrical Failure and the Novel* (Princeton, NJ: Princeton University Press, 2012).

12. Nancy Armstrong, *How Novels Think: The Limits of Individualism from 1719–1900* (New York: Columbia University Press, 2005), 48. While the breadth of this claim means one can always find instances to counter it, Armstrong's overall account from the eighteenth to the nineteenth century is one of a novel that aged into its conservatism, emptying itself of political projects broader than disciplining the individual.

13. Jacques Rancière, *The Politics of Aesthetics*, trans. and ed. Gabriel Rockhill (London: Bloomsbury, 2006), 29.

14. Bauman, *Liquid Love*, 141. Bauman discusses the contemporary condition of refugees in temporary camps, as neither permanently settled nor nomadic in *Liquid Love*. As effectively non-citizens their political disenfranchisement extends out to their being rendered not only invisible but also beyond ken. "In a world filled to the brim with imagined communities, they are the *unimaginables*" (ibid.).

15. On the productive role that Victorian misanthropes, curmudgeons, and antisocialites played in thinking about hypocrisy and other social ills, see Christopher Lane, *Hatred and Civility: The Antisocial Life in Victorian England* (New York: Columbia University Press, 2004). Lane has brought out strong countercurrents to the received accounts of the centrality of Victorian sympathy and communitarian thought in ways consonant with my own thinking. What distinguishes my notion of antisociality and Lane's is encapsulated by the central place of "hatred" and "enmity" in his accounts. Where Lane tends to see representations of "aggression as inseparable from society," I discover less phobic flights from the social than efforts know it by taking leave of those nearby for the comfort of strangers, the affective qualities of anonymity (ibid., 85). For a development of antisociality's relation to the novel, see John Plotz, "Antisocial Fictions: Mill and the Novel," *Novel: A Forum on Fiction* 43 (Spring 2010): 38–46. Jeff Nunokawa's thinking on social distance and the novel, as well as a sense of society as an end itself, is the other half of the conversation that this book hopes in some small measure to uphold. See Jeff Nunokawa, "Speechless in Austen," *Differences* 16, no. 2 (2005): 1–36 and "Eros and Isolation: The Antisocial George Eliot," *ELH* 69 (Winter 2002): 835–60.

16. J. S. Mill, "On Liberty," in *On Liberty and Other Essays* (Oxford: Oxford University Press, 1991), 9.

17. Mark Granovetter, "The Strength of Weak Ties," *American Journal of Sociology* 78 (May 1973): 1360–80.

18. Leo Bersani, *A Future for Astyanax: Character and Desire in Literature* (Boston: Little, Brown, 1976), 51–88.

19. Goffman, *Behavior in Public Places*, 69–75.

20. Émile Durkheim, *Selected Writings*, ed. Anthony Giddens (Cambridge: Cambridge University Press, 1972), 64. Durkheim's theorization of the social and of social facts as external to and independent of individuals—social rules and practices whose power is felt upon these precepts' violation—is the founding conceptualization of a disciplinary object for classical social theory. Hannah Arendt's influential if idiosyncratic account of

the social differs from Durkheim's in important ways, in particular, in her sense of the social as a fallen version of the public realm, one that is tainted by the interests of the private. For Arendt, the social is an ever-increasing realm under modernity, a realm that "devour[s] the older realms of the political and the private as well as the more recently established sphere of intimacy." Hannah Arendt, *The Human Condition*, 2nd ed. (1958; repr., Chicago: University of Chicago Press, 1998), 45.

21. Erving Goffman, *Relations in Public: Microstudies of the Public Order* (New York: Harper & Colophon, 1971), 255. I turn to Jonathan Crary's arguments about attentiveness and modernity more extensively in chapter 2, where I discuss transient forms of interest in George Eliot. See Jonathan Crary, *Suspensions of Perception: Attention, Spectacle, and Modern Culture* (Cambridge, MA: MIT Press, 2001).

22. The account I give of the undirected, ephemeral, or evanescent qualities of stranger sociality shares an interest with recent queer work on forms of social relationality without institutional or narrative issue, forms that might fall short of, or outside, realist figuration. See, along with Bersani's *A Future for Astyanax*, his essay "Sociability and Cruising," in Leo Bersani, *Is the Rectum a Grave?: And Other Essays* (Chicago: University of Chicago Press, 2010), 45–62. In my chapter on Oscar Wilde, I elaborate on my work's relation to the anti-futurity strain of queer theory, expanding on the ways in which work by Bersani, Michael Moon, and Michael Warner, among others, has influenced my understanding of the relations among sexuality, social form, and literary form. That chapter also articulates the space I want to open up for a better understanding of the productive ways in which queer theory and sociological thought might be read together, as well as a formal account of sociability without issue, a contentless relationality, whose proper coordinates are neither circumscribed by nor entirely apart from the sexual.

23. A few works I have in mind: Kurnick's *Empty Houses*; Audrey Jaffe, *Scenes of Sympathy: Identity and Representation in Victorian Fiction* (Ithaca, NY: Cornell University Press, 2000); Kent Puckett, *Bad Form: Social Mistakes and the Nineteenth-Century Novel* (New York: Oxford University Press, 2008); Mary Ann O'Farrell, *Telling Complexions: The Nineteenth-Century English Novel and the Blush* (Durham, NC: Duke University Press, 1997); Alex Woloch, *The One vs. the Many: Minor Characters and the Space of the Protagonist in the Novel* (Princeton, NJ: Princeton University Press, 2003); Jeff Nunokawa, *Tame Passions of Wilde: The Styles of Manageable Desire* (Princeton, NJ: Princeton University Press, 2009); Bersani, *A Future for Astyanax*; and D. A. Miller, *Jane Austen; or, The Secret of Style* (Princeton, NJ: Princeton University Press, 2000). This book might have turned, say, to embarrassment or social mistakes in the novel, as a way of marking out how a self-consciousness about good form, a local version of sociological knowledge, is intertwined with nineteenth-century realist literary form. See O'Farrell and Puckett for two recent accounts that take up these arguments. Especially useful for my thinking of both sociology and the novel as formalizing projects has been Puckett's account of how a self-consciousness about good social form, and the necessary gap between one's blunder-prone self and an ideally socialized self, registers and extends a wish for formal coherence that structures the novel.

24. For example, see the claim that in "the purely documentary sense, one can see the novel as dealing with much the same, economic, and political textures as sociology." Diana T. Laurenson and Alan Swingewood, *The Sociology of Literature* (London: MacGibbon and Kee, 1971), 12, quoted in Mark McGurl, *The Novel Art: Elevations of American Fiction after*

Henry James (Princeton, NJ: Princeton University Press, 2001), 188n56. I will later treat in more detail the critical history around sociological thought and the British novel in the nineteenth century.

25. The phrase "significant form" comes from Bersani, "Realism and the Fear of Desire," in *A Future for Astyanax*, 55.

26. Wilkie Collins, *The Woman in White*, ed. John Sutherland (Oxford: Oxford University Press, 1996), 20.

27. Goffman, *Behavior in Public Places*, 85.

28. Elaine Hadley, *Melodramatic Tactics: Theatricalized Dissent in the English Marketplace, 1800–1885* (Stanford, CA: Stanford University Press, 1995), 19.

29. Ferdinand Tönnies makes the foundational distinction for classical social theory in the late nineteenth century between *Gemeinschaft* and *Gesellschaft*, roughly corresponding to traditional and modern forms of social organization. Ferdinand Tönnies, *Community and Civil Society* (Cambridge: Cambridge University Press, 2001). First published as *Gemeinschaft und Gesellschaft* in 1887.

30. Collins, ibid., 22.

31. My understanding of this scene as a condensation of modernity and of the right to be let alone draws directly on conversations with Jeff Nunokawa. See also D. A. Miller's reading of this moment in *The Novel and the Police* (Berkeley: University of California Press, 1989), which figures it as a primal scene that momentarily threatens Walter Hartright's masculinity (as well as that of the implicitly male reader's), a masculinity the novel then labors across the rest of its plot to restore. That the stranger here is a young woman alone, accosting a single young man is, of course, significant to the plot of the novel and to Walter Hartright's anxiety in this social scene. However, the right to be let alone, of course, is precisely what a woman of any class might not be able to count upon if walking the streets unaccompanied in nineteenth-century London. On women in public and, in particular, on women as spectators in the Victorian streets, see Deborah Nord, *Walking the Victorian Streets: Women, Representation, and the City* (Ithaca, NY: Cornell University Press, 1995), and Judith R. Walkowitz, *City of Dreadful Delight: Narratives of Sexual Danger in Late-Victorian London* (Chicago: University of Chicago Press, 1992). On the historical gendering of modernity as feminine, see Rita Felski, *The Gender of Modernity* (Cambridge, MA: Harvard University Press, 1995).

32. Sennett, *The Fall of Public Man*, 3, 27.

33. Bauman, *Liquid Love*, 148. Elsewhere in Bauman, strangers are a source of anxiety in modernity that never dissipates, a social homology to Derrida's *pharmakon*; not containable within philosophical binaries, strangers resist and disorganize those binaries as "undecidable." Zygmunt Bauman, *Modernity and Ambivalence* (Ithaca, NY: Cornell University Press, 1995), 55. Bauman locates the "liquid" in the later twentieth and early twenty-first centuries, but the modernity he finds emblematized in the stranger is already arriving in the nineteenth century. The stranger as bearer, but also occasion for the theorization, of modernity finds its most lurid formulation in Mark Seltzer's *Serial Killers*. In Seltzer's account "stranger killing" exemplifies the crises of agency in modernity, the epoch in which the freedom of self-invention is experienced as the demand to make up a self without recourse to any grounds upon which to do so, to make up a self from oneself. Seltzer roots the precondition for "stranger killing," the original term for serial killing, in the everyday "stranger-intimacy" that emerged with the advent of urbanization in the

twentieth century. In Seltzer's account of stranger intimacy and reflexivity, from which this book has learned a great deal, the serial killer's experience of a crisis of identification amongst strangers—unable to differentiate self-identity from a self-identification with strangers—induces a violent compulsion to mimesis, serial killing (30–62). For Seltzer, the serial killer, along with other forms of death on a broad scale, instance the "pathological public sphere," the modern form of public sociality that is constituted around the witnessing of mass violence. More recently Seltzer has adduced Erving Goffman and the "averted sociality" of "awayness" to further a link between modern sociality and the violently pathological. However, Seltzer does so by putting to the side Goffman's abiding interest in the seemingly inconsequential social encounters of everyday life, the microsociology not just of psychiatric institutions, but of moments on train platforms, in living rooms, at sidewalk cafes—everyday, rather than pathological, modernity. Seltzer has suggestively described recent interest in literary and cultural studies in Goffman's microsociology as part of the "incrementalist turn"—a turn to the scaled down, to minor characters and minor feelings, to small scale resistances—which is itself companion to the contemporary humanities own scaled down institutional status. However, as this study suggests, a turn to the apparently minor quality of weak ties, strangers, and the microsociology of everyday life might also index an aspiration as much maximalist as minor, an interest in the vast dark matter than constitutes our social universe. "Official World," *Critical Inquiry* 37 (Summer 2011): 724–53. Anthony Giddens, by contrast with Seltzer, understands the normally unremarkable quality of life lived amidst strangers as evidence of the trust we place in strangers and chance acquaintances, a stabilizing means of managing the ontological insecurity of modernity. "Civil inattention is a fundamental aspect of trust relations in the large-scale anonymous settings of modernity. It is the reassuring 'noise' in the backdrop of the formation and dissolution of encounters." Anthony Giddens, *The Consequences of Modernity* (Stanford, CA: Stanford University Press, 1990), 88. Giddens argues at another point, however, that "it is simply not true that in conditions of modernity that we live increasingly in 'a world of strangers.'" Rather, "we live in a *peopled* world, not merely one of anonymous blank faces" (ibid., 143). Giddens oscillates between an account of the world as both vast beyond our ken and "peopled." This oscillation or toggling between the expansively multitudinous and the stranger nearby is part of the dynamic I mean to bring out in the literature of social density (ibid., 142). For Walter Benjamin's classic and influential account of urban shock, see "On Some Motifs in Baudelaire," in *Illuminations*, 155–94.

34. William Wordsworth, *The Prelude* ((New York & London: Penguin, 1996), 7:608–12, 616–17. I quote here from the 1805 version of the poem.

35. Jaffe, *Scenes of Sympathy*, 83. On spectatorship in the nineteenth century, see also Nord, *Walking the Victorian Streets*. Jacques Khalip's study of anonymity in romanticism emphasizes new forms of unrepresentable subjectivity in literary forms that discard conventional markers of social identity. Jacques Khalip, *Anonymous Life: Romanticism and Dispossession* (Stanford, CA: Stanford University Press, 2009). In this study's terms, Khalip's work constitutes an interesting pre-history to Victorian anonymity, but his emphasis on a radically dispossessed subjectivity coheres with understandings of the stranger as alienating Other (in this case, an Other within oneself) that are closer to those of Jaffe and Seltzer, ones I am hoping to counter. Catherine Gallagher suggests fictional characters themselves are appealing precisely for their seeming intimacy for readers and

their ultimate unknowability, their lack of a real-world referent. Catherine Gallagher, "The Rise of Fictionality," in *The Novel*, 1:336–63.

36. For examples of an understanding of the novel as particularly concerned with sympathy as a form of feeling or pity, see Janice Carlisle, *The Sense of an Audience: Dickens, Thackeray, and George Eliot at Mid-Century* (Athens: University of Georgia Press, 1981); David Marshall, *The Surprising Effects of Sympathy: Marivaux, Diderot, Rousseau, and Mary Shelley* (Chicago: University of Chicago Press, 1988); as well as Catherine Gallagher's account of sympathetic capability fostered by the novel in the creation of a speculative, commercial subject, in *Nobody's Story: The Vanishing Acts of Women Writers in the Marketplace, 1670–1820* (Berkeley: University of California Press, 1994). For recent works quite different from one another that view sympathy in the novel as a psychic structure, through which a subject negotiates his or her own identity, see Jaffe, *Scenes of Sympathy*, and Rachel Ablow, *The Marriage of Minds: Reading Sympathy in the Victorian Marriage Plot* (Stanford, CA: Stanford University Press, 2007). Rae Grenier's recent reconsideration of sympathy not as reproductive feeling, but a cognitive act, one central to realism, resonates with the forms of nearly contentless sociality I trace here. For Grenier, sympathy's "fellow-feeling" is a "form[ ] of . . . engagement without demanding that particular feelings become manifest," sympathy as a social fantasy of "going along with others" (in Adam Smith's phrase) "in a kind of contentless companionship." Rae Grenier, *Sympathetic Realism in Nineteenth-Century British Fiction* (Baltimore, MD: Johns Hopkins University Press, 2012), 10.

37. *The Sociology of Georg Simmel*, 10.

38. Charles Dickens, *Bleak House* (New York: Penguin, 1996), 256.

39. Charles Dickens, *Sketches by Boz* (New York: Penguin, 1995), 166.

40. Ibid., 167.

41. Ibid., 168.

42. Dickens's frequent turn to a theatrical idiom in *Sketches by Boz*, in which Boz raises and lowers the curtain upon the scene at hand, chimes with Goffman's dramaturgical accounts of the self in public and, in particular, of sociality as performance and ritual. "In a public place, the individual appears to be indifferent to the strangers in his presence; but actually he is sufficiently oriented to them so that, among other things, should he need to perform corrective rituals, he can transform the strangers around him into an audience to receive his show." Goffman, *Relations in Public Places*, 154. In the light of Goffman, Boz's role as master of ceremonies, ushering otherwise unremarkable public social activities on and off the stage, imagines a world in which the performance of self in everyday life would be an occasional act, one requiring a showman like Boz to turn it into theater, rather than the nearly ceaseless and mandatory performance public social life is in Goffman's account. In Goffman, unlike *Sketches by Boz*, we are each our own stage manager.

43. Gerard Genette, *Narrative Discourse: An Essay in Method*, trans. Jane E. Lewin (Ithaca, NY: Cornell University Press, 1980), 121–35. I am grateful to an anonymous reader for Oxford University Press for pressing me here to think about the pseudo-iterative.

44. Moretti, *The Way of the World*, 35.

45. Dickens, *Sketches by Boz*, 137.

46. Woloch, *The One vs. the Many*, 188–90. My account of "Greenwich Fair" here draws upon Woloch's discussion of this sketch.

47. Dickens, *Sketches by Boz*, 168.

48. Franco Moretti, *Atlas of the European Novel, 1800–1900* (New York: Verso, 1998), 51.

49. Dickens, *Sketches by Boz*, 170.

50. Or realized. Locating the Neutral in a variety of experiences, principles, stances, and more, the Neutral as elaborated by Barthes is always just a verb form away from being its opposite, an affirmative or codifiable philosophical position, "practiced" rather than "realized." Roland Barthes, *The Neutral: Lecture Course at the College de France (1977–1978)*, trans. Rosalind Krauss and Denis Hollier (New York: Columbia University Press, 2005), 27. See Anne-Lise Francois, *Open Secrets: The Literature of Uncollected Experience* (Stanford, CA: Stanford University Press, 2008), for a discussion of Barthes's notion as a category of experience that fails to rise to the level of affirmation or narrative consequentiality. I will return later in this book, in chapters 2 and 4, to a discussion of free indirect style as not only articulating but also bearing neutral kinds of sociality.

51. Ibid., 35.

52. Georg Simmel, "Sociability," in *On Individuality and Social Forms*, ed. Donald Levine (Chicago: University of Chicago Press, 1971), 130, 128.

53. *The Sociology of Georg Simmel*, 50.

54. Dickens, *Bleak House*, 37–38.

55. Ibid., 83.

56. Marcus, *Apartment Stories*, 11. While Marcus refers here to what she calls the "apartment-house" plots of a set of nineteenth-century novels, I am suggesting the principle of narrative convergence typifies novelistic plot in the nineteenth-century more generally. Marcus's own study of urban space and the novel traces out the less familiar plot and narrative dynamic by which kin are converted into strangers, intimates made into ghosts amidst the blurred lines that divide and define street and home, public and private.

57. Georg Lukács, "Narrate or Describe?" in *Writer and Critic: And Other Essays*, trans. and ed. Arthur Kahn (New York: Grosset & Dunlap, 1971), 135.

58. Amanda Anderson, *The Powers of Distance: Cosmopolitanism and the Cultivation of Detachment* (Princeton, NJ: Princeton University Press, 2001); James Buzard, *Disorienting Fictions: The Autoethnographic Work of Nineteenth-Century British Novels* (Princeton, NJ: Princeton University Press, 2005); and Andrew Miller, *The Burdens of Perfection: On Ethics and Reading in Nineteenth-Century British Literature* (Ithaca, NY: Cornell University Press, 2008). I engage with the arguments of these works in greater detail in later chapters of this book. See also David Wayne Thomas, *Cultivating Victorians: Liberal Culture and the Aesthetic* (Philadelphia: University of Pennsylvania Press, 2003).

59. Ibid., 40.

60. Elaine Hadley, *Living Liberalism: Practical Citizenship in Mid-Victorian Britain* (Chicago: Chicago University Press, 2010), 55, 14.

61. On the carnal appeals of detachment, and the novel as offering its own forms of partial participation to promiscuous readers, see David Kurnick, "An Erotics of Detachment: *Middlemarch* and Novel-Reading as Critical Practice," *ELH* 74 (Fall 2007): 583–608.

62. Along with Anderson, Buzard's *Disorienting Fictions* and Christopher Herbert's *Culture and Anomie: Ethnographic Imagination in the Nineteenth Century* (Chicago: University of Chicago Press, 1991) have been especially generative for me in their understanding the mutual inflections of literary form and the human sciences in the nineteenth century, in particular, ethnography, anthropology, and emergent sociology.

In the long critical tradition that has seen the novel and sociological thought as having overlapping terrains, major works would include Raymond Williams, *Culture and Society: 1780–1950* (New York: Columbia University Press, 1983), and Georg Lukács, *The Theory of the Novel* (Cambridge, MA: MIT Press, 1991), as well as the work of Fredric Jameson. Suzanne Graver's work on George Eliot and the sociology of Ferdinand Tönnies also understands the realist novel as the central site for exploring the great sociological divide between modernity and tradition. Suzanne Graver, *George Eliot and Community: A Study in Social Theory and Fictional Form* (Berkeley: University of California Press, 1984). I treat the relation between literature and the rise of sociology in my first chapter, but other recent works that have drawn literature within close range of ethnographic, anthropological, and sociological projects include Susan Mizruchi, *The Science of Sacrifice: American Literature and Modern Social Theory* (Princeton, NJ: Princeton University Press, 1998); Nancy Bentley, *The Ethnography of Manners: Hawthorne, James & Wharton* (Cambridge: Cambridge University Press, 1995); Mark McGurl, "The Posthuman Comedy," *Critical Inquiry* 38 (Spring 2012): 533–53; and Elsie Michie, *The Vulgar Question of Money: Heiresses, Materialism, and the Novel of Manner from Jane Austen to Henry James* (Baltimore: Johns Hopkins University Press, 2011). See also the essays in "New Sociologies of Literature," special issue, *New Literary History* 41, no. 2 (2010), for a sense of the range and heterogeneity of current approaches to literary study that are informed by a relation to sociological thought.

63. Two examples of works that trace such influences in great detail are Nancy Paxton, *George Eliot and Herbert Spencer: Feminism, Evolutionism, and the Reconstruction of Gender* (Princeton, NJ: Princeton University Press, 1991), and Sally Shuttleworth, *George Eliot and Nineteenth-Century Science: The Make-Believe of a Beginning* (Cambridge: Cambridge University Press, 1984).

64. Mary Poovey, *Making a Social Body: British Cultural Formation, 1830–1864* (Chicago: University of Chicago Press, 1995), 17.

65. See chapters 2 and 4 for my fuller discussion of free indirect style as a social mode. I also note there the relevant critics whose work informs my account of free indirect style, including Ann Banfield, *Unspeakable Sentences: Narration and Representation in the Language of Fiction* (Abingdon, Oxon: Routledge & Kegan Paul, 1982); Miller, *Jane Austen*; and Francois, *Open Secrets*.

66. Adela Pinch, *Thinking about Other People in Nineteenth-Century British Writing* (Cambridge: Cambridge University Press, 2010), 11.

67. See "New Sociologies of Literature" (in particular, Heather Love, "Close But Not Deep: Literary Ethics and the Descriptive Turn," in "New Sociologies of Literature," special issue of *New Literary History* 41, no. 2 (2010): 371–91) as well as a range of other works, including data-driven work such as Franco Moretti's practices of "distant reading," and work in the sociology of literature, of which Mark McGurl's *The Program Era: Postwar Fiction and the Rise of Creative Writing* (Cambridge, MA: Harvard University Press, 2011) is a powerful recent example.

Chapter 1

1. Matthew Arnold, *'Culture and Anarchy' and Other Writings*, ed. Stefan Collini (Cambridge: Cambridge University Press, 1993), 185–86. All subsequent citations will be

from this edition and will hereinafter be abbreviated as *CA* in the text. Gustave Le Bon, *The Crowd: A Study of the Popular Mind*, 2nd ed. (Marietta, GA: Cherokee Publishing Company, 1982), xv. I am grateful to the editors of *Victorian Poetry*'s special issue on science and poetry for their suggestions on portions of this chapter which appeared in that issue. *Victorian Poetry* 44 (Spring 2003).

2. In June 1866 Arnold delivered a lecture, entitled "Culture and Its Enemies," which would later become chapter 1, "Sweetness and Light," in the collection that he entitled *Culture and Anarchy* upon publication in 1869. Arnold's revision of "enemies" to "anarchy" only after the Reform League riot in Hyde Park, which took place in July 1866, suggests that "anarchy" was able to perform important rhetorical and figurative functions in his work that "enemies" could not.

3. For a recent attempt to understand the genesis of disinterestedness in Arnold in light of Agamben and Kant, one that, like my understanding here, turns to the projects undertaken in Arnold's lyric poetry in order to give a revised account of Arnoldian disinterest, see Kevin McLaughlin, "Culture and Messianism: Disinterestedness in Arnold," *Victorian Studies* 50 (Summer 2008): 615–39. See also Herbert Tucker's "Arnold and the Authorization of Criticism," which also reads Arnold's poetry alongside his essays, showing how Arnold the critic, but not the poet, works to "institutionalize disinterestedness" by detaching criticism from interpretation. *Knowing the Past: Victorian Literature and Culture*, ed. Suzy Anger (Ithaca, NY: Cornell University Press, 2001), 100–120.

4. In the most general terms, the project of sociology has been understood as "generating knowledge about modern social life which can be used in the interests of prediction and control." Anthony Giddens, *The Consequences of Modernity* (Stanford, CA: Stanford University Press, 1990), 15. My interest here is less in drawing a fully comprehensive portrait of early sociology, or successfully characterizing the entire project of sociology, than in bringing out the modes by which criticism is enlisted by Arnold as a means of managing the challenges of the social world of modernity, and, in particular, the ways in which the crowd's enlistment in that project finds an earlier history in Arnold's poetic work.

5. Matthew Arnold, *The Complete Prose Works of Matthew Arnold*, ed. R. H. Super (Ann Arbor: University of Michigan Press, 1973), 9:161. Hereinafter works from this edition will be abbreviated as *CPW* in the text and noted by volume and page number.

6. The narrative of the historical intersection of literature and sociology in this period that my argument follows is that of Wolf Lepenies in *Between Literature and Science: The Rise of Sociology*, trans. R. J. Hollingdale (Cambridge: Cambridge University Press, 1988). For a recent account of the disciplinary formations of the later nineteenth century, and the effects of the rising prestige of the human sciences, in particular, and scientific practices, in general, see Amanda Anderson and Joseph Valente, eds., *Disciplinarity at the Fin de Siècle* (Princeton, NJ: Princeton University Press, 2002). See also Amanda Anderson, *The Powers of Distance: Cosmopolitanism and the Cultivation of Detachment* (Princeton, NJ: Princeton University Press, 2001), for a discussion of detachment that has influenced my understanding of Arnoldean "disinterest," as well as for the role of natural science in Arnold's work. My reading of the social aspects of Arnold's project has benefited from Chris Baldick's history of criticism in this period, *The Social Mission of English Criticism, 1848-1932* (Oxford: Oxford University Press, 1983). Arnold's summary argument on behalf of literature in this early version of a contest of the faculties can be found in "Literature and Science" in *CPW* 10:53–73.

7. It is precisely culture as an oblique version of social control that Arnold's commentators tend to turn to. Terry Eagleton notes Arnold's tendency to take all the tendencies of human nature and "harmonise them within a cohesive conflict-free order—within, in a word, Culture." *Criticism and Ideology: A Study in Marxist Literary Theory* (London: NLB, 1976), 106. Edward Said suggests that Arnold views "society as a process and perhaps also an entity capable of being guided, controlled, even taken over." *The World, the Text, and the Critic* (Cambridge, MA: Harvard University Press, 1983), 10. I will be tracing here the consonance, and ensuing complications, between proto-sociological efforts in the nineteenth-century to define, understand, and control the social realm and the modes by which Arnold assigns that same task to culture in the form of crowd management.

8. Philip Abrams, *The Origins of British Sociology, 1834-1914* (Chicago: University of Chicago Press, 1968), 48. The history of British sociology, a discipline whose institutionalization was slow in coming as a result of numerous factors, is complicated by the wide variety of practices—moral statistics, amelioration-oriented social reports, and theories of social evolution, to name just a few—that went on both in and outside of the academy, and which were characterized by their practitioners as sociology. In addition to Abrams, see Simon Joyce, "Victorian Continuities: Early British Sociology and the Welfare of the State" and Lauren M. E. Goodlad, "Character and Pastorship in Two British 'Sociological' Traditions: Organized Charity, Fabian Socialism, and the Invention of New Liberalism," in Anderson and Valente, eds., *Disciplinarity at the Fin de Siècle*, 235–80. Both building on and departing from Abrams, these two more recent accounts offer histories and pre-histories of sociology and proto-sociological practice in nineteenth-century England which stress the heterogeneity of its early stages. M. S. Hickox traces the absence of "classical," or theoretical, sociology in England to a gap between the speculative evolutionary theory of Spencer, which provided the raw material for theoretical work, and the tendency of social investigation to be narrowly interested in social reform rather than creating an autonomous field of inquiry. Hickox is also interesting on the effect of the absence of a coherent intelligentsia in England upon the development of classical sociology. "The Problem of Early English Sociology," *Sociological Review* 32 (Feb. 1984): 1–17. My thinking about culture draws upon Christopher Herbert's coherent account of the incoherences brought on by efforts to figure "culture" as a totality in early anthropology in *Culture and Anomie: Ethnographic Imagination in the Nineteenth Century* (Chicago: University of Chicago Press, 1991). Spencerian organicism and social evolution, of course, comprise one well-known instance of an early effort to develop a science of society which did labor to develop a theory of the social whole. See Sally Shuttleworth's illuminating study of the language of organicism as it is variously employed in nineteenth-century social theory and literature, *George Eliot and Nineteenth-Century Science: The Make-Believe of a Beginning* (Cambridge: Cambridge University Press, 1984).

9. Perry Anderson, *English Questions* (London: Verso, 1992), 92.

10. Herbert Spencer, *The Study of Sociology*, 9th ed. (London: Williams & Norgate, 1872-73), 71.

11. The history of writing on crowds as a new phenomenon of modern urban life does not, of course, begin with Arnold. Space does not allow for a more thorough account than I can give briefly here of the variety of literary, historical, and social scientific texts on the crowd that inform Arnold's own warnings. Le Bon's claim in 1896 that the "Era of the Crowd" had arrived registers a panic about the political power of crowds that emerges,

largely in the wake of the French Revolution, over the course of the nineteenth century (*Popular Mind*, xv). Reaction to the bread riots, the deaths of working-class demonstrators at Peterloo in 1819, and the dawning of the era of the Mass Platform in England with the organized, national Chartist congregations of the late 1830s and 1840s underscore the long history of crowd politics that Le Bon registers only belatedly. John Plotz's *The Crowd: British Literature and Public Politics* (Berkeley: University of California Press, 2000) has been invaluable to my own project as both an illumination of the varied aesthetic and political dimensions of the crowd in the first half of the nineteenth century, and as suggestive of later structural possibilities for the crowd, which I pursue through sociology and Arnold. Plotz marks the crowd's radical new representational claims in the years of the Chartist movement, one development of which was that the congregation of bodies in public became visible as itself a coherent demand for political power on behalf of a larger group, that of the working class. By 1839, Plotz argues, "the age of the organized crowd had arrived" (130). Most important for my own discussion is the transformation of the conditions in which crowds of earlier decades that were viewed as isolated eruptions of irrational, undirected fervor could by the 1840s successfully represent by metonymy a broader social order—in the case of Chartism, that of the working class. Only after the crowd comes to be understood as metonymic of social order, its disruption as well as its maintenance, can it then become the crucial object of, and offer opportunities for, the theorizations of the social realm that sociologists undertake later in the nineteenth century.

A partial list of other works which have labored to recover a coherent political history of crowds from its historical and popular representations as a faceless mob, and which I have drawn on here, include George Rudé, *The Crowd in History: A Study of Popular Disturbances in France and England, 1730-1848*, rev. ed. (London: Lawrence & Wishart, 1981), and E. P. Thompson, "The Moral Economy of the English Crowd in the Eighteenth Century," *Past & Present* 50 (Feb. 1971): 76–136. Mark Harrison emphasizes the less violent crowds at royal events and festivals in the first part of the nineteenth century, uncovering their crucial role as figures of social cohesion and order in ways instructive for me, albeit to the neglect of the important political claims of these crowds. *Crowds and History: Mass Phenomena in English Towns, 1790-1835* (Cambridge: Cambridge University Press, 1988).

12. In his account of crowd theory, J. S. McClelland writes that after the nineteenth century, any social theory "which did not make room for the crowd at its centre looked makeshift, mistaken or willfully obtuse." *The Crowd and the Mob: From Plato to Canetti* (London: Unwin Hyman, 1989), 3. Mary Ryan has elaborated upon the collective structures of parades as a "syntax" of legible social order in American urban areas in ways useful for my own reading of crowds as metonym of social order more broadly. "The American Parade: Representations of the Nineteenth-Century Social Order," in *The New Cultural History*, ed. Lynn Avery Hunt (Berkeley: University of California Press, 1989).

13. Catherine Gallagher, *The Industrial Reformation of English Fiction: Social Discourse and Narrative Form, 1832-1867* (Chicago: University of Chicago Press, 1985).

14. For illuminating and imaginative treatments that have opened up the possibilities of reading the crowd as a political and aesthetic form, in addition to Plotz, see Michael Tratner, *Modernism and Mass Politics: Joyce, Woolf, Eliot, Yeats* (Stanford, CA: Stanford University Press, 1995). For mass culture and the crowd's self-spectacularization in a continental context, see Vanessa Schwartz, *Spectacular Realities: Early Mass Culture*

in Fin-de-Siècle Paris (Berkeley: University of California Press, 1998). While Plotz and Tratner each offer studies of the crowd's appeal for early to mid-nineteenth century and modernist writers, respectively, they each put to the side the discipline whose attention the crowd most garnered, that of sociology. Although each acknowledges that the crowd first caught, and continues to hold, the attention of sociologists, they see the relationship as primarily one of mutual interest between social theorists and writers. Viewed through a lens of disciplinary competition in this chapter, I hope to show one historical reason for the fascination that the crowd exerted on the poet and literary critic in the nineteenth century. The lure of the crowd both as a political force and an aesthetic experience manifest across numerous nineteenth-century works—including Thomas De Quincey's *Confessions of an English Opium Eater* (London: Penguin Books, 2003) and Wordsworth's book 7 of *The Prelude*, as well as many other texts—might usefully be reconsidered, in part, through the crowd's centrality as a figure in the early stages of a disciplinary contention between literature and proto-social theory.

15. Elaine Hadley, *Living Liberalism: Practical Citizenship in Mid-Victorian Britain* (Chicago: Chicago University Press, 2010), 4n5. Hadley's study provides an important revision of many accounts of political liberalism as the era of a declined public sphere and laissez-faire by attending to liberalism less as theory than as practice, underscoring the ambivalences that attend liberal ideals of individuated subjectivity, such as disinterestedness and character. For Hadley, while liberalism clearly thought in terms of individual subjects rather than groups, its interest in the practice of its ideals means that how stances of individual disinterested reflection and judgment can be made to bear upon lived experience and the social world are crucial.

16. Ibid., 53, 47–48.

17. For the nineteenth-century public sphere as nostalgia, see Terry Eagleton, *The Function of Criticism* (New York: Verso, 1984). For illuminating and very useful analyses of the withdrawal of affective investment in the nineteenth-century public sphere, see Athena Vrettoes, *Somatic Fictions: Imagining Illness in Victorian Culture* (Stanford, CA: Stanford University Press, 1995); John Kucich, *Repression in Victorian Fiction: Charlotte Brontë, George Eliot, and Charles Dickens* (Berkeley: University of California Press, 1987); and Ann Cvetkovich, *Mixed Feelings: Feminism, Mass Culture, and Victorian Sensationalism* (New Brunswick, NJ: Rutgers University Press, 1992). For the definitive account of the bourgeois public sphere in the eighteenth century, see Jürgen Habermas, *The Structural Transformation of the Public Sphere: An Inquiry into a Category of Bourgeois Society*, trans. Thomas Burger with Frederick Lawrence (Cambridge, MA: MIT Press, 1991).

18. The argument for the existence of the public sphere in the nineteenth century that my thinking draws upon is found in Geoffrey Eley, "Nations, Publics, and Political Cultures: Placing Habermas in the Nineteenth Century," in *Habermas and the Public Sphere*, ed. Craig Calhoun (Cambridge, MA: MIT Press, 1992), 289–339. For recent considerations of an expanded conception of the public sphere, see the essays collected in *The Phantom Public Sphere*, ed. Bruce Robbins (Minneapolis: Minnesota University Press, 1993).

19. Eric Hobsbawm, "Mass-Producing Traditions: Europe, 1870–1914," in *The Invention of Tradition*, ed. Eric Hobsbawm and Terence Ranger (Cambridge: Cambridge University Press, 1983), 263–307.

20. Arnold does not acknowledge even the right to existence for the crowd in Hyde Park; instead, he draws upon dispersed figurations of the crowd's collective structures to engage its power. Arnold's texts differ in this manner from such direct engagements of the crowd as Thomas Carlyle's essay "Chartism" earlier in the century. In that text, Carlyle asserts the critic's role of speaking for the crowd which cannot articulate its own desires: "Bellowings, inarticulate cries as of a dumb creature in a rage and pain; to the ear of wisdom they are inarticulate prayers: 'Guide me, govern me! I am mad and miserable, and cannot guide myself.'" "Chartism," in *Selected Writings*, ed. Alan Shelston (New York: Penguin, 1986), 189. For a suggestive reading of the crowd as a discursive entity in competition with Carlyle's own place as a critic, see Plotz, *The Crowd*. For an analysis of Carlyle's silencing of the monstrous crowd as enabling the critic's own speech, as well as ensuring its fitness for a place in a universal discourse, see Baldick, *Social Mission of English Criticism*.

21. More contemporary work on the crowd also figures the public and the crowd as interrelated. Robert E. Park follows Le Bon when he writes of the crowd as defined by social contagion rather than spatial factors: "Individuals can be designated a crowd not because they are together, but because they mutually infect each other with their thoughts or feelings." *The Crowd and the Public, and Other Essays* (Chicago: University of Chicago Press, 1972), 18. Le Bon writes, "An entire nation, without having visible connections, can become a crowd under the action of certain influences." *Popular Mind*, 3. Sociological and social-psychological work on the crowd and the specific nature of crowd phenomenon in the nineteenth and early twentieth centuries coincides with reflections on what constitutes "the public" to such a degree that "public-ation" itself might best describe the types of action in the passages above. Theorists like Le Bon refine the study of the crowd away from spatial definitions, and in doing so begin to describe "the public" and "the crowd" as interrelated if not coincident entities.

22. Siegfried Kracauer, "The Group as Bearer of Ideas," in *The Mass Ornament: Weimar Essays*, trans. Thomas Levine (Cambridge, MA: Harvard University Press, 1995), 143–72.

23. Arnold, *Culture and Anarchy*, 107. Unlike the public sphere as described by Habermas, "the mid-Victorian public sphere is by no means the object or organ of valued public discourse, but rather a phantasmagoric threat to given realities of liberal status." Hadley, *Living Liberalism*, 45. In this sense, my analysis of Arnold's "monster processions" follows readings of monstrosity in Romanticism, such as the mob of the French Revolution and Frankenstein's monster, that trace the disruptive effects of monstrous entities upon representation. For these arguments, see Christopher Baldick, *In Frankenstein's Shadow: Myth, Monstrosity, and Nineteenth-Century Writing* (Oxford: Oxford University Press, 1987), and Fred Botting, "*Frankenstein* and the Language of Monstrosity," in *Reviewing Romanticism*, ed. Philip W. Martin and Robin Jarvis (London: Macmillan, 1992). Rather than finding proleptically deconstructive capacities in the crowd, a "monstrous overflow of meaning," as Fred Botting does, I want to explore the modes by which the crowd enables the representation of an ambivalently desired social sphere (ibid., 53).

24. On this historical relationship, along with Lepenies's *Between Literature and Science*, see also Herbert's *Culture and Anomie*, which treats the borrowings and mutual incoherences brought about by the theory of culture for both nineteenth-century sociology and literature. These two works have much in common, with Lepenies's study being explicitly one of disciplinary competition, while Herbert's work focuses on the attempts

of nineteenth-century anthropologists, sociologists, novelists, literary critics, and jour-nalists to accommodate or make sense of the term "culture." See also James Buzard, *Disorienting Fictions: The Autoethnographic Work of Nineteenth-Century British Novels* (Princeton, NJ: Princeton University Press, 2005).

25. Thomas H. Huxley, "Science and Culture," in *Collected Essays*, vol. 3, *1854* (New York: D. Appleton, 1910), 150.

26. Herbert Spencer, "What Knowledge Is of Most Worth?" in *Essays on Education and Kindred Subjects*, ed. Ernest Rhys (New York: E. P. Dutton, 1910), 32.

27. Lepenies, *Between Literature and Science*, 170.

28. See Ian Hacking's account of the "avalanche of printed numbers," in the nineteenth century. Statistical analyses of all manner of social phenomena, Hacking argues, helped to erode notions of physical determinism and enabled accounts of chance as being governed by natural or social laws. *The Taming of Chance* (Cambridge: Cambridge University Press, 1990). See also, Theodore Porter, *The Rise of Statistical Thinking, 1820-1900* (Princeton, NJ: Princeton University Press, 1988).

29. Hacking, *Taming of Chance*, 1. Huxley, "On the Educational Value of the Natural History Sciences," in *Collected Essays*, 3:58.

30. Émile Durkheim, *Selected Writings*, ed. Anthony Giddens (Cambridge: Cambridge University Press, 1972), 64.

31. Émile Durkheim, "What Is a Social Fact?" in *Sociological Debates: Thinking about "The Social,"* ed. Floya Anthias and Michael P. Kelly (Kent: Greenwich University Press, 1995), 130–31.

32. Susanna Barrows's book, *Distorting Mirrors: Visions of the Crowd in Late Nineteenth-Century France* (New Haven, CT: Yale University Press, 1981), has been invalu-able to me as a guide to the history of continental crowd psychology.

33. Ibid., 117.

34. John Stuart Mill, *On Liberty*, in *On Liberty and Other Essays* (Oxford: Oxford University Press, 1991), 17–18.

35. Isobel Armstrong, *Victorian Poetry: Poetry, Poetics, and Politics* (London: Routledge, 1993), 173. Arnold's formations under the "pressure" of colonial others and, in par-ticular, the centrality of racial difference to Arnold's formulations of culture are detailed in instructive fashion by Robert Young's "The Complicity of Culture: Arnold's Ethnographic Politics," chap. 3 in *Colonial Desire: Hybridity in Theory, Culture, and Race* (London: Routledge, 1995). For comprehensive studies of Arnold's poetry, see A. Dwight Culler, *Imaginative Reason: The Poetry of Matthew Arnold* (New Haven, CT: Yale University Press, 1966), and David G. Riede, *Matthew Arnold and the Betrayal of Language* (Charlottesville: University of Virginia Press, 1988). Riede is especially illuminating on the disabling effects of Arnold's efforts to elaborate a language of criticism and poetry that is at once scientific, socially purposeful, and poetic.

36. Matthew Arnold to Arthur Hugh Clough, 23 September 1849, in Nicholas Murray, *A Life of Matthew Arnold* (London: Hodder & Stoughton, 1996), 99.

37. Matthew Arnold to Jane Arnold, 10 March 1848, in Park Honan, *Matthew Arnold: A Life* (New York: McGraw Hill, 1981), 135.

38. *The Poetical Works of Matthew Arnold*, ed. C. B. Tinker and H. F. Lowry (Oxford: Oxford University Press, 1950), 52–60. Subsequent citations of poems will be from this edition, which will be hereinafter be abbreviated in the text as *PW*.

39. Roland Barthes, *The Neutral: Lecture Course at the College de France (1977–1978)*, trans. Rosalind Krauss and Denis Hollier (New York: Columbia University Press, 2005), 35.

40. "Public intimacy" is drawn from Lauren Berlant and Michael Warner, "Sex in Public," in *Intimacy*, ed. Lauren Berlant (Chicago: University of Chicago Press, 2000), 311–30. The multitude's lack of any specific markers of class, political interest, or nationality—its condition as a general rather than a particularized crowd—further position it here not as particularized collectivity, but as a proving ground for Arnoldean detachment.

41. For a more complete consideration of Arnold's lyric "moments," see Virginia Carmichael, "The Moment of Lyric in Matthew Arnold's Poetry," in "Centennial of Matthew Arnold: 1822–1888," special issue, *Victorian Poetry* 26, no. 1–2 (1988): 61–74.

42. In this respect, "The Buried Life" departs from the text it seems to be echoing, Book 7 of Wordsworth's "The Prelude." There, the speaker also plunges into the London crowd: "How often in the overflowing streets / Have I gone forwards with the crowd and said / Unto myself 'The face of everyone / That passes by me is a mystery!' " Rather than propelling a desire for self-knowledge, as in Arnold, the confusion induced by "Living amid the same perpetual flow / Of trivial objects, melted and reduced / To one identity by differences / That have no law, no meaning, and no end" is identified with a self-dissolution brought on by the crowd (ll. 701–4). For an acute and more extended reading of Wordsworth's legacy as reworked by Arnold in his poetry, see U. C. Knoepflmacher, "Dover Revisited: The Wordsworthian Matrix in the Poetry of Matthew Arnold," in *Matthew Arnold: A Collection of Critical Essays*, ed. David J. DeLaura (Englewood Cliffs, NJ: Prentice-Hall, 1973), 46–53.

43. "The Buried Life" rewrites the terms of the encounter with the modern world envisioned in "The Scholar-Gipsy." There, in "isolation" sequestered from the "strange disease of modern life" in which "each half lives a hundred different lives," the legendary scholar-gipsy has "*one* aim," "*one* desire." The envied autonomy and concentration of the individual, however, are allied again with the immersion in a collective, here the ahistorical group of the "gipsy-tribe." Kracauer diagnoses precisely this relay between autonomy and concentration as a condition of modernity in his essay "The Group as Bearer of Ideas": "so long as man comports himself as an individual entity, thousands of urges arise in him," but once he becomes a part of a group, he is concentrated and transformed into an "extratemporal group individuality." The crowd produces the contradictory effect of nullifying the individual subject and lending the individual a satisfyingly concentrated group individuality. *The Mass Ornament*, 152–58.

44. The consonance of the general mass of men's silence in public with the erotic spur to self-knowledge underlines the poem's seeming location of desire as an inward state premised upon a rejection of the social. The initial turn from the erotic pair to the "hidden self," what might be described as an erotics of repression and self-exploration on the part of the speaker underlines the libidinal aspects of repression that Kucich explores in *Repression and Victorian Fiction*. Kucich describes a "productive repression" in the nineteenth-century novel in which repression is not a barrier to erotic life, but rather a mode of its intensification. Repression in Kucich's analysis is a self-negation that causes the novelistic subject to turn away from erotic investments in intersubjective relations, and instead locate affective investment inwardly. Producing a libidinalized heightening

of interior life which becomes the object of desire, self-negation itself is a modality of desire. Thus the richly interiorized life of the subject of the Victorian novel, as well as the subject outside the novel, is a product of the withdrawal from public emotion that is most generally associated with repression. This libidinal dynamic, in which silence is valued over expression, reserve over display, also serves to highlight what Kucich describes as a systematic deflection of desire away from any relationship to collective identity, a deflection made evident in part by the primarily negative representations of crowds in the nineteenth century (ibid., 24). By this light, "The Buried Life" is exemplary of Kucich's "productive repression." The effect of the self-negating silence of the great mass of men is to exalt interiority, to heighten an erotics of the self, to produce as alluring the "mystery of this heart which beats / So wild, so deep in us" (ll. 52–53). The stated desire of the speaker to "unlock this heart" to his beloved is, in such a reading, instead a turn away and inward toward an erotic of self-repression.

While Kucich's reading of negation illuminates the productive aspect of the inward turn that repression elicits in this poem, I want to retain something of the letter of his argument, if not the spirit. Kucich diagnoses a general "emptying of the public sphere of desire" in Victorian repression that correlates to a turn away from collective affect in general (ibid., 289). By contrast, I have been trying to argue for something like the retention, albeit an ambivalent one, of an aftereffect or artifact of that investment in collective life through the figure of the crowd. One important distinction between my own analysis and Kucich's argument is my focus on the aspect of publicity that remains more crucial for a critic such as Arnold than for the novelists that Kucich treats. Publicity, as a necessary adjunct to Arnold's public works project for culture, is retained as a necessary quantity even as, or even because, the public sphere is so devalued. The crowd is both figure and metonymy for the social sphere, thus underlining the potentially anarchic and monstrous qualities of that sphere for Arnold, but as well its phantasmatic, if disavowed, retention. The "productive repression" in this poem, the heightening of an inward subjectivity called "the genuine self," I argue in contrast to Kucich, is best analyzed not as a turn *from* the crowd, but as crucially dependent on incorporating the *presence* of the crowd. Against the sequestration Kucich proposes as crucial to nineteenth-century subjectivity, I stress the necessary public, social engagement—the incorporation of public affect into private subjectivity—although it may be only fleeting or ultimately derogated, offered by the crowd.

45. See Anderson, *The Powers of Distance*, 91–118, for an account of the contradictory forms of detachment Arnold both promotes and cautions against.

46. David DeLaura notes the development of "culture" in the sense of self-cultivation in the nineteenth century, and Arnold's attempts to elaborate for this self-development a more public inception. "Matthew Arnold and Culture: The History and the Prehistory," in *Matthew Arnold in His Time and Ours: Centenary Essays*, ed. Clinton Machann and Forrest D. Burt (Charlottesville: University Press of Virginia, 1988), 1–16.

47. See Pierre Bourdieu, *Distinction: A Social Critique of the Judgement of Taste* on the struggle to maintain the difference between "disinterest" and "indifference" (Cambridge, MA: Harvard University Press, 1984), 34.

48. "Collective tendencies," Durkheim asserts, "have an existence of their own," and "are forces as real as cosmic forces." *Suicide: A Study in Sociology*, ed. George Simpson, trans. John A. Spaulding (New York: Free Press, 1951), 309.

49. Frances Ferguson, *Solitude and the Sublime: Romanticism and the Aesthetics of Individuation* (New York: Routledge, 1992), 97.

50. Max Weber, *The Protestant Ethic and the Spirit of Capitalism*, trans. Talcott Parsons (London: Routledge, 1992).

51. Theodor Adorno, "On Lyric Poetry and Society," in *Notes to Literature*, vol. 1, ed. Rolf Tiedemann, trans. Shierry Weber Nicholsen (New York: Columbia University Press, 1991), 37–54.

Chapter 2

1. George Eliot, *Middlemarch* (New York: Penguin, 1994), 141. All quotations will be from this text and will be given in the text.

2. A. V. Dicey, review in *Nation* (October 1786), quoted in *George Eliot: The Critical Heritage*, ed. David Carroll (New York: Routledge, 1971).

3. Adam Phillips, *Monogamy* (New York: Random House, 1996), 96.

4. The historical genesis of the problems of attention and absorption in modernity—what this chapter takes up as a question of what society feels like in Eliot, and the effects of the novel's own sociological imagination—is the subject of Jonathan Crary's *Suspensions of Perception: Attention, Spectacle, and Modern Culture* (Cambridge, MA: MIT Press, 2001). Crary shows that the various scientific attempts to describe the attentive subject and the conditions, environmental and physiological, for attention in the later part of the nineteenth century found that attention contained "the conditions for its own undoing" and was "continuous with states of distraction, reverie, dissociation and trance" (45–46). The narration's intervention upon its own over-attentiveness here, a sneak attack on itself, as it were, confirms John Dewey's contention that "a shock of surprise is one of the most effective methods of arousing attention." *Psychology* (New York, 1887), 127, quoted in Crary, *Suspensions of Perception*, 49. The centrality of surprise and shock in Eliot's account of sympathy, as well as narrative interest, will be taken up later in this chapter.

Stephen Arata has recently traced out in fascinating detail the retooling of attention, and the investment of attentive reading with the Victorian virtue of work, in the latter part of the nineteenth century amidst demands for attentiveness brought on both by the sense of a world as increasingly distracting, full of stimulation, and by modern office and factory work. His account of William Morris's interest in producing by contrast "works that could be read without effort or concentration," which would resist what Arata calls a "bureaucratization—of reading, its assimilation into structures of self-discipline and self-control" offers an image of losing interest as well, though one distinct from Eliot's narrator's more effortful disattending. Stephen Arata, "On Not Paying Attention," *Victorian Studies* 46, no. 2 (2004): 203, 202. A recent account of theories of novel reading in the nineteenth century by Nicholas Dames shows a reader characterized as much by distraction and inattentiveness as by forms of deliberate involvement most familiar to us, showing this reader to be both utterly immersed within and responsive to as well as oddly detached from the fictional world of the novel. The conjunction of involvement and detachment, immersion and disattending that Dames recovers through the physiological models of reading developed by Victorian theorists of the novel exemplifies the readerly affect and stance that I am suggesting are responsive to the crowded and potentially overwhelmingly populous fictional environment of Eliot's novel. Nicholas Dames,

The Physiology of the Novel (Oxford: Oxford University Press, 2007). Concerns about the status of readerly absorption in fictional worlds were at the heart of Victorian cases both for and against the novel. Those eager to cast reading as improving and exemplary of mindful, purposive attentiveness, as well as those who thought fiction reading lent itself to dangerous daydreaming, pointed to a reader's absorption as evidence for their cases. See also Deb Gettelman, "Reading Ahead in George Eliot," *NOVEL: A Forum on Fiction* 39, no. 1 (Fall 2005): 25–47. On absorption and antitheatricality as a central dynamic in painting from Diderot onward, see Michael Fried, *Absorption and Theatricality: Painting and Beholder in the Age of Diderot* (Chicago: University of Chicago Press, 1988).

  5. Erving Goffman, *Behavior in Public Places: Notes on the Social Organization of Gatherings* (New York: Free Press, 1963), 256.

  6. I have lifted the phrase "Here Comes Everybody" from Zadie Smith's essay on *Middlemarch* in *Changing My Mind: Occasional Essays* (New York: Penguin, 2009).

  7. Henry James, "The Novels of George Eliot," chap. 1 in *Views and Reviews* (Boston: Ball Pub. Co., 1908).

  8. James Buzard, *Disorienting Fictions: The Autoethnographic Work of Nineteenth-Century British Novels* (Princeton, NJ: Princeton University Press, 2005), 10. Buzard's work emphasizes the marking of the boundaries of cultures, and the boundary between discourse and story space in the novel, by the novel's delimiting moves. In Buzard's account, this shows how the mobility of the nineteenth-century novel's narrator and the elaboration of partial forms of participation in the fictional world coheres with the emergent science of ethnography's notion of a participant observer. The far-flung reaches of a global British empire are evoked by novels, Buzard suggests, only to negate them, to turn them into a standpoint from which to take in England as a discrete nation and culture; that is, novels gesture outside England in order to emphasize the boundedness of England (148). See also Harry Shaw, *Narrating Reality: Austen, Scott, Eliot* (Ithaca, NY: Cornell University Press, 1999), for an account of Eliot's historicist realism as insisting upon characters staying local, being bound by one's place, an insistence driven by Eliot's concern about the socially dispersive effects of modernity.

  9. While sociological theory shares proto-anthropology's or ethnography's interest in social structures, its broader concern with the social, rather than culture, makes open-ended sociality an object of interest in itself. The nature of the social bond, as early sociological theory begins to explore it, is less codified and boundary-defining than the "culture concept" of the proto-ethnography that Buzard brilliantly shows to have shaped the novel in this period, in particular, the ways its narration is shaped by the "inward conceptual rhythm" of anthropology's insider–outsider distinction (39).

  10. Michael Wood elegantly describes the realist novel's own counterfactual bent, amidst its otherwise hard-to-shake effect of historical realism, in similar terms: "And in novels the different, unperformed action will, if we let it, do more than linger in our minds. It will become part of the texture of the work, an embodiment of the writer's and the reader's sense of what Henry James called 'operative irony,' which 'implies and projects the possible other case.'" Michael Wood, "Time and Her Aunt," in *A Companion to Jane Austen*, ed. Claudia Johnson and Clara Tuite (West Sussex: Wiley-Blackwell, 2009), 195–205. The Henry James quote is from "The Art of Fiction" (Longman's Review, 1884).

  11. Franco Moretti, *The Way of the World: The Bildungsroman in European Culture* (London: Verso, 2000), 215.

12. This chapter is in part an effort to take up Woloch's compelling account of the realist novel as it begins to feel the pressures of its own socially dense fictional space, being torqued by its attention to the one and the many. In finding the art of losing interest within Eliot, I am suggesting another means of contending with social density, one available both to narrators and to readers. That *Middlemarch* is especially shaped by the tension between the singularizing, individualizing energies of a protagonist and its aspiration to deflect its own energy toward a more inclusive social field is apparent in the broad range of those who might equally plausibly be thought the novel's central character or simply one among many protagonists. The novel's effort to render Dorothea one among many protagonists, as well as its reluctance to fully make good on such a democratizing move—its unwillingness to do much more than ask "Why always Dorothea?"—reflects, Woloch suggests, the changing conditions of political representation in nineteenth-century England. Written following the second Reform Bill of 1867, but set on the eve of the first Reform Bill in 1832, *Middlemarch* thus registers with particular acuity the tensions between impulses to expand the franchise in the period, and the continued existence, even deepening, of forms of class division and social stratification amidst such movements toward human equality. The concern Eliot's novel displays with the inequalities of narrative registers "the competing pull of inequality and democracy within the nineteenth-century bourgeois imagination." Alex Woloch, *The One vs. the Many: Minor Characters and the Space of the Protagonist in the Novel* (Princeton, NJ: Princeton University Press, 2003), 31.

13. Ibid., 30-42.

14. Andrew Miller, *The Burdens of Perfection: On Ethics and Reading in Nineteenth-Century British Literature* (Ithaca, NY: Cornell University Press, 2008), 191–96.

15. Woloch, *The One vs. the Many*, 26.

16. "Unacted possibility" is from Barbara Hardy, *The Novels of George Eliot: A Study in Form* (New York: Oxford University Press, 1967), 143, quoted in A. Miller, *Burdens of Perfection*, 197.

17. In what follows, I am drawing upon thinking about forms of experience that are important less for actually being lived by a character than they are for the formal qualities of the novel, or forms of experience that do not rise to the level of being articulated in speech or thought. For the former, see Theo Davis, *Formalism, Experience, and the Making of American Literature in the Nineteenth Century* (Cambridge: Cambridge University Press, 2007). For the latter, see Anne-Lise Francois, *Open Secrets: The Literature of Uncollected Experience* (Stanford, CA: Stanford University Press, 2008).

18. Omniscient narration itself being built upon a fantasy of the transcendence of the limitations of novelistic character, in whom vision and knowledge is always incomplete. On omniscient narration as establishing its unboundedness, mobility, and transcendence of identity and bodily being by constructing, and transcending character, see Audrey Jaffe, *Vanishing Points: Dickens, Narrative, and the Subject of Omniscience* (Berkeley: University of California Press, 1991).

19. For a discussion of "frequency" in the sense of sound in this passage, and the acoustic dimensions of Victorian culture more generally, see John Picker, *Victorian Soundscapes* (New York: Oxford University Press, 2003). In this section my thinking about the relation between sociological expansiveness and feeling has been helped by and is in conversation with David Kurnick's notion of "sociological eros," in which knowledge or embodiment of the social, or typicality or commonness, is effected through an eroticized relation to

that knowledge. For Kurnick, as for me, "frequency" operates as a kind of passageway between individual and common experience, or between the personal and the sociological. See David Kurnick, "The Erotics of Large Numbers: The Novel and the Sociological Imagination of the Novel" (lecture).

20. *Oxford English Dictionary Online*, s.v. "frequency."

21. Émile Durkheim, "What Is a Social Fact?" in *Sociological Debates: Thinking about "The Social,"* ed. Floya Anthias and Michael P. Kelly (Kent: Greenwich University Press, 1995), 130–1.

22. The first occurrence of frequency in the statistical sense I adduce here is given as 1854 by the *Oxford English Dictionary*. "The number of times an event or character occurs in a given sample; also (the *relative* or *proportionate frequency*), this number expressed as a proportion of the total possible number of occurrences."

23. Audrey Jaffe, *The Affective Life of the Average Man: The Victorian Novel and the Stock-Market Graph* (Columbus: Ohio State University Press, 2010), 26. Jaffe's powerful account of *Middlemarch* as saturated with the effects of statistical modes of imagining society, and as particularly concerned with typicality at the level of character, in which to be a central character in Eliot is to try to avoid being like everyone else, shares some of this book's interest in the aesthetic modes and effects of social complexity. Her argument that Eliot takes up the notion of character as Lukácsian type, creating an individual fictional character to represent the many who might share certain social or personal traits with many others locates Eliot's engagement with the problem of social multiplicity at the level of character and characterization. A book as singularly concerned with the representative completeness of "this particular web" as *Middlemarch*, however, suggests that Eliot's characterological mode should be read in tandem with the notion of the novel as a network of individuals, as well as with a sensitivity to moments in which the experience of typicality or ordinariness is less something either embraced by characters we are meant to not especially like (as Jaffe suggests with the character Chettham, who is often described as thinking of himself as "a fellow like Chettham"), or to be avoided, even if unsuccessfully as with Lydgate.

24. George Eliot, "The Natural History of German Life" (Oxford: Oxford University Press, 1992), 263.

25. Carolyn Williams's thinking on the force of type and typification in Eliot has helped me think through the sociological qualities of this passage, its sense that individual social forms can be understood only in relation to larger, generalized group formations. Carolyn Williams, "Moving Pictures: George Eliot and Melodrama," in *Compassion: The Culture and Politics of an Emotion*, ed. Lauren Berlant (New York: Routledge, 2004), 105–44. As two recent readers of Eliot have noted, such a carnal experience of non-singularity is one way to describe what it feels like to be a central character in Eliot, who often take shape through their epic precedents, carrying a trail of classic or mythic precursors behind them. See Catherine Gallagher, "George Eliot: Immanent Victorian," *Representations* 90, no. 1 (Spring 2005): 61–74, and David Kurnick, "Abstraction and the Subject of Novel Reading: Drifting through Romola," *Novel* 42, no. 3 (Fall 2009): 490–96. The most influential work on character and types in realism is that of Georg Lukács.

26. I am paraphrasing here Buzard's account of realist form as taking shape in the nineteenth century by differentiating itself from such social scientific texts: "the novel comes very self-consciously to assert a form of textual organization sharply distinguished

from that of the catalogue, the list, the encyclopedia, the state-sponsored blue book or statistical table." *Disorienting Fictions*, 45.

27. For Eliot's narrator as having to keep in check its own Midas-like powers, see Buzard, *Disorienting Fictions*.

28. I am sampling here from Mark McGurl's discussion of scale and the way literary form facilitates a sense of the "proper" scale of perception, making the world seem manageable, human sized. Mark McGurl, "The Posthuman Comedy," *Critical Inquiry* 38 (Spring 2012): 533–53. The maximalist vision of *Middlemarch* I am drawing out, its orientation toward expansiveness and social extensivity, should be seen in dialectical relation to the more familiar minimalist or miniature *Middlemarch*: a novel focused on the limited and diminutively scaled social formation of a provincial town.

29. See *New Sociologies of Literature*, the recent special issue of *New Literary History* 41, no. 2 (Spring 2010), ed. James English.

30. Franco Moretti, "Conjectures on World Literature," *New Left Review* 1 (January–February 2000): 55–57.

31. My critique of Moretti here complements Audrey Jaffe's own account of "distant reading" as novelistic at the level of character, since it simply names a general practice of relating to oneself. The "inscription of the self within any collective coherent narrative requires distant reading: the evaluation of one individual's position in relation to that construction; an apprehension of the self as both participating in and differing from a consolidated and coherent image of the whole." *The Affective Live of the Average Man*, 113. On the scale of the social sublime in Eliot, and the question of sympathy's relationship to political agency, see Bruce Robbins's excellent "The Sweatshop Sublime," *PMLA* 117, no. 1 (January 2000): 84–97.

32. *George Eliot and Her Readers: A Selection of Contemporary Reviews*, ed. John Holstrom and Lawrence Lerner (New York: Barnes and Noble, 1966), 94.

33. Ibid., 102. Carroll notes the character lists appeared regularly in reviews of Eliot's novels. *George Eliot: The Critical Heritage*, 28.

34. These lists take their place among the variety of non-novelistic contexts, such as anthologies of aphorisms drawn from her novels, or passages appearing on civil service exams in later nineteenth-century culture, that Leah Price has recently shown were primary sites of engagement with Eliot for many in the nineteenth-century. As with Alexander Main's collection, *Wise, Witty, and Tender Sayings [of] George Eliot*, which allowed readers Eliot's wisdom disembedded from its fictional context, enumerative character lists might float free of the novel to achieve some quasi-independent status, affording readers Eliot's novel's social scope, but recast in catalogue form, an anthology of characters, as it were. Leah Price, *The Anthology and the Rise of the Novel: From Richardson to George Eliot* (Cambridge: Cambridge University Press, 2000). Alexander Main, *Wise, Witty, and Tender Sayings in Prose and Verse: Selected from the Works of George Eliot* (Edinburgh: W. Blackwood and Sons, 1875). The serial or transient nature of the interest generated by these character lists, in which moving from one to the next is part of the pleasure, marks these lists as, in their own minor way, responsive to the forms of social and formal complexity that mark the modernity of Eliot's novels: a means of managing a potentially overwhelming diffusiveness or superabundance of fictional life. On serial art and the open-endedness of the aesthetic judgment of "interesting," which Henry

James suggested is the only quality that could characterize a genre as diffuse as the novel, see Sianne Ngai, "Merely Interesting," *Critical Inquiry* 34, no. 4 (Summer 2008): 777–817.

35. Wolf Lepenies, *Between Literature and Science: The Rise of Sociology*, trans. R. J. Hollingdale (Cambridge: Cambridge University Press, 1988). The critical history that understands Eliot's fiction as a form of historical sociology is extensive. For Eliot's novels' engagement with early sociology, see Steven Marcus, who finds in Eliot's fiction a spontaneous social theory, the fractures and tensions of which I am hoping to demonstrate here. Steven Marcus, "Literature and Social Theory: Starting in with George Eliot," in *Representations: Essays on Literature and Society* (New York: Random House, 1975), 182–213. Suzanne Graver traces out in masterly detail Eliot's engagement with classical sociology's central interest in modernization. Suzanne Graver, *George Eliot and Community: A Study in Social Theory and Fictional Form* (Berkeley: University of California Press, 1984). See Philip Fisher, *Making Up Society: The Novels of George Eliot* (Pittsburgh: University of Pittsburgh Press, 1981), and Daniel Cottom, *Social Figures: George Eliot, Social History, and Literary Representation* (Minneapolis: University of Minnesota Press, 1987). Amanda Anderson's and James Buzard's more positive accounts of detachment and social insight might be productively read against Cottom's more critical assessment of Eliot's normative vision. Nancy Paxton reconstructs the influence of Herbert Spencer and George Eliot's writings upon one another in *George Eliot and Herbert Spencer: Feminism, Evolutionism, and the Reconstruction of Gender* (Princeton, NJ: Princeton University Press, 1991). Graver views a cultivated or distanced stance toward social identities and forms, found in proto-sociology and elsewhere, as responsive to both the dispersive, alienating, heterogeneous aspects of modernity and the suffocating, unreflective attachments of traditional social formations within Eliot's work. I am bringing to light not only the continuities between Eliot and sociology, as these critics do, but also important and productive frictions between sociological thought and literary form in her work.

36. What I am describing here as a metropolitan narrative "overlay" on the geographic locale of provincial Middlemarch indicates that, contrary to Franco Moretti's recent suggestion that narrative form takes its shape from the geography of the social space it represents, a novel might narrate the provincial as if it were a city, and vice versa. Franco Moretti, *Atlas of the European Novel, 1800–1900* (New York: Verso, 1998). Indeed, Moretti's confession in an earlier work that he "nursed for a long time a strong disappointment that *Middlemarch* takes place where it does, and not in London" suggests that even narrative structures as finely attuned to the fictional territory of its represented world as *Middlemarch* might open up spaces within itself, or its readers, for narrative disjunctions such as the one I am suggesting here, eliciting momentary confusion or regret over the novel's geographic milieu. Moretti, *The Way of the World*, 220. In arguing for urbanity's reach well beyond the city limits, Sharon Marcus also has pointed out that novelistic narrative should not be seen as determined by settings. Part of our pleasure in novels may well be in their transmutations, in fact, presenting urban buzz on a country lane and making a city feel as intimate as a small town. Sharon Marcus, "Sophisticating the Provinces" (paper presented at "Urbanism, Urbanity, and the Novel," UC Santa Cruz, Dickens Universe Conference 2006).

37. Anthony Giddens, *The Consequences of Modernity* (Stanford, CA: Stanford University Press, 1990), 83–88.

38. Goffman, *Behavior in Public Places*, 83–137.

39. In "The Natural History of German Life," Eliot emphasizes the novel's capacity to surprise even its obliviously self-absorbed readers, startling them into sympathy. In *Middlemarch* as well, surprise is the sign of a new or renewed capacity for attending to the social world. On distraction and susceptibility as central to sympathy in Eliot, see Mary Ann O'Farrell, "Provoking George Eliot," in *Compassion: The Culture and Politics of an Emotion*, ed. Lauren Berlant (New York: Routledge, 2004).

40. The phrase "weak ties" is from Mark S. Granovetter's 1973 essay, "The Strength of Weak Ties," *American Journal of Sociology* 78, no. 6 (1973): 1360–80. Sharon Marcus, *Apartment Stories: City and Home in Nineteenth-Century Paris and London* (Berkeley: University of California Press, 1999) (see intro, n. 10).

41. Georg Simmel, "The Metropolis and Mental Life" in *The Sociology of Georg Simmel*, trans. and ed. Kurt H. Wolff (New York: Free Press, 1950), 409–16.

42. Simmel, *The Sociology of Georg Simmel*, 9.

43. Unfocused interaction is Goffman's term for the ways people who are within one another's visual or aural range, but not interacting directly, still signal their awareness of being around others. "Street behavior" is a primary form of unfocused interaction. Goffman, *Behavior in Public Places*, and *Interaction Ritual: Essays in Face to Face Behavior* (Chicago: Aldine, 1967), 133.

44. Daniel Siegel, "Preacher's Vigil, Landlord's Watch: Charity by the Clock in 'Adam Bede,'" *NOVEL: A Forum on Fiction* 31, no. 5 (Fall 2005): 48–74. Elizabeth Deeds Ermarth also underscores the sense of social contingency as grounds for sympathy, but marks a shift from Eliot's earlier work, in which sympathy arises between those well-acquainted, to her later work, such as *Middlemarch*, in which sympathy connects those who are "more casually related." Elizabeth Deeds Ermarth, "George Eliot's Conception of Sympathy," *Nineteenth-Century Fiction* 40, no. 1 (June 1985): 23.

45. My thinking here draws on and combines two senses of noise, one from Goffman's sociology and one from information theory, in order to show the various dimensions in which the novel registers what I earlier discussed as "frequency" of "all ordinary life." In Goffman, civil inattention amidst strangers in the anonymous settings of modernity form noise not in the sense of random sounds, but rather the carefully calibrated social rhythms of public life. Thus, strangers form "a reassuring 'noise' in the backdrop" of the "formation and dissolution" of more sustained, face-to-face encounters. Giddens, *The Consequences of Modernity*, 88. Thus, the "noise" of strangers enables more sustained encounters to acquire consequence in distinction from that noise. In a recent cybernetic account by William Paulson, literature might be considered as a kind of system self-organized from noise, with noise being anything introduced into a transmitted message that was not part of that message, like static on a phone call. "Literature is a noisy transmission channel that assumes its noise so as to be something other than a transmission channel." This sense of reading literature as providing a cognitive experience of an encounter with complexity is also suggestive for my reading of social and narrative complexity in Eliot. William Paulson, *The Noise of Culture: Literary Texts in a World of Information* (Ithaca, NY: Cornell University Press, 1988), ix.

46. This understanding of the dual nature of narrative is fundamental to narratology, going by various terms such as discourse and story-world, *fabula* and *sjuzhet, histoire* and *recit*. See Mieke Bal, *Narratology: Introduction to the Theory of Narrative* (Toronto: University of Toronto Press, 1985). The sense of this scene as an anticipatory figuration of social

convergence has been explored in a theatrical register by David Kurnick in *Empty Houses*. Thank you to Theo Davis for helping me think about the nature of experience here in this passage. My phrasing of this point alludes to what Anne-Lise Francois calls the "literature of uncounted experience," moments of "thoughts and desires to which we cannot or will not give consequence or empirical result." *Open Secrets*, 32.

47. Caroline Levine, *The Serious Pleasures of Suspense: Victorian Realism and Narrative Doubt* (Charlottesville: University of Virginia Press, 2003).

48. On the indeterminacy produced by *Middlemarch*'s interconnectedness, see Fredric Jameson, "The Experiments of Time: Providence and Realism," in *The Novel*, Volume 2: *Forms and Themes*, ed. Franco Moretti (Princeton, NJ: Princeton University Press, 2006).

49. Dorrit Cohn, *Transparent Minds: Narrative Modes for Presenting Consciousness in Fiction* (Princeton, NJ: Princeton University Press, 1978), 100. Cohn's and Banfield's are the classic studies of free indirect style. Ann Banfield, *Unspeakable Sentences: Narration and Representation in the Language of Fiction* (Abingdon, Oxon: Routledge & Kegan Paul, 1982). On free indirect style as the narrative technique most suited to the compromise between bourgeois values and conservativism that the novel enacts in its form, see Franco Moretti, "Serious Century," in *The Novel*, Volume 1: *History, Geography, and Culture*, ed. Franco Moretti (Princeton, NJ: Princeton University Press, 2006), 364–400. My account here is informed by and responsive to particularly those of Moretti and D. A. Miller, *Jane Austen; or, The Secret of Style* (Princeton, NJ: Princeton University Press, 2000). Frances Ferguson offers a different account of ideology and free indirect style in Austen than that of Miller. Frances Ferguson, *Solitude and the Sublime: Romanticism and the Aesthetics of Individuation* (New York: Routledge, 1992). Some critics have inclined toward Foucauldian accounts of free indirect style's rise alongside the impersonal techniques of power, in which the invisibility and "neutrality" of a narrative voice that speaks the voice of a character is homologous (and historically simultaneous) with the rise of the subjectivizing power of the penitentiary, rendered ubiquitous by the invisibility and "naturalness" of free indirect style's narrative presence. See John Bender, *Imagining the Penitentiary: Fiction and the Architecture of Mind in Eighteen-Century England* (Chicago: University of Chicago Press, 1987). Harry Shaw and Andrew Miller each offer suggestive philosophical accounts of free indirect style as constituting the promise of unmitigated access to another's thoughts, granted in novels but not in life, and the ethical practice of attempting to understand others. In ways that resonate with my own sense of free indirect style as the narrative technique suited to social neutrality or distance, Michael McKeon emphasizes the "narrative objectification" of interiority through free indirect style and allies it, at the level of sentence and style, "with the condition of detachment or distance to which the theory of the novel is itself notably attentive." *Theory of the Novel: A Historical Approach*, ed. Michael McKeon (Baltimore: Johns Hopkins University Press, 2000), 485–91.

50. Moretti, "Serious Century," 395–96, emphasis in original. Anne Waldron Neumann and D. A. Miller, along with Moretti, all describe the relation between the voice of the narrator and that of the character as "neutral." Moretti qualifies that neutrality with "perhaps" in his account of free indirect style as the instrument of socialization, in which a character begins to see herself with the detached, "objective" eyes of the narrator. Anne Waldron Neumann, "Characterization and Comment in Pride and Prejudice: Free

Indirect Discourse and 'Double-Voiced' Verbs of Speaking, Thinking, and Feeling," *Style* 20 (Fall 1986): 390.

51. Miller, *Jane Austen*, 59–60.

52. This, I want to note, is not the same thing as arguing that omniscient narration is itself neutral or without distinguishing qualities, or that omniscient narrator's own rhetorical conventions are not marked by social qualities like gender. For a comprehensive argument about gender's important role in narration, and in particular female narration's restriction to the act of witnessing, "by her exclusion from the active shaping of narrative form and meaning" in the novel, see Alison Case, *Plotting Women: Gender and Narration in the Eighteenth- and Nineteenth-Century British Novel* (Charlottesville: University of Virginia Press, 1999), 4.

53. Banfield, *Unspeakable Sentences*.

54. Similarly, Francois finds within free indirect style a putting into question of whether the thoughts and feelings expressed in free indirect style are the property of the character or narrator. What I am proposing here is a socialization of the indeterminacy Francois finds at the level of thought and expression.

55. By a different light, the migration of social relationality from plot to narrative space might be seen as a measure of the ubiquity of Eliot's socialization imperative, extending even beyond the depicted social world of the novel to include the space of its narration. In such an extension, however, sociality itself is transmuted into forms unrecognized as such by novelistic plot.

56. For an extended reading of the effects of *Middlemarch*'s narrator as defined by its difference from mere social correctness, the narrator's timeless style as distinct from the merely fashionable, one that my own understanding of the interaction between narrator and character has benefited from, see Kent Puckett, *Bad Form: Social Mistakes and the Nineteenth-Century Novel* (New York: Oxford University Press, 2008).

57. Georg Simmel, "Sociability," in *On Individuality and Social Forms*, ed. Donald Levine (Chicago: University of Chicago Press, 1971), 127–41.

58. Georg Simmel, "Flirtation," in *On Women, Sexuality, and Love*, trans. Guy Oakes (New Haven, CT: Yale University Press, 1984), 145. Simmel finds in flirtation a means of registering the socially extensive environments of the modern city without being overwhelmed by them; its commitment to non-commitment, to not settling on a single person, suit it to navigating crowded social fields. See also Adam Phillips, *On Flirtation: Psychoanalytic Essays on the Uncommitted Life* (Cambridge, MA: Harvard University Press, 1994), and D. A. Miller's discussion of flirtation in *Narrative and Its Discontents: Problems of Closure in the Traditional Novel* (Princeton, NJ: Princeton University Press, 1981), 21. Richard Kaye's *The Flirt's Tragedy: Desire without End in Victorian and Edwardian Fiction* (Charlottesville: University of Virginia Press, 2002) illuminates the extensive history of flirtation within the extensive history of sexuality and the marriage plot in the novel. To Kaye's understanding of flirtation as a form of "managed desire," I add a sense of flirtation as a sophisticated stance toward social forms, as well as adduce an episode in *Middlemarch* where such management of social forms fails.

59. Contrary to characterizations of social relations as waning, or becoming less cohesive in modernity, such as is found in Ferdinand Tönnies's typology, Durkheim's sociology understands the division of labor under modern conditions as bringing about increased

social solidarity. Describing the transition from traditional to modern forms of social organization, Durkheim writes: "Social relationships . . . become more numerous. Thus the division of labour progresses the more individuals there are who are sufficiently in contact with one another to be able mutually to act and react upon one another . . . We agree to call dynamic or moral density this drawing together." The actual density of England in 1832 is less crucial here than the density of the novelistic community that Lydgate inhabits; that is, the degree to which anything he says or does will have multiple effects upon others, or, as he puts it "so many threads pulling at once." Émile Durkheim, *The Division of Labor in Society* (New York: Free Press, 1984), 201.

60. On gossip as an instrument of community formation in *Middlemarch*, see Patricia Meyer Spacks, *Gossip* (New York: Knopf, 1985). D. A. Miller also discusses gossip in *Middlemarch* in *Narrative and Its Discontents*, 110–29.

61. Jeff Nunokawa has illuminated the antisocial dividends of erotic attraction and the isolation this attraction sanctions, or at least provides an alibi for, in Eliot and others in two recent essays. Jeff Nunokawa, "Eros and Isolation: The Antisocial George Eliot," *ELH* 69 (Winter 2002): 835–60, and "Sexuality in the Victorian Novel," in *The Cambridge Companion to the Victorian Novel*, ed. Deirdre David (Cambridge: Cambridge University Press, 2001), 125–48. While Lydgate and Rosamond also find being alone together enough to provide an erotic charge, the sociality of their public flirtation provides its own seemingly more manageable thrill in being conducted under the watchful eyes of others. Such social management, however, consistently proves more elusive in practice than in theory in this novel.

62. Simmel, *The Sociology of Georg Simmel*, 405–7, emphasis in original.

63. Simmel, *Women, Sexuality, and Love*, 136.

64. Kaye, *The Flirt's Tragedy*, 18.

65. John Stuart Mill, "Thoughts on Poetry and its Varieties," *The Crayon* 7, no. 4 (April 1860): 93–97. And, the "game-like" quality of their flirtation turns their social engagements into play, as ungrounded, as engrossing as any game. Simmel underscores the self-grounding of sociability, its apartness from "the real world," in these terms: "In the game [of sociability], they lead their own lives; they are propelled exclusively by their own attraction." *The Sociology of Georg Simmel*, 50.

66. My understanding of publicity as not merely a site but also a condition of speech is guided by Michael Warner's discussion of discursive publics in *Publics and Counterpublics* (New York: Zone Books, 2002), 65–124.

67. Lydgate understands tact here as a lightness of touch that bespeaks a knowledge worn easily, embodied in everyday actions. But he also counts on tact as guiding an "appropriate" social reticence on Rosamond's part. See Simmel on the impersonal, neutral qualities of "tact" in "Sociability," in *The Sociology of Georg Simmel*, p. 45. On the amorous qualities of tact, nonetheless "'unhooked' from the desire-to-possess," discussed in this book's introduction, see Roland Barthes, *The Neutral: Lecture Course at the College de France (1977–1978)*, trans. Rosalind Krauss and Denis Hollier (New York: Columbia University Press, 2005), 35. Puckett's discussion of social mistakes in the novel has been particularly helpful for my thinking about the relationship among social smarts, narration, and character in this section.

68. For the argument I am drawing on here, that the omniscience narrator gains its coherence as an effect of its being defined by its difference from and negation of fictional

character, which is always represented as limited, see Jaffe, *Vanishing Points*. For the particularly acute form such a relationship between narrator and narrated takes in the registers of social and aesthetic form, as well as style, see Puckett, *Bad Form*, and D. A. Miller, *Jane Austen*.

69. Craig Calhoun, "Indirect Relationships and Imagined Communities: Large Scale Social Integration and the Transformation of Everyday Life," in *Social Theory for a Changing Society*, ed. Pierre Bourdieu and James S. Coleman (Boulder, CO: Westview Press, 1991), 95–120. On *Middlemarch* and community, see also William Deresiewicz, "Heroism and Organicism in the Case of Lydgate," *Studies in English Literature* 38 (1998): 723–40. As I am, Deresiewicz is concerned with the social causes of Lydgate's obduracy, as well as with powers of resistance put forward by complex social structures (apart from any one individual's particular feelings) found in such a town as Middlemarch. I want to bring out here the dimension of epistemology that vexes any account by Eliot of social knowledge, an aspect absent from Deresiewicz's penetrating argument which in many other ways coheres with my own reading of Lydgate's troubles.

70. Alan Mintz discerns a temporary fusing of the narrative voice with the figure of Lydgate in the passages describing his scientific imagination (97–102). Alan Mintz, *George Eliot and the Novel of Vocation* (Cambridge, MA: Harvard University Press, 1978), 97–102. The novel's suggestion, over and again, that things might have been different if only Lydgate had applied his highly refined powers of apprehending the human body to the social body of Middlemarch, imagines a continuity between medical and sociological knowledge. But his failure to succeed in doing so, a failure predicated in part on the lack of transferability between knowledge of the human and the social bodies that this analogy papers over, offers a miniature portrait of something like a contest of the faculties, between the character of the scientist—here implicitly a scientist of the social—and the social's great novelist, Eliot herself.

Chapter 3

1. Oscar Wilde, "The Decay of Lying," in *The Artist as Critic: Critical Writings of Oscar Wilde*, ed. Richard Ellmann (Chicago: University of Chicago Press, 1982), hereinafter this essay is cited in the text as DL. All subsequent references to Wilde's essays will be to this edition.

2. In *Dorian Gray*, we find the peculiar social magic of fame or infamy that allows an entire city to be miniaturized, with its scale reduced from a geographic terrain to a social scene, one in which Dorian would often be stared or pointed at, and talked about while walking the vast city's streets. So, by novel's end, the city has all the claustrophobic qualities of life in a small town. Reversing the usual geographic alignments of anonymity in the city and cozy familiarity in the country, Dorian escapes his own ubiquity and familiarity in London by losing himself in the anonymity of village life. "Half the charm of the little village where he had been so often lately was that no one knew who he was." Oscar Wilde, *The Picture of Dorian Gray* (Oxford: Oxford University Press, 1974), 219, hereinafter cited in the text as *DG*. Subsequent references will be to this edition. One wonders what the other half of the charm is, and in doing so, remarks how much the country here resembles the anonymity-granting social space of its urban other.

3. Oscar Wilde, "The Soul of Man under Socialism," in *Artist as Critic*, 260, hereinafter cited in the text as SMS.

4. See Mark Granovetter, "The Strength of Weak Ties," *American Journal of Sociology* 78 (May 1973): 1360–80. This chapter is in part an effort to make good on the innumerable ways in which Jeff Nunokawa has shaped my thinking about the varieties of attachment and desire found in Wilde's work. See Jeff Nunokawa, *Tame Passions of Wilde: The Styles of Manageable Desire* (Princeton, NJ: Princeton University Press, 2009). David Alderson reads ephemerality in Wilde, instanced by the centrality to his work of the term "moment," as primarily a dissident mode of release from the moral implications of action. David Alderson, "Momentary Pleasures: Wilde and English Virtue," in *Sex, Nation and Dissent in Irish Writing*, ed. Éibhear Walshe (Cork: Cork University Press, 1997), 43. Such release, paradigmatically the male same-sex act in Alderson's understanding in which the "pristine intensity of the moment [is] divorced from any moral implications," is taken to be a form of anti-familial sexual practice in Wilde's work (ibid., 54). My analysis reads ephemerality as constitutive of a far broader means of escape from the claims of others, not only from normative structures such as marriage and the family but also from the constraining powers associated with the social in general.

5. The *OED* describes a shift in definitions of the epigram, from poetic wit and brevity, "a short poem ending in a witty or ingenious turn of thought" in 1596, to something more aggressive, "a pointed or antithetical saying," by 1796. That Wilde was cross-examined in his first trial on seven of the thirty-five epigrams that comprise "Phrases and Philosophies for the Use of the Young" might suggest that, in Wilde's hands, the epigram form itself could be cause for suspicion of immorality or sexual scandal. Years later, Somerset Maugham would be asked to remove all epigrams from a play for fear the form might scandalize his audience, which may indicate that the epigram became sufficiently associated with the scandal of homosexuality to be subject to such excisions by the early twentieth century. I am grateful to Richard Kaye for this anecdote about Maugham.

6. Oscar Wilde, *De Profundis and Other Writings* (New York: Penguin, 1986), 151. It is worth noting that within *De Profundis* itself, which is both a letter to Lord Alfred Douglas and plausibly intended for eventual publication, as well as being a far more discursive text than anything else he wrote, this is about as close as Wilde gets to an epigram. If it is one, it is the final one, as it were, the epigram that condensed all other epigrammatic condensations.

7. This chapter draws some of its motivation from an effort to see what becomes of the form of confident speech embodied most perfectly in the nineteenth century by the narrators of Jane Austen when that confidence is asserted within rather than about a fictional world. The effects and attitude of the certainty embedded within the epigram, and possibly loaned to its speaker, take their force in no small part from what D. A. Miller has called "Austen's attitude." "Austen's Attitude," *Yale Journal of Criticism* 8, no. 1 (1995): 1–5. Miller's consideration of omniscient narrative, aphoristic pronouncements, and the good form of "style," have helped me see what Wilde and Austen might, and might not, have in common. My hope is to give some texture to the broad historical conditions of modernity to which certainty is one compensatory response. See also D. A. Miller, *Jane Austen; or, The Secret of Style* (Princeton, NJ: Princeton University Press, 2000).

8. J. S. Mill, *On Liberty* (Oxford: Oxford University Press, 2008). Mill's 1859 essay employs terms to describe the relation between the individual and the society that

Wilde's essay also draws upon. In Mill, society acts upon the individual as "interference," "encroachment," "restraint," "compulsion," and "control" (ibid., 9–18). As with Wilde, the powers of the social in Mill exceed those of the merely judicial or political: "When society itself is the tyrant—society collectively, over the separate individuals who compose it—its means of tyrannizing are not restricted to the acts which it may do by the hands of its political functionaries. Society can and does execute its own mandates" (ibid., 8). For Wilde, however, unlike Mill, no measures but the most extreme forms of social renovation will suffice to protect the individual from society's impinging effects. For a reading that traces Wilde's indictments of the public in this essay back to his obsession with negative reviews of *Dorian Gray*, see Lawrence Danson, *Wilde's Intentions: The Artist in His Criticism* (Oxford: Oxford University Press, 1997), 148–67.

9. Oscar Wilde, "Lord Arthur Savile's Crime," in *Oscar Wilde: The Major Works*, ed. Isobel Murray (Oxford: Oxford University Press, 1980), 27.

10. Amanda Anderson, *The Powers of Distance: Cosmopolitanism and the Cultivation of Detachment* (Princeton, NJ: Princeton University Press, 2001), 158, 148. While Anderson stresses Wilde's epigrams, and their embodiment in the denaturalizing, critical habits of the dandy, as containing the fundamental contradiction between detachment and self-realization in Wilde, I want to explore how such a mode of speech as the epigram functions as much to clear a room as to realize a self, or to save someone else's self in its ethical mode. David Wayne Thomas looks at the problem of freedom in Wilde amidst Victorian liberalism's practices of self-reflection. David Wayne Thomas, *Cultivating Victorians: Liberal Culture and the Aesthetic* (Philadelphia: University of Pennsylvania Press, 2004), 156–86.

11. Erving Goffman, *Interaction Ritual: Essays in Face to Face Behavior I* (Chicago: Aldine, 1967), 2–3.

12. "The only difference between a caprice and a lifelong passion is that a caprice lasts longer" (*DG*, 23).

13. The distinction I am quickly sketching here between indifference and the forms of transient, seemingly negligible interest in Wilde draws upon Pierre Bourdieu's notion of "interest" (even and especially disinterested interest) as the requirement for entry into any field, such as the aesthetic field, or game. "The notion of interest is opposed to that of disinterestedness, but also to that of indifference. One can be interested in a game (in the sense of not indifferent), while at the same time being disinterested. The indifferent person 'does not see why they are playing,' it's all the same to them; they are in the position of Buridan's ass, not making a distinction. Such a person is someone who, not having the principles of vision and division necessary to make distinctions, finds everything the same, is neither moved not affected." Pierre Bourdieu, *Practical Reason: On the Theory of Action*, trans. Randall Johnson (Stanford, CA: Stanford University Press, 1998), 77.

14. I am grateful to an anonymous reader for Oxford University Press for helping me clarify my understanding of Wilde's relation to Mill.

15. Walter Pater, *The Renaissance: Studies in Art and Poetry*, ed. Adam Phillips (Oxford: Oxford University Press, 1986), 153.

16. Regenia Gagnier's study of Wilde's publics, for example, while noting the ways in which Wilde's epigrams signal his attentiveness to a middle-class reading and viewing public, as well as the cover paradox would provide for the views of a queer Irishman writing at the end of the nineteenth century in England, attends to the epigram only

passingly. Regenia Gagnier, *Idylls of the Marketplace: Oscar Wilde and the Victorian Public* (Stanford, CA: Stanford University Press, 1986). Jonathan Freedman points to Wilde's epigrams' capacity to express the contradictions of conventional Victorian thought in the form of an antinomy, which Wilde then revises by reversing one of the terms of the antinomy. For Freedman, however, such contradictions underscore Wilde's own powerlessness, his "inability to transcend the forms of the culture in the very means by which he satirizes them." Jonathan Freedman, *Professions of Taste: Henry James, British Aestheticism, and Commodity Culture* (Stanford, CA: Stanford University Press, 1990), 8. See also Stefan Collini's account of the difficulty posed by the writing of "Victorian moralists" such as Thomas Carlyle for twentieth-century literary criticism, which assimilated such propositional writing as non-propositional, emphasizing irony and ambiguity rather than discursive statements. Stefan Collini, "From 'Non-Fiction Prose' to 'Cultural Criticism,'" in *Rethinking Victorian Culture* Juliet John and Alice Jenkins, eds., (New York: St. Martin's, 2000), 13–28. Wilde's high-profile status in strands of queer criticism that emphasize the denaturalizing powers of his irony, however, suggest that his assimilation to twentieth-century criticism has been as the inverse of that Victorian moralist tradition, non-propositional and ironic, a "Victorian Anti-Moralist." See, for instance, Christopher Craft, *Another Kind of Love: Male Homosexual Desire in English Discourse, 1850-1920* (Berkeley: University of California Press, 1994), and Jonathan Dollimore, *Sexual Dissidence: Augustine to Wilde, Freud to Foucault* (Oxford: Oxford University Press, 1991). Anderson's focus on the ethical dimensions of the epigram might be seen as an attempt to rectify the problem Collini identifies, though in her conclusion that the epigram in Wilde ultimately "lacks a specific normative dimension that can sufficiently respond to the needs of others" feels to me that it travels too far back in the other direction, asking the epigram to say what it can only say by not saying. Anderson, *Powers of Distance*, 173.

17. Sianne Ngai, "The Cuteness of the Avant-Garde," *Critical Inquiry* 31 (Summer 2005): 811–47. In this paragraph and the following, I am drawing on Ngai's account of cuteness as an expression of an Adornian understanding of art's most acute power as lying in its capacity to theorize its own circumscribed, limited power in modernity.

18. Oscar Wilde, *The Importance of Being Earnest*, in *The Importance of Being Earnest and Other Plays*, ed. Peter Raby (Oxford: Oxford University Press, 1995), 268, hereinafter cited in the text as *Earnest*. All citations of Wilde's plays will be from this edition.

19. As Joseph Bristow notes, Wilde's epigrammatic style also could, to some, interfere with a work's overall shape. "In [one reviewer of *An Ideal Husband*'s] view, this 'very able and entertaining piece of work' suffered because several scenes were overburdened with witticisms of the kind that 'threaten[ed] to become all trademark and no substance.'" William Archer, "An Ideal Husband," in *The Theatrical "World" of 1895* (London: Walter Scott, 1896), 18, quoted in Joseph Bristow, ed., introduction to *Wilde Writings: Contextual Conditions* (Toronto: University of Toronto Press, 2003), 5. A complaint that Wilde's trademark epigrammatic style overwhelms the substance of a play suggests, in the language of commercial property, both how tightly associated the epigram ("witticisms") became with Wilde, as well as the epigram's ubiquity.

20. Oscar Wilde, *An Ideal Husband*, in *Earnest and Other Plays*, 212, hereinafter cited in the text as *Husband*.

21. "The Critic as Artist," in *The Artist as Critic*, 380, hereinafter cited in the text as CA.

22. In this passage, Wilde mocks those members of the small upper class of English society who would regard, with a Malthusian eye, the vast numbers at the lower end of the social stratum as so much "surplus population." The snob's hand-wringing over the expanding membership of the upper reaches of society with the decline of the aristocracy becomes itself a target of such Malthusian visions in Wilde's satire here.

23. Émile Durkheim, "What Is a Social Fact?" in *Sociological Debates: Thinking about "The Social,"* ed. Floya Anthias and Michael P. Kelly (Kent: Greenwich University Press, 1995), 1–13.

24. Georg Simmel, *The Philosophy of Money*, ed. David Frisby, trans. Tom Bottomore and Frisby (New York: Routledge, 1991), 298.

25. Michael Warner, *Publics and Counterpublics* (New York: Zone Books, 2002), 285.

26. Michael Moon, "Solitude, Singularity, Seriality: Whitman vis-à-vis Fourier," *ELH* 73 (Summer 2006): 305. Whitman's poetry is more interested in such scenes of intimate attachment as, in Moon's words, a "series of shared recognitions between and among actual and potential lovers" (ibid.). I want to suggest that Wildean ephemerality, even as, like Whitman's, it refuses to specify the nature of the attachments between men, encompasses a broader sense of an attachment to transient sociality itself, to an iteration of what Simmel calls sociability, as I will discuss in more detail below.

27. Ibid., 308. Here too we should note the resonance of Whitman's catalogues with Wilde and his epigrams, which often appear as series or lists—in the Preface to Dorian Gray, and the two works comprised entirely by epigrams, "Phrases and Philosophies for the Use of the Young," and "A Few Maxims for the Instruction of the Over-Educated." Wilde often composed lists of epigrams in his working notebooks, producing page after page of epigrams (often reworked many times over) which could then be used in various works as necessary, a sort of well to which he might return again and again. As I suggested in my discussion of character lists drawn from George Eliot's novels, the form of the list bespeaks its own rearrangeability, the possibility that future relations and new configurations that cannot be anticipated, could be generated out of the list.

28. The gothic qualities of *The Picture of Dorian Gray*, in which the wish to be alone is nearly coterminous with the varieties of narcissism and pathologies ascribed to Dorian Gray, is one measure of both how thoroughly social Wilde's fictional environments are, as well as the extreme measures necessary, measures cast as pathologies, to be on one's own in Wilde's world. See Nunokawa, *Tame Passions of Wilde*. Douglas Mao treats the powerful influence thought to be exercised by the "environment" upon the development of the self in aestheticist understandings in *Fateful Beauty: Aesthetic Environments, Juvenile Development, and Literature, 1860-1960* (Princeton, NJ: Princeton University Press, 2010).

29. *The Complete Letters of Oscar Wilde*, ed. Merlin Holland and Rupert Hart-Davis (New York: Henry Holt & Co., 2000), 425.

30. Paul Saint-Amour, *The Copywrights: Intellectual Property and the Literary Imagination* (Ithaca, NY: Cornell University Press, 2003), 94. Ivan Kreilkamp has also recently studied the status of orality in nineteenth-century print culture, finding in the voice, and trope, of the Victorian storyteller the back-construction of a Victorian realist novel anxious about its own fully mediatized print modernity. Ivan Kreilkamp, *Voice and the Victorian Storyteller* (Cambridge: Cambridge University Press, 2005). In a different tact on Wilde's relation to modern media, Daniel Novak has argued in compelling terms for how photography becomes a means of defining a particular set of literary techniques

known as realism, showing just how central photography is to Wilde. Daniel Novak, *Realism, Photography and Nineteenth-Century Fiction* (Cambridge: Cambridge University Press, 2008).

31. See, e.g., a book comprised of stories told by Wilde at various social occasions, printed and bound as *Echoes* by Gabrielle Enthoeven, British Library's Eccles Bequest, 1890.

32. The following passages are only two of many instances of Wilde reusing lines in different works. "[Society] feels instinctively that manners are of more importance than morals" (*DG*, 142), versus, "My dear Windermere, manners before morals" (Oscar Wilde, *Lady Windermere's Fan*, in *Earnest and Other Plays*, 51). "[Insincerity] is merely a method by which we can multiply our personalities" (*DG*, 142–43), versus, "What people call insincerity is simply a method by which we can multiply our personalities" (*CA*, 351).

33. As Linda Dowling notes, when Wilde's "Soul of Man under Socialism" was first published in the *Fortnightly Review* in 1891, there were thirty-two epigrammatic sentences or passages that Wilde italicized, an effect that all but announces their extractability and rearrangement, instantiating, in a typographic form that thus echoes his social program, the wish expressed by "all association must be quite voluntary" (SMS, 296). These epigrams, however, were restored to roman type when the essay was reprinted in Wilde's collection of essays, *Intentions*, as if to limit the fragmenting powers of the endlessly circulatable, recontextualizable epigram. Oscar Wilde, *The Soul of Man under Socialism and Selected Critical Prose*, introduction by Linda Dowling (London: Penguin, 2001).

34. For studies of Wilde that stress the modes by which he illuminates the figurative dimensions of language, finding within his work the insights of deconstruction before its day, see, among others, Craft, "Alias Bunbury," in *Another Kind of Love*, 106–39; William Cohen, *Sex Scandal: The Private Parts of Victorian Fiction* (Durham, NC: Duke University Press, 1996), 191–236; and Joel Fineman, "The Significance of Literature: The Importance of Being Earnest," in *Critical Essays on Oscar Wilde*, ed. Regenia Gagnier (New York: G. K. Hall, 1991), 108–18.

35. In other places, Wilde seems to have nearly run out of proper names altogether, as with Adrian Singleton in *Dorian Gray*, the opium-addicted youth corrupted by Dorian, who now, named as a condition of isolation—"Singleton"—remarks "I have had too many friends" (*DG*, 188). The multiple lives and free play critics have discovered encrypted within Wilde's character's names is countered here by one thoroughly circumscribed by a name and condition of not multiplication, but isolation. Other imaginative readings pursue the tendencies toward authorial self-inscription and the multivalency of names and naming in Wilde, readings I hope to complement by drawing out the opposing current of the severe rationing of names elsewhere in Wilde. On Wilde's use of his own name within his work, see Karl Beckson, "The Autobiographical Signature in *The Picture of Dorian Gray*," *Victorian Newsletter* 69 (Spring 1986): 30–32; and Cohen on the self-revealing/self-concealing properties of names in Wilde's "The Portrait of Mr. W. H." (*Sex Scandal*, 197–210).

36. Aaron Kunin, "Characters Lounge," *Modern Language Quarterly* 70 (September 2009): 291–317.

37. For a reading of the recursive qualities of twentieth-century fiction as it has been shaped by the system of creative writing programs and the university, and from which my sense of Wilde as instantiating a literary ecosystem of his own borrows, see Mark

McGurl, *The Program Era: Postwar Fiction and the Rise of Creative Writing* (Cambridge, MA: Harvard University Press, 2011).

38. Deidre Lynch, *The Economy of Character: Novels, Market Culture, and the Business of Inner Meaning* (Chicago: University of Chicago Press, 1998), 13.

39. Georg Simmel, "Sociability," in *On Individuality and Social Forms*, ed. Donald Levine (Chicago: University of Chicago Press, 1971), 128.

40. Ibid., 133, 137.

41. Ibid., 45.

42. Leo Bersani, "Sociability and Cruising," in Leo Bersani, *Is the Rectum a Grave?: And Other Essays* (Chicago: University of Chicago Press, 2010), 45–62. "The danger associated with cruising is not that it reduces relations to promiscuous sex, but rather that promiscuity may stop. Few things are more difficult to block than our interest in others, to prevent them from degenerating into a 'relationship'" (57). And here, Lord Henry from *The Picture of Dorian Gray*: "The difference between a caprice and a life-long relationship is that a caprice lasts longer" (23). In Bersani's own epigrammatic echo of Wilde, we can see Wilde's epigrammatic promiscuity as a response at the level of literary form to constraints of "relationships," though Bersani, unlike Wilde, emphasizes the difficulty of preventing interest from "degenerating into a 'relationship.'" In Wilde the problem of more durable relations, one feature of what has come to be called anti-futurity in queer theory, is overcome rhetorically through paradox rather than in the negations of anti-futurity, by the elan and certitude of the aphorism. Wilde helps us to see that the force of queerness's negation of the social is not to be confused with a negation of *sociability*. Rather, sociability bears its participants away from futurity, from character, from any purpose other than itself, though in ways so mild as to be hard to recognize next to the punk allure of negation or the violence of self-shattering that is central elsewhere in Bersani's accounts of queer sociality. It is in the difference between a violent self-shattering and the lighter-than-air quality of sociability that I would mark out the difference with, and overlap of, my account of Wilde and the "anti-social thesis" of queer theory. For the most bracing polemical version of the political stakes of anti-futurity and an urge toward negation, see Lee Edelman's *No Future: Queer Theory and the Death Drive* (Durham, NC: Duke University Press, 2004). See also the recent *PMLA* forum for a recent re-evaluation of "The Antisocial Thesis in Queer Theory," *PMLA* 121 (May 2006): 8+19–28. On sociability and queer theory, see Jeff Nunokawa, "Queer Theory: Postmortem," in *After Sex?: On Writing since Queer Theory*, ed. Janet Halley and Andrew Parker (Durham, NC: Duke University Press, 2011).

43. Leo Bersani, *A Future for Astyanax: Character and Desire in Literature* (Boston: Little, Brown, 1976), 61.

44. Edelman, *No Future*, 7.

45. Amanda Anderson and David Wayne Thomas on Wilde are notable exceptions to this characterization. And, of course, work on sexuality and literature, particularly in its queer dimensions is precisely where so much powerful thinking about the social in literary study has taken place, in particular, in Eve Sedgwick's *Between Men*. Eve Sedgwick, *Between Men: English Literature and Male Homosocial Desire* (New York: Columbia University Press, 1985). The recent work of Heather Love on Erving Goffman and stigma points toward the queer critical resources for thinking about literature and the social

that might be found in sociological writing. See Heather Love, "Safe," *American Literary History* 25 (Spring 2013): 164–75.

46. Richard Sennett, *The Fall of Public Man* (New York: W. W. Norton, 1992), 36.

47. The formal independence and force of the Wildean sociable scene, and its atomic unit, the epigram, that I am discussing here bears comparison with Mark Seltzer's recent systems-theory-inflected argument about the autonomization of social life in the "indoor social world" of Patricia Highsmith, which he identifies as part of a broader "autopoietic moment": "the moment at which sociation stands free of external reference, like a game, and at the same time achieves the objectivity of a social system. . . . The first world yields to the second; it is as if reference were a foreign concept and self-reference the default position—that is, the self reference of the system, irrespective of persons." Mark Seltzer, "The Official World," *Critical Inquiry* 37 (Summer 2011): 724–53. Under the sociable aesthetic of Wilde's own conspicuously indoor social world, the social system becomes primary and characters become secondary to it, a social system that is almost irrespective of persons.

48. Anthony Giddens, *The Consequences of Modernity* (Stanford, CA: Stanford University Press, 1990), 38, 176.

49. Simmel, "Sociability," 139.

Chapter 4

1. Raymond Williams, "The Knowable Community," in *The Country and the City* (Oxford: Oxford University Press, 1974), 169–70. This chapter has taken shape through many helpful discussions of Henry James with Karen Swann, Theo Davis, Tanya Agathocleous, Stuart Burrows, and David Kurnick, who brought this moment in Raymond Williams to my attention.

2. Williams, "The Knowable Community," 170. For a more detailed description of what Williams calls "structures of feeling," see chapter 9 in *Marxism and Literature* (Oxford: Oxford University Press, 1978), 128–35.

3. Henry James to his father, May 1869, in Leon Edel, *Henry James: A Life* (New York: Harper & Row, 1985), 97.

4. James, *The Aspern Papers and Other Stories*, ed. Adrian Poole (Oxford: Oxford University Press, 1983), 1; hereinafter cited in the text as *Aspern*.

5. Leo Bersani, *A Future for Astyanax: Character and Desire in Literature* (Boston: Little, Brown, 1976), 128; Ross Posnock, *The Trial of Curiosity: Henry James, William James, and the Challenge of Modernity* (Oxford: Oxford University Press, 1991), 137; and Sharon Cameron, *Thinking in Henry James* (Chicago: University of Chicago Press, 1989), 33.

6. Bersani, *Future*, 138–39.

7. "Distanciation creates the possibility of media, which become both means and ends in themselves—not the default substitute for an absent object. If this were not the case, we would be unable to explain the pleasure of talking on the telephone, reading novels, or even accumulating money as the medium of exchange. Pleasure in mediation may have grown out of the need to relieve the anxiety attached to the dispersion of persons in social space, but this pleasure now spurs the creation of new media where there is no compelling social necessity for their existence." John Guillory, "Genesis of the Media Concept,"

Critical Inquiry 36 (Winter 2010): 358. James's critical essays are not, of course, new media, but I am suggesting they offer the modern appeals of social mediation as an end in itself that Guillory identifies.

8. Mark Goble, "Wired Love: Pleasure at a Distance in Henry James and Others," *ELH* 74 (Summer 2007), 397-427.

9. Henry James, *The Critical Muse: Selected Literary Criticism*, ed. Roger Gard (New York: Penguin, 1987), 290-94.

10. Dorothy Hale, *Social Formalism: The Novel in Theory from Henry James to the Present* (Stanford, CA: Stanford University Press, 1998), 5. Hale's powerful account of James's novel theory, one that proposes social relationality as a feature of novelistic form, has shaped the interest of this chapter and is one I will be drawing on it throughout.

11. Ibid., 14.

12. Henry James, "George Eliot," *Essays on Literature, American Writers, English Writers* (New York: Library of America, 1984), 1:922.

13. My interest here in writing's, and in particular the essay's, affordance of a space of relationality apart from the press of embodied intimacy thus overlaps with Cameron's understanding of the externalization of consciousness of James to the extent that this might be understood as a socialization of mental activity (though I diverge from Hale's understanding of the social in James's novel theory as primarily mystification). I am interested, however, in the mediation and non-mediation of sociability, rather than consciousness, as a problematic in James. The impersonal intimacy I will explore in more detail in what follows also resembles the ways in which, especially in the later fiction, the words or thoughts of one character can become hard to tell from another, or even from James himself, but without the accompanying sense for a reader of what Ruth Bernard Yeazell, in discussing that porousness, calls "a kind of epistemological vertigo." Ruth Bernard Yeazell, "Talking in Henry James," *PMLA* 91 (January 1976): 69. Barbara Hochman discusses "James's life-long concern with the text as a basis for contact between unseen and distant partners in a shared endeavor." Barbara Hochman, "Disappearing Authors and Resentful Readers in Late Nineteenth-Century American Fiction: The Case of Henry James," *ELH* 63 (Spring 1996): 191-92.

14. For this account of remediation as "thickening" the medium, see Guillory, "Genesis of the Media Concept," 340. Garrett Stewart's account of readerly address in nineteenth-century realist fiction, the means by which the novel conscripts a reader in the act of reading into its narration, resonates here as well in the notion of the novel reader/novel relationship as "mediate but intimate." With each moment of "Dear Reader," the novel narrates to the reader a form of mediated intimacy. Garrett Stewart, *Dear Reader: The Conscripted Audience in Nineteenth-Century British Fiction* (Baltimore, MD: Johns Hopkins University Press, 1996), 7.

15. I am drawing here on McGurl's account of James's effort to remake the novel into the "art novel" in Mark McGurl, *The Novel Art: Elevations of American Fiction after Henry James* (Princeton, NJ: Princeton University Press, 2001). On the legacy of James's theory of the novel for contemporary criticism, along with McGurl and Hale, see Mary Poovey, "Beyond the Current Impasse in Literary Studies," *American Literary History* 11 (Summer 1999): 354-77. For an account of "pre-Jamesian" novel theory, see Nicholas Dames, *The Physiology of the Novel* (Oxford: Oxford University Press, 2007). My account here has also benefited from Jonathan Freedman's work on James and the emergence of professionalism

and aestheticism in *Professions of Taste: Henry James, British Aestheticism, and Commodity Culture* (Stanford, CA: Stanford University Press, 1990).

16. Henry James, review of *Life of George Eliot*, by John Cross, chap. 2 in *Partial Portraits* (London: Macmillan, 1899), quoted in Rosemarie Bodenheimer, *The Real Life of Mary Ann Evans: George Eliot, Her Letters and Fiction* (Ithaca, NY: Cornell University Press, 1996), 56.

17. As Mary Ann O'Farrell points out, Eliot's preference for staying home also allows her to avoid the possibility that she and George Henry Lewes, unmarried and living together, would not be admitted to the home of those on whom they might call for fear of scandal in doing so. See O'Farrell's essay as well for the idea of "susceptibility" in Eliot's characters and the capacity to be distracted by others as scandals that dwell close to the heart of her ethics of responsiveness to other people. Mary Ann O'Farrell, "Provoking George Eliot," in *Compassion: The Culture and Politics of an Emotion*, ed. Lauren Berlant (New York: Routledge, 2004), 145-58.

18. James, "Middlemarch," *The Critical Muse*, 75, hereinafter cited in the text as M.

19. Henry James, "Preface to *Roderick Hudson*," in *The Art of the Novel: Critical Prefaces* (Chicago: University of Chicago Press, 2011), 14.

20. Leah Price, commenting on the large size of passages typically quoted in nineteenth-century reviews, describes the review as, in effect, a miniaturized version of the work under review, a commonplace book of quotations: "[the review occupies] a middle ground between the two book-length genres [the anthology and the collection] that competed to represent other texts in miniature." Leah Price, *The Anthology and the Rise of the Novel: From Richardson to George Eliot* (Cambridge: Cambridge University Press, 2000), 139. See also Price's discussion of Victorian readers' understandings of Eliot's novels as paradoxically both "peculiarly quotable" and incapable of being adequately represented by the synecdochic logic of quotation (ibid., 137-49).

21. Some reviewers of Eliot bucked against the Victorian review's standard procedure of quoting at length, claiming that to do so would violate that organic unity of the text being reviewed, a unity James saw as missing in *Middlemarch*. Still other reviewers such as A. V. Dicey found that the many quotable maxims and aphorisms within Eliot's work (epigraphs at the chapter headings, the ostentatiously quotable sayings of particular characters) so fragmented it as to themselves get in the way of comprehending the novel as a whole. Rather than regarding *Middlemarch* as a kind of anthology of sorts, awaiting extraction and quotation, as Price suggests her readers did, James makes his critique of the extractable qualities of *Middlemarch* by refusing to take the book up on its quotability.

22. Henry James, "The Future of the Novel," in *The Critical Muse*, 338. James associates the emergence of a mass readership with a vocabulary that rhymes with his concerns about *Middlemarch* here, a readership whose very "mass" appears as a problem for the novelist in "The Future of the Novel." On the social and aesthetic consequences of population paranoia in James, visible in James's effort to remake the novel's audience into a smaller, "smarter" one distinct from the "mass," see chap. 1 in McGurl's *The Novel Art*. James's focalizations through a single character's consciousness might be seen as one of efforts to make the art novel distinct from the "traditional" realist novel of Eliot, which usually features dispersed, multiple centers of narrative interest. One could never imagine James's narrator interrupting himself to wonder "Why always Isabel?"

23. James, *Art of the Novel*, 5. Among the ways we might mark the difference between Eliot and James as novelists of the social, then, is less in different degrees of sensitivity to the

social's extensiveness, than in the gestures toward social amplitude of Eliot's *Middlemarch* by which individuals come alive to the felt powers of the social, and James's identification of the curtailing of the unbounded nature of the social with novelistic form itself, even as we can detect in him a wish to write a novel as broad as everyone he does not know in London.

24. Dorothea is from the novel's opening sentence identified with the forms of relief that James here mimes both tonally and structurally: "Miss Brooke had that kind of beauty which seems to be thrown into relief by poor dress.... Her stature and bearing seemed to gain the more dignity from her plain garments, which by the side of provincial fashion gave her the impressiveness of a fine quotation from the Bible,—or from one of our elder poets,—in a paragraph of to-day's newspaper." *Middlemarch*, 7. Dorothea's beauty is all the more evident in relief against the plain clothing she wears. But, like James's review, the opening combines this sense of relief as contrast with the emotional sense of relief, relief generated by particularity amidst too-muchness: a reader's own relief at coming across a biblical or poetic quotation amidst the massive, information-oriented prose otherwise contained by the newspaper.

25. The reverberations of Eliot's novel within James's review might be thought of as simply endemic to the essay form itself, whose flexibility and miscellaneous qualities allows it to house within itself different styles, genres, modes of speech, etc. In Adorno's understanding, the essay's formal fluidity and capaciousness also means that it is irreducible to any single principle of inquiry or limited to any finite subject matter. "[The essay's] self-relativization is inherent in its form: it has to be constructed as though it could always break off at any point. It thinks in fragments, just as reality is fragmentary, and finds its unity in and through breaks and not by glossing them over.... Discontinuity is essential to the essay; its subject matter is always a conflict brought to a standstill." Theodor Adorno, "The Essay as Form," in *Notes to Literature*, vol. 1, ed. Rolf Tiedemann, trans. Sherry Weber Nicholsen (New York: Columbia University Press, 1991), 16. The shape-shifting talents of the essay would suggest that "genre-envy" of the sort I find in James's review would not be one of its affects, since the essay can assimilate anything it likes. However, James's taste for formal coherence, which we might phrase in Adornian terms as a *distaste* for fragments, also leads him in this review into the style and language of Eliot's novel, ventriloquizing, critiquing, and rewriting it all at once.

26. James, *Art of the Novel*, 328.

27. Ibid., 342. My sense that James's essay might be read as a revision, even a joint rewriting, of Eliot's novel looks forward to James's New York Edition Prefaces, interpretative prefaces to his own work that effectively constitute a "reconception" of those novels. He looks forward, albeit in the very different terms of author to author, rather than author to prior work, as with the Prefaces. For the notion of James's prefaces as a "reconception," rather than rewriting, of the novels, see Cameron, *Thinking in Henry James*, 37. Hale describes this as James's "altruism" to his earlier novels, his sense of the "ongoing alterity of the objects whose interest generated his novels" (*Social Formalism*, 50). See also Jerome McGann, who describes James's revisions to the New York edition as a rereading rather than rewriting, "revelations—clarifications—of what was always and originally true." Jerome McGann, "Revision, Rewriting, Rereading; or, An Error [Not] in *The Ambassadors*," *American Literature* 64 (1992): 95.

28. Andrew Miller, *The Burdens of Perfection: On Ethics and Reading in Nineteenth-Century British Literature* (Ithaca, NY: Cornell University Press, 2008), 191-217.

29. James, *Art of the Novel*, 37-38. Hales also discusses James's "vampiric" identifications in his social conceptualization of the relation between novelist and character.

30. Posnock, *The Trial of Curiosity*, 10.

31. D. A. Miller, *Jane Austen; or, The Secret of Style* (Princeton, NJ: Princeton University Press, 2000), 58.

32. Ibid., 58.

33. Ibid., 59-60.

34. Andrew Miller, *Burdens of Perfection*, 84-91. Miller draws upon Harry Shaw's insight about Eric Auerbach's criticism as a kind of critical free indirect discourse to think about other critics who exemplify the uncertainty produced in writing about a literary work, the critic "poised uncertainly both within and beyond the writing he is studying," among them D. A. Miller and Neil Hertz (ibid., 85).

35. Anne-Lise Francois, *Open Secrets: The Literature of Uncollected Experience* (Stanford, CA: Stanford University Press, 2008), 19.

36. See my discussion of "The Neutral" and "the familiar" in this book's introduction.

37. Andrew Miller, *Burdens of Perfection*, 85.

38. Both Eliot's fiction and Eliot herself, as I suggested in this chapter's opening, have operated as particularly strong sites for thinking about realism, identification, and what might be called forms of social surrogacy. In an influential account of the effects of characters' conscription as surrogates for Eliot's anxieties about authorship, Neil Hertz describes a related moment of authorial identification between Eliot herself and the character Hetty Sorrel from *Adam Bede*. "Poor Hetty," chap. 5 in Neil Hertz, *George Eliot's Pulse* (Stanford, CA: Stanford University Press, 2003). Hetty becomes the singular locus of Eliot's authorial investment by the book's end, a move signaled by a series of passages in its final pages when Hetty suddenly, unexpectedly becomes much more interesting than previously, acquiring an interior life that seems incommensurate with her as we have known her. This authorial identification with a character who is "too fragile a vessel" to bear this consciousness for long, a "flooding" of a character as Hertz calls it, is a moment of sublimity that brings Eliot to what he calls an "end of the line" moment of authorial reflection (ibid., 110). James's softer, lightened channeling of Eliot and his fantasy of meeting Dorothea are far removed from the dramas of uncertain agency that Hertz identifies with the "end of the line," but this moment where James sounds like the author he is reviewing echoes Eliot's characters' own tendency to echo, at crucial moments, their narrator or their creator. In this way, James's critical free indirect style also returns us to Raymond Williams's own rhetorically abrupt moment of becoming possessed, as it were, by Eliot mid-essay, a possession that nonetheless does nothing to lessen Williams's own critical agency.

39. Henry James, *The Middle Years* (New York: Charles Scribner's Sons, 1917), 72, hereinafter cited in the text as *MY*.

40. René Wellek, "Henry James's Literary Theory and Criticism," *American Literature* 30 (November 1958): 293-321.

41. My account of the essay form itself as a site of social neutrality and an openness to other forms of tactful relationality shares a set of interests and coordinates with David Russell's compelling account of the Romantic essays of Charles Lamb. Lamb's essays

offer a "tactful social style" amidst growing urban populousness, an "ethical and aesthetic response to the beginnings of urban modernity" that makes the essay "a middle space of social relation." David Russell, "'Our Debt to Lamb': The Romantic Essay and the Emergence of Tact," *ELH* 79 (Spring 2012): 179-209.

42. Erving Goffman, *The Presentation of Self in Everyday Life* (New York: Anchor, 1959), 49.

43. Eliot to Madame Bodichon, October 2, 1876, in *The George Eliot Letters*, ed. Gordon S. Haight (New Haven, CT: Yale University Press, 1954), 6:290.

44. Ibid., 33.

45. James, *The Critical Muse*, 186-87.

46. Ibid., 293.

47. "The Art of Fiction" was written by James in response to Walter Besant's earlier talk of the same name, largely to refute Besant's sense of the novel as having some sort of pedagogical usefulness in inculcating morality, and his effort to lay out a set of terms by which one might judge a novel good or bad, as well as to codify the criteria by which a critic might evaluate a novel. In James's dissent from Besant, he lightly mocks those who would limit novels to either being "instructive or amusing"; instead, the novel's rationale is its own "search for form," and its "only obligation to which in advance we may hold a novel . . . is that it be interesting" (191). That is, James refutes Besant, but declines to give anything by way of a positive definition of the novel.

48. Nancy Bentley, *The Ethnography of Manners: Hawthorne, James & Wharton* (Cambridge: Cambridge University Press, 1995), 8. Bentley historicizes James's fiction within the nineteenth-century science of ethnography and a new interest in manners and customs, demonstrating the forms of social authority that would accrue to a novel form that made the cultural power of manners intelligible. The migration of manners into Jamesian criticism, in this light, would also be a means of securing status and power of novel criticism as its own specialized practice.

49. Kent Puckett, *Bad Form: Social Mistakes and the Nineteenth-Century Novel* (New York: Oxford University Press, 2008), 8-9. On sociability and the novel of manners, see also Susan Winnett, *Terrible Sociability: The Text of Manners in Laclos, Goethe, and James* (Stanford, CA: Stanford University Press, 1999). See also Bentley, *The Ethnography of Manners*. I hope to extend and in some ways retexture Puckett's arguments about the novel and bad form by thinking through not the relation between the mistake-prone realist novel character and the narrative omniscience whose ostensibly perfect form is lent coherence by its difference from and negation of character, but through the language of relationality and tact in James's criticism. To say that an entire novel shows bad form, a "want of tact throughout," indicates a global range of effects distinct from the formal coherence secured by an individual character's social mistake, but also shows how self-consciously a novelist might utilize the language of tact to secure for novel criticism its own coherence and good form.

50. For the most complete discussion of culture and taste as "classification struggle" in Pierre Bourdieu, *Distinction: A Social Critique of the Judgement of Taste* (Cambridge, MA: Harvard University Press, 1984).

51. This understanding thus accords with Adorno's description of tact as an (impossible) "reconciliation . . . between the unauthorized claims of convention and the unruly

ones of the individual." *Minima Moralia: Reflections from Damaged Life*, trans. E. F. N. Jephcott (London: Verso, 1974), 36.

52. Sara Blair traces the relation of authorship and "mastery" to gender in James. The "regulatory impulses" of the Prefaces, in which James claims the "power to codify as literary doctrine the dynamic of the novel," are exemplary of the ways in which, as with James's novel *The Portrait of a Lady*, he "sacrifice[s] the ideal of freedom for its heroine to the exercise of a higher authorial consciousness of failed and incomplete forms of mastery." "In the House of Fiction: Henry James and the Engendering of Literary Mastery," in *Henry James's New York Edition: The Construction of Authorship*, ed. David McWhirter (Stanford, CA: Stanford University Press, 1995), 66. James's reviews of Eliot, as occasional pieces, strike me as less exemplary of mastery than fantasized co-authorship. These reviews are also distinctive in that it is not James's own work at stake here in these essays, at least not directly. See also Sarah B. Daugherty, "Henry James and George Eliot: The Price of Mastery," *Henry James Review* 10 (Fall 1989): 153-66. Lindsey Traub makes the case for understanding James's writing on Eliot, the elder author about whom he wrote the most in his career as a book reviewer, as a laboratory in which he might explore and stake out his own professional territory by way of both identification and dis-identification with Eliot, using his sense of her as rival as a means of pressing himself further. "Beyond the Americana: Henry James Reads George Eliot," in *Special Relationships: Anglo-American Affinities and Antagonisms 1854-1936* (Manchester: Manchester University Press, 2002), 160-77. Amanda Claybaugh reads the James-Eliot rivalry as being constituted in part through their common interests in the legacy of Anglo-American reformist writings upon the realist novel. She makes the persuasive argument that James's career-long engagement with Eliot, in his reviews, his prefaces, and his visits to her home, are crucial to the ways in which his own formal principles and practices evolved. Reading and writing about Eliot enabled him to differentiate the social commitments of Anglo-American realism, exemplified by Eliot's sense that the realist novel should have some effect upon the world, from its continental counterpart's inclination to see realism as an end in itself. Amanda Claybaugh, *The Novel of Purpose: Literature and Social Reform in the Anglo-American World* (Ithaca, NY: Cornell University Press, 2007), 115-51.

53. Henry James to Grace Norton, March 5, 1873: "To produce some little exemplary works of art is my narrow and lowly dream. They are to have less 'brain' than *Middlemarch*; but (I boldly proclaim it) they are to have more form."

54. "*Daniel Deronda*: A Conversation," in *The Critical Muse*, 104.

55. Joseph Litvak, *Strange Gourmets: Sophistication, Theory, and the Novel* (Durham, NC: Duke University Press, 1997), 6. Kent Puckett argues that Eliot's narrator in *Middlemarch* defines good narrative form by its distance from the mere social correctness of Middlemarchers. I am suggesting here that James finds Eliot's sententiousness and Deronda's Good Guy act to be itself an overly fussy "want of tact."

56. James, *The Critical Muse*, 115.

57. Percy Lubbock's theorizations of the novel, developed as a codification of James's own accounts of the "art of fiction," would emphasize just this quality of "tact" as indirection in the best novelists. "The famous 'impersonality' of Flaubert and his kind lies only in the greater tact with which they express their feelings—dramatizing them, embodying them in living form, instead of stating them directly." Percy Lubbock, *The Craft of Fiction* (New York: Charles Scribner's Sons, 1921), 67-68.

58. Pierre Bourdieu, *The Logic of Practice*, trans. Richard Nice (Stanford, CA: Stanford University Press, 1992), 66-79. The phrase "feel for the game" is Bourdieu's.

59. Adorno, "The Essay as Form," 1:6. See also Georg Lukács, "On the Nature and Form of the Essay," in *Soul and Form*, ed. John T. Sanders and Katie Terezakis, trans. Anna Bostock (London: Merlin Press, 1974).

60. Donald N. Levine, ed., *Georg Simmel On Individuality and Social Forms* (Chicago: Univeristy of Chicago Press, 1971), 137. In the suggestion that form itself might become the democratizing and "self-sufficient concern" of "sociable" conversation, sociable talk might enable us to better recognize other effects of authorial surrogacy within James. In moments when James's characters seem to speak in the voice or the style of their narrators, or one another even, we might find in these not the awkward overbrimming consciousness that Williams and Hertz associate with Eliot's identification with characters, but potentially utopic moments, expressive of a dream of a fully democratized, shared Jamesian style of speech possessed not just by the lucky few, but by all. For this last point, see David Kurnick, "What Does Jamesian Style Want?" *Henry James Review* 28 (Fall 2007): 213-22.

61. Bersani, *Future*, 139.

62. James, "Preface to *Portrait of a Lady*," in *The Critical Muse*, 485-86.

63. Cameron, *Thinking in Henry James*, 54.

64. James, "Preface to *Portrait of a Lady*," 491. We can note too how far this language of contractual sociality, the account of the social as a party undertaken freely, is from *Middlemarch*'s strong sense of social interdependence and obligation.

65. See Cameron, *Thinking*, for James's contractual language. On freedom as the "recurrent Jamesian subject," see Bersani, "The Jamesian Lie," in *Future*, 128-55.

66. Simmel, *Individuality and Social Forms*, 45.

67. James's language describing this moment resonates with the Prefaces in their evocation of the affect of shame and exposure of an author being confronted by his own work: the book returned by Lewes "had jumped with violence, under the touch of accident, straight up again into my own exposed face" (*MY*, 84).

68. My brisk reading of shame here could be unfolded in more detail with reference to Eve Sedgwick's reading of the Prefaces as themselves a performance of queer sexuality through shame, turning them into a space across which James can establish a relationship with his younger self. Sedgwick works through the complex dynamics by which James's Prefaces turn upon shame, staging a return by the older James to the younger James and in turn to the readable signs of his experiences of his sexual shame in order to then master them. James's Prefaces, however, also produce a countervailing cathexis of that shame, allowing the older James's Prefaces to function "as a way of coming into a loving relation to queer or 'compromising' youth." Sedgwick marks the space between the writing James and his younger self, one that is temporal but also intersubjective, and is in turn spatialized, as an erotic site. The story I adduced here tracks a similar trajectory by which shame is productive, here transmuted into an interest not without its erotic dimensions, but is cooler, more neutral than the shame that marks the Prefaces and its writing subject. Eve Sedgwick, "Shame, Theatricality, and Queer Perfomativity: Henry James's *Art of the Novel*," in *Touching Feeling: Affect, Pedagogy, Performativity* (Durham, NC: Duke University Press, 2003), 41.

69. Simmel, *Individuality and Social Forms*, 136-37.

70. Mill's well-known and widely circulated condensed description of lyric address emphasizes lyric as speech that is indifferent to its listener: "Eloquence supposes an audience; the peculiarity of poetry appears to us to lie in the poet's utter unconsciousness of a listener. Poetry is feeling confessing itself to itself, in moments of solitude. . . . All poetry is of the nature of soliloquy." J. S. Mill, "Thoughts on Poetry and its Varieties," *The Crayon* 7 (April 1860): 93–97.

Afterword

1. Henry James, *The Middle Years* (New York: Charles Scribner's Sons, 1917), 69.

2. Michael Fried, *Why Photography Matters as Art as Never Before* (New Haven, CT: Yale University Press, 2008), 231.

3. Heather Love, "Close But Not Deep: Literary Ethics and the Descriptive Turn," in "New Sociologies of Literature," special issue of *New Literary History* 41, no. 2 (2010): 371–91. On description as a method of reading, see also Stephen Best & Sharon Marcus, "Surface Reading: an Introduction," *Representations* 108, no. 1 (Fall 2009): 1–21.

4. See, *New Literary History*, "New Sociologies of Literature" for the range of works mentioned here, especially the essays by James English, Heather Love, David Alworth, and Mark McGurl. Franco Moretti, *Distant Reading* (New York: Verso, 2013).

5. The Underground New York Public Library project refers us back at least to Walker Evans subway photographs of the late 1930s, in which, as with these photographs, the space of the subway feels like an imaginary theater, one comprised of strangers whose absorption in book is at once a means of getting away from and being with others. One could go on to think through what such a photographic project might tell us about the perceived decline of literary reading (the people photographed are reading books, not magazines, newspapers, electronic readers, or looking at their phones), the aesthetic aura of a fading world in which the act of reading is bathed, even the civic eros of public space amidst the rise of dating apps in the early 21ˢᵗ century.

6. Peter Malone, "On Kawara's Polite Conceptualism," http://hyperallergic. com/194375/on-kawaras-polite-conceptualism.

7. See Sianne Ngai, *Ugly Feelings* (Cambridge: Harvard University Press, 2005) for a discussion of the combination of the sublimity of the vast amount of time in Kawara's work, and the bureaucratic blandness of the ledgers, which Ngai allies with the astonishing and stupefying affective category she calls "stuplimity" (294-95).

{ INDEX }